Machine Translation:

A Knowledge-Based Approach

Machine Translation:

A Knowledge-Based Approach

Sergei Nirenburg
Jaime Carbonell
Masaru Tomita
Kenneth Goodman

Morgan Kaufmann Publishers
San Mateo, California

Sponsoring Editor   Michael B. Morgan
Production Editor   Yonie Overton
Cover Designer   Patty King
Copyeditor   Leslie Tilley

Morgan Kaufmann Publishers, Inc.
Editorial Office:
2929 Campus Drive, Suite 260
San Mateo, CA 94403

Library of Congress Cataloging-in-Publication Data is available for this book.

Contents

List of Figures

List of Tables

Preface

Machine translation has come of age as a scientific, intellectual and technological discipline. Several paradigms have developed, with both earlier and more mature ones yielding commercial machine translation systems. Research continues unabated, focused primarily on producing translations of greater accuracy. Nowhere is the accent on accuracy more pronounced than in the knowledge-based approach. Although the new paradigm has been amply described in technical reports, journal articles and conference papers, this is the first monograph devoted exclusively to theoretical and methodological issues in knowledge-based machine translation.

The book surveys major recent developments, compares knowledge-based machine translation to other approaches and presents a paradigmatic view of MT component processes: natural language analysis, natural language generation, text meaning representation, ontological modeling and so forth. Separate chapters are also devoted to machine-aided translation, to translation of spoken language and to our anticipations of the future of machine translation. A "Reader's Guide" to the individual chapters appears at the end of chapter 1.

This book has a companion volume, *The KBMT Project: A Case Study in Knowledge-Based Machine Translation* (Goodman and Nirenburg 1991). That volume describes in significant detail a substantial knowledge-based machine translation project at Carnegie Mellon University's Center for Machine Translation.

As with any science in ferment, it is difficult to obtain a freeze-frame image of machine translation in general. Our goal in this book is to describe the conceptual "lay of the land" in knowledge-based machine translation. The monograph is not intended as a complete survey or a comprehensive history of the field, there being various such accounts available elsewhere. Rather, the idea is to present and evaluate particularly *theoretical* and *methodological* issues in a cohesive framework and to focus on the component technologies required for knowledge-based machine translation.

■

Several people were especially helpful in the preparation of this book. Candace Sidner, Erich Steiner, Alex Waibel and Yorick Wilks provided valuable comments on an earlier version. Christine Defrise, Ajay Jain, John Leavitt, Lori Levin, See-Kiong Ng and Eric Nyberg were involved in research directly connected to topics in this book and in several instances offered help on its contents. Raman Chandrasekar, Peter Cousseau, Katherine Cox, Bobb Menk, Barbara Moore and Inna Nirenburg helped in various ways with preparation of the final version, including the Bibliography. Radha Rao provided much-appreciated administrative support.

Some passages in chapter 5, on aspects of LR parsing, are adapted with thanks from Tomita 1986a, 9ff.

Sergei Nirenburg, Jaime Carbonell, Masaru Tomita and Kenneth Goodman
Pittsburgh, 1991

Chapter 1

MT in a Nutshell

1.1 Introduction

Translation among languages is economically, sociologically and politically vital in the modern world. Translation among the European languages, for instance, is a requirement for the unified Europe of 1992. The American and Japanese economies rely on export markets in a large number of languages; English alone does not suffice. *The New York Times* estimated in 1989 that the world market for translation was at least $20 billion and was growing rapidly. The potential market is much larger, as the majority of documents and communications whose translation may be of significant benefit go untranslated due to the high cost and unavoidable delays of human manual translation.

Given the indisputable need for massive, timely and inexpensive translation, the dream of many computational linguists and computer scientists has been to develop fully automated machine translation (MT). A practical, but scaled-back objective is machine-aided translation (MAT), where the computer aids the human translator increase his or her throughput via electronic terminology banks, orthography and grammar checkers, and text production facilities. This book focuses on the more ambitious grand objective of fully automated MT, and more specifically on the modern school of knowledge-based machine translation.

Over 30 years ago Yehoshua Bar-Hillel published an analysis of the state of the MT research of his day (Bar-Hillel 1960) and correctly concluded that translation requires text comprehension and that then current MT efforts were bound to fail with respect to their stated task of developing high-quality fully automated translation systems because they did not treat the semantic stratum of language. Bar-Hillel was absolutely right in his judgment of those MT efforts. Unfortunately, the 1960 state of the art in linguistics, artificial intelligence and computer software and hardware, and the virtual nonexistence of computational linguistics as a field, was such that computer comprehension of text was not feasible at that time. Machine translation, therefore, proceeded in a semantic vacuum and met with serious difficulties. One reaction to these difficulties was the report by the Automatic Language Processing Advisory Committee (ALPAC 1966), which caused government funding for MT to be drastically curtailed in the United States.

At present, however, MT is back with a vengeance. Two and a half decades have passed since ALPAC and the widely publicized demise of the large-scale first generation effort in MT. But rumors about the death of the field were, indeed, exaggerated. The intensity and diversity of research and development in machine translation decreased for a time, but have gradually regained momentum and are now at an all-time high. Among the factors contributing to this renascence are the enormous improvement in computer hardware and software quality, realistic expectations and progress in theoretical and computational linguistics and artificial intelligence. Advances in these areas are essential prerequisites for the success of MT. At present MT is a vibrant research and development topic, actively pursued in Japan, Europe and the United States. A number of good surveys of the history of machine translation are available (Zarechnak 1979; and especially Hutchins 1986). Still, a brief account of the history of the field is in order.[1]

1.2   A Concise History of MT Research

In the late 1940s MT seemed a very attractive and feasible application of computer technology. This opinion was bolstered by the following considerations. First, in the era of information explosion translation becomes a very important business. As in every other business, automation should, in principle, enhance efficiency. Second, translation is a common task regularly performed by humans. Therefore, the specification of the task is relatively straightforward: the conceptual design of a potential MT system can be modeled after the organization of the translation process performed by humans. Third, dictionary look-up, which may account for a very significant part of the time spent by human translators, can be reduced to an insignificant level when on-line dictionaries are used. Finally, the spectacular

---

[1]See JEIDA 1989 for a Japanese perspective on the ALPAC report and its consequences.

successes of cryptography during World War II called for applying its methods to other fields. Translation could in some sense be understood as a code-breaking task. ("When I look at an article in Russian, I say: 'This is really written in English, but it has been coded in some strange symbols. I will now proceed to decode'," wrote Warren Weaver [1955].) Feasibility considerations tended to be influenced by the perception of translation as a common, everyday task, performed with relative ease by humans.[2] The above considerations formed the rationale behind the exciting development of MT research from the late 1940s until the early 1960s.

It is customary to consider the so-called Weaver Memorandum as the starting point of research in MT. In 1949 Weaver, then a vice president of the Rockefeller Foundation, distributed 200 copies of a letter in which he suggested the concept of MT to some of the people who were likely to have an interest in its development. Even though the memorandum was predominantly a strategic document, several important theoretical and methodological issues were discussed, including the problem of multiple meanings of linguistic units, the logical basis of language, the influence of cryptography and the need to analyze language universals. Not all of the scientific ideas in the memorandum were appropriate and useful (notably, the entire cryptographic angle proved to be inapplicable), but it aroused significant scientific and public interest in the concept of MT. In 1948, a University of London team led by Andrew Booth and Richard Richens was the world's only MT research and experimentation center. In the first two years after the Weaver Memorandum, work on MT started in earnest at a number of scientific research institutions in the United States, including the Massachusetts Institute of Technology (MIT), the University of Washington, the University of California at Los Angeles, the RAND Corporation, the National Bureau of Standards, Harvard University and Georgetown University.

The major concepts, topics and processes of MT—such as morphological and syntactic analysis, pre- and postediting, homograph resolution, interlingua representation of meaning, work in restricted vocabularies, automating dictionary look-up, and so on—were first defined and debated at that time. The first scientific conference on MT was held in 1952 at MIT, and the first public demonstration of a translation program took place in 1954 at Georgetown University.

The Georgetown experiment involved translating about 50 Russian sentences, selected from texts on chemistry, into English. The dictionary included some 250 words, and the Russian grammar consisted of just six rules. No pre-editing

---

[2]It was only in the 1970s that the field of artificial intelligence came to the understanding that it is precisely the actions easy for humans that often prove the most difficult to model with computers.

of the source language sentences was required, and the output was of adequate quality. This experiment was perceived by the general public and sponsors of scientific research as strong evidence for the feasibility of MT. The wide publicity and resonance of this experiment has also led to the establishment of MT projects outside the United States, notably in the Soviet Union.

Through the 1950s and into the following decade, research in MT continued and grew. The requirements of MT gave an impetus to significant theoretical developments in linguistics and what would later become known as the disciplines of computational linguistics and artificial intelligence. Attempting to scale upwards from the initial Georgetown experiment, however, proved very difficult, as translation quality declined with expanded coverage. In the ensuing years, the quality of actual translations remained largely below an acceptable level and required extensive human postediting, as can be seen from the following example, an excerpt from the output of a 1962 demonstration of the Georgetown GAT system, one of the best examples of MT from Russian to English:

> By by one from the first practical applications of logical capabilities of machines was their utilization for the translation of texts from an one tongue on other. Linguistic differences represent the serious hindrance on a way for the development of cultural, social, political, and scientific connections between nations. Automation of the process of a translation, the application of machines, with a help which possible to effect a translation without a knowledge of a corresponding foreign tongue, would be by an important step forward in the decision of this problem. (Hutchins 1986, 76, quoting Dostert 1963)

Still, researchers in MT remained largely optimistic about the prospects of the field. "The translation machine . . . ," wrote Emile Delavenay in 1960, "is now on our doorstep. In order to set it to work, it remains to complete the exploration of linguistic data" (Hutchins 1986, 151). When Yehoshua Bar-Hillel published his critique of contemporary MT research (Bar-Hillel 1959, 1960), his was a minority opinion. Bar Hillel's central claim was that fully automatic high-quality machine translation was unattainable with the technology of the times because of the inability to develop computer programs for lexical disambiguation. His now-famous example was the following:

(1.1)   Little John was looking for his toy box. Finally, he found it. *The box was in the pen.* John was very happy.

The word *pen* in the emphasized sentence above has at least two meanings—a writing pen and a playpen. Bar-Hillel's conclusion was that "no existing or imaginable program will enable an electronic computer to determine that the word *pen* in the given sentence within the given context has the second of the above meanings." He had not, of course, envisioned subsequent scientific developments that focused precisely on the resolution of such ambiguities, as discussed, for instance, in Carbonell et al. 1981.

Since Bar-Hillel was one of the early champions of MT and had intimate knowledge of the research in the field, his critique has had a wide resonance in public attitudes toward MT, as well as among its sponsors in the U.S. government and industry. Coupled with the increased difficulty of problems facing MT research after the initial successes, and notwithstanding the fact that many of the then-current projects (notably, at Georgetown University and IBM) pursued exactly the type of MT research recommended by Bar-Hillel—namely, a combination of machine translation with human postediting—this criticism started the process of reassessment of attitudes toward the field. The reassessment culminated in the publication in 1966 of the influential ALPAC report. ALPAC had been organized in 1964 by the U.S. National Academy of Sciences, and its report was critical of the state of the art in MT and recommended drastic reductions in the level of support for MT research.

The ALPAC report was sharply—and appropriately—criticized as biased and inaccurate. Many of its assessments, however, were correct, especially those dealing with the evaluation of practicality of the contemporary MT research. In retrospect, the strongest negative effect of ALPAC was not so much the reduction in funding as the damage to the status of MT as a scientific endeavor in the United States, where government-sponsored MT research came to a virtual standstill, although projects in Europe and later in Japan flourished.

The early MT projects, indeed, failed to reach their goal of building systems of fully automated high-quality machine translation (FAHQMT, as it was labeled in Bar-Hillel 1960). The principal mistake of the early MT workers was, however, that of judgment: the complexity of the conceptual problem of natural language understanding was underestimated. The variety and the sheer amount of knowledge necessary for any solution to this problem proved to be enormous, so that the success of MT as an application became dependent on the solution to the problem of knowledge acquisition and integration. It would take more than 15 years for MT to start a scientific comeback in the United States.

While the ALPAC report reduced American efforts in MT, research and development continued in several scientific groups in the Soviet Union, Canada, Germany, France and Italy, as well as in a small number of commercial institutions in the United States. Notable MT achievements in the 15 years after the ALPAC report included the development and everyday use of the first unquestionably successful MT system, TAUM-METEO, developed at the University of Montreal and used routinely since 1977 to translate weather reports from English into French (Isabelle 1987). The MT program SYSTRAN was used during the Apollo-Soyuz space mission in 1975, and in the following year was officially adopted as a translation tool of the European Economic Community (EEC).

The beginning of the revival of MT as a scientific discipline and an application of linguistic and computer technology must, however, be traced to the establishment of the Eurotra project and the MT efforts in Japan. Begun in 1978, Eurotra is an ambitious, well-supported project aimed at providing MT capability among all official EEC languages (Danish, Dutch, English, French, German, Greek, Italian, Portuguese and Spanish) . At present, Eurotra employs about 160 researchers in a number of national groups and at the project headquarters in Luxembourg. (For an overview of the Eurotra program, see the articles in *Machine Translation*, vol. 6 (1991), nos. 2 and 3.) The current generation of Japanese MT efforts started around 1980, supported both by the government and industry, most notably with the Mu project at Kyoto University (see, e.g., Nagao et al. 1985) laying the foundation for the current extensive Japanese industrial MT projects. The proceedings of the MT Summit conference, held in Hakone, Japan, in 1987 (Nagao 1989) contain a good survey of the major Japanese experimental MT systems.

These developments gradually led to a revival of MT research in the United States. MT activities at various scientific meetings have significantly intensified, and several conferences devoted specifically to MT have been organized in the past five years. New research groups have been set up, the largest being the Center for Machine Translation at Carnegie Mellon University, with a research staff of about 35. The new importance of MT has been shown at the international conferences on machine translation—MT Summits I (Hakone, 1987), II (Munich, 1989) and III (Washington, D.C., 1991), which attracted researchers, users and sponsors of MT from all over the world; members of academia; governmental institutions; industrial entities; and multinational bodies such as the EEC. The general mood of the conferences reflects a new optimism based on modern scientific advances and the fact that the need for MT in the 1990s is vastly more pressing than in the world of 40 years ago.

The new optimism of MT researchers and sponsors is based on spectacular advances in computer technology (drastic improvements in processing speed and memory capacity, advances in computer architecture, emergence of database technology, development of high-level programming languages and interactive programming environments, etc.) and computational linguistics (in particular, techniques for morphological and syntactic analysis and synthesis of natural language texts). Advances in automatic processing of meaning and techniques of human-computer interaction are also an important component of the current MT paradigms. With the knowledge of the past difficulties, and, therefore, with a realistic assessment of the possibilities of MT technology application, the current MT projects are well equipped to produce a new wave of scientifically sound and practically useful machine translation systems. These systems are being designed both to compete and to cooperate with humans in translating a wide variety of scientific, industrial, official, journalistic and other texts. And, most significantly, low-cost, rapid-response MT systems promise to increase the volume of timely translations manyfold, addressing an unmet societal need for timely delivery of currently untranslated quality information whose source may be in a number of different languages.

1.3 The Mandate of Machine Translation, as Viewed by Users

Machine translation technology is economically and sociologically necessary in the modern world. This may be the ultimate external justification for the existence of the field. This understanding of the mandate of MT is summarized by Slocum (1985, 2): "Academic debates about what constitutes 'high quality' and 'fully-automatic' are considered irrelevant by the users of machine translation and machine-aided translation systems; what matters to them are two things: whether the systems can produce output of sufficient quality for the intended use (e.g., revision), and whether the operation as a whole is cost-effective or, rarely, justifiable on other grounds, like speed."

A major additional rationale must, however, be defined for work in machine translation. The latter constitutes a convenient and realistic testbed for evaluating the quality of a variety of knowledge bases, linguistic theories and language descriptions. It can also serve as the basis for software engineering experiments in designing and implementing large software systems. Components of a comprehensive MT system can be readily adapted for service in other applications of computational linguistics and artificial intelligence. Indeed, machine translation is a hybrid scientific field stretching across the boundaries of science and engineering, basic research and development, computer science, linguistics, artificial intelligence and software engineering. It is one of the most natural applications for theoretical linguistics (grammar theory, the lexicon, semantics, pragmatics and

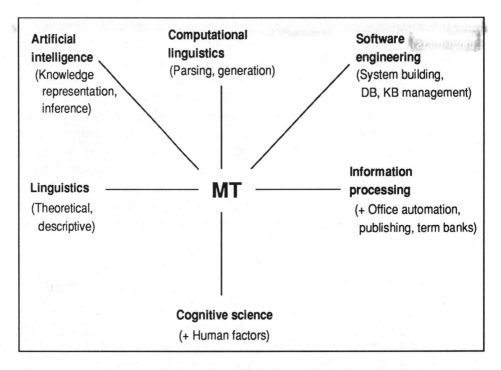

Figure 1.1: **Relation of MT to other disciplines. Machine translation is truly an interdisciplinary enterprise combining science and technology, inquiry into the nature of language and of computational algorithms and data structures, study of human-computer interaction and general information processing.**

discourse), computational linguistics (algorithms for parsing, semantic interpretation and generation) and descriptive linguistics (lexicon and grammar acquisition). Most of all, however, the operational computational aspects (language analyzers and generators) must be fully developed to integrate the knowledge sources into functional and robust translation systems.

The general task of machine translation can be described very simply:

> *Feed a text in one language (SL, for source language) into a computer and, using a computer program, produce a text in another language (TL, for target language), such that the meaning of the TL text is the same as the meaning of the SL text.*

The simplicity of this problem statement allows even a nonspecialist immediately to understand what MT is about. This simplicity is, however, somewhat deceptive—there are many points in the above description that can be interpreted in a number of ways and require careful discussion. To name just a few:

- Can *any* text be used as input to a machine translation system? Should one have the ability of processing arbitrary texts as a research objective?

- Is it a worthwhile goal to strive to preserve the *form* (in addition to the meaning) of the source language text in the translation? If so, is it an attainable goal?

- How difficult is it to increase the number of source and target languages once a system for a given pair of languages is developed?

- How difficult is it to adjust a translation system to a different subject domain once a system for a given subject domain is developed?

- What are the constraints on the medium (speech, electronic texts, etc.) in which translation is rendered?

- How can one determine the quality of a translation?

- How does one determine the economic or scientific value of MT?

- What should be done when an MT system fails to produce an adequate translation?

Some of the above questions should interest MT customers—governments, international organizations, industrial and other corporations, including translation agencies. Other questions relate more directly to the concerns of designers and implementors of MT systems. In this section we address typical concerns of MT customers and other interested "outsiders." The next section will be devoted to the "inside" views of the field.

1.3.1   What Do We Translate?

The purpose of machine translation is, on the one hand, to relieve the human translator of the need to work with tedious, repetitive and aesthetically unsatisfying material and, on the other, to speed up and facilitate worldwide information dissemination. It is hardly necessary to argue for the fundamental importance of the ability to disseminate information across linguistic borders. The volume of such information is already very large and is bound to increase with the growth of international trade and international political cooperation. The case of Japan and the Pacific Rim countries is an example of the former.[3] The EEC, especially the EEC after 1992, provides an example of the latter.

Translating fiction and poetry is not a task for machine translation. Also, additional types of texts may be deemed too idiosyncratic or inappropriate for automatic processing—for instance, political campaign speeches or advertising copy. Therefore, the focus is on translating technical technical texts and other expository texts.

Real-time translation of dialogues between two humans (possibly even translation of spoken language to spoken language), especially when constrained to well-defined topics such as medical advice or travel arrangements, is definitely within the larger scope of MT.

1.3.2   Tradeoffs in MT

The definition of machine translation at the beginning of this section tacitly presupposes that the whole process is to be carried out automatically and that, if the meaning of the source language text is preserved, then the high quality of the target text is guaranteed. Therefore, this definition applies to fully automated high-quality machine translation, which is not yet a reality. Machine translation systems today regularly encounter difficulties in translating certain texts. What can be done in such cases to render the system immediately usable? Clearly, some constraints on the definition of the task should be relaxed. The principal avenues of relaxation are (i) adjusting downward the acceptability threshold of MT output, (ii) allowing the translation process to be only partially automated, and (iii) making sure that the texts selected for translation can, in fact, be automatically processed by the system. Each type of relaxation is closely coupled with a translation paradigm, as discussed in Carbonell and Tomita 1987. As will be seen from the discussion below, some approaches actually use a combination of the above relaxation techniques.

1.3.2.1   Modifying the Acceptability Threshold

In many cases, especially when a machine-translated text is not intended for publication, the quality standards for MT can be effectively lowered without tangible

---

[3]One study (JEIDA 1989, 19-20) estimates the size of the translation market in Japan in 1988 as being close to a trillion yen annually (about $8 billion), calculated as about 240 million pages of translation at ¥ 4,000 per page, a page containing 400 characters of kana or 125 English words. The market was expected to increase about twofold in the following two years.

harm. This situation arises, for instance, when an expert in a scientific field would like to read an article in his or her field of expertise but that is in a language he or she does not know. In the best case, a medium-quality machine-translated text will suffice for understanding the content. At worst, a decision could be made on the basis of such a translation whether the article is interesting enough for it to be translated by other means, such as a more costly human translation. Intermediate positions, such as human postediting of the rough translation may prove economically superior to a complete retranslation. Other situations in which this approach is satisfactory are illustrated in King 1989 and Henisz-Dostert 1979.

A crucial cautionary note, however, is in order when discussing the acceptability of low-quality translation. Translation quality may be low on stylistic or semantic grounds. The former is acceptable when not producing publishable text, but the latter is almost never acceptable. The decision to produce "rough and dirty" translations bypassing semantic analysis can be misleading. Consider a cookie jar with 100 delicious freshly baked chocolate-chip cookies, 95 of which are not poisoned. Such a cookie jar could be worse than useless; it could be tempting and therefore actively dangerous. Such is the case of knowledge-free translation. Statistically, a large part may be correct, but unidentified portions could be semantically wrong, to the point of being actively misleading disinformation. Just as in the cookie analogy, there are acceptable errors (too large, slightly stale chocolate chips—or too verbose, suboptimal lexical selections), and completely unacceptable ones (laundry detergent used instead of flour, or translating "check tires for wear and damage" as instructions to check for wear and then to damage the tires, if "damage" is interpreted as a verb instead of a noun).

1.3.2.2 Partial Automation in MT

Until very recently human intervention in the MT cycle came predominantly in the form of *postediting*—a human editor improving the results of machine translation before it is submitted to publication or otherwise disseminated. This approach allows MT systems with relatively shallow levels of input text understanding to be usable in practice. Among such systems are SYSTRAN (e.g., Gachot 1989) and its direct predecessor, GAT (Zarechnak 1979), SPANAM (Vasconcellos and Leon 1985), HICATS/JE (Kaji 1989) and some others. A major objective in systems relying on postediting is to make human involvement as painless as possible in comparing source and target texts and correcting any translation errors. Many professional posteditors report serious difficulties in improving machine-translated output compared to that of human translators. The computer interfaces used by posteditors must be improved; at present, posteditors use a simple and unstructured screen editor. Moreover, some posteditors actively dislike "cleaning up the mess that the machine made" when coping with translations of poor quality.

One of the main research and development objectives in the field is to enhance the power of MT systems so that the extent of postediting is reduced and, eventually, the need for it eliminated. Postediting is needed because current systems cannot understand the input text well enough and must, therefore, make guesses about the appropriate translation correlates for source language lexical units and grammatical constructions. In many cases, naturally, these guesses turn out to be wrong. If we eliminate the need for such guesses, then the system should be able to generate adequate target language texts. One way to eliminate this guesswork is to invoke human help not *after* the guesses were made but *instead* of them. This means using people to help the machine understand the source language text well enough for the generation component of a machine translation system to produce texts of a quality similar to that of human translators. In this way, no substandard texts are produced.

1.3.2.3   Restricting the Ambiguity of SL Text

The most straightforward way of restricting the source text ambiguity is by choosing a sufficiently narrow subject domain. The corresponding terminological inventory should then also be limited and circumscribable. This attitude to MT has come to be known as the *sublanguage* approach (e.g., Kittredge and Lehrberger 1982; Grishman and Kittredge 1986; Kittredge 1987). In fact, many current MT systems are of this type since it is not quite within the state of the art to build very large dictionaries that would cover all sublanguages.

The best example of the sublanguage approach is the operational MT system TAUM-METEO (see, e.g., Isabelle 1987), developed at the University of Montreal and delivered to the Canadian Weather Service for everyday routine translations of stylized weather reports from English into French. The system operates very successfully, practically without human intervention. Its vocabulary consists of about 1,500 items, about half of which are place names. The syntactic constructions that occur in the variant of English used as SL in TAUM-METEO constitute a relatively small subset of English syntactic constructions. There is very little semantic ambiguity in the system because potentially ambiguous words are expected to be used in only one of their meanings—namely, the one that belongs to the subworld of weather phenomena. For instance, the word *front* in TAUM-METEO will be understood unequivocally as a weather front.

Finding well-delineated, self-sufficient and useful small sublanguages is a very difficult task, and this is one of the reasons why the success of TAUM-METEO has not yet been repeated by any other operational system. Unfortunately, most subworlds are not as constrained with respect to vocabulary size, semantic ambiguity and syntactic diversity as repetitive weather forecasts. Translating computer manuals, for instance, is another practical domain whose structure is richer than weather forecasts in all three dimensions: lexical, syntactic and semantic. This domain is being actively investigated by many projects, including those at the IBM Tokyo Research Laboratory and at Carnegie Mellon University.

In the richer constrained domains, enhanced semantic and pragmatic analysis and/or additional human help may be required for the system to ensure good-quality output. This is because within any sizeable sublanguage, texts can contain lexical units and syntactic constructions that a system is incapable of processing. In addition, a certain number of errors (e.g., typographical ones) and unusual phenomena (e.g., special symbols or symbols from other alphabets) can be encountered. In order to prepare texts for machine translation a human *pre-editor* may be employed. A human pre-editor reads the input text and modifies it in such a way that the MT system is able to process it automatically. Difficult and overly ambiguous words and phrases are replaced with those the editor knows that the program will handle. Pre-editing (or *controlling inputs to MT*, as it has also been known) has been employed in a number of projects, for instance, by the MT project at Xerox Corporation (see Hutchins 1986, 292ff., for a discussion of the issue). Like interactive editors, pre-editors must also be supplied with interfaces and tools. A major task in pre-editing is developing memory and decision aids for the user to make a correct decision to retain or change an element of input and, if the latter, whether to propagate a change to all occurrences of the textual element.

1.3.3 Bilingual or Multilingual Machine Translation?

Although translation between a single source and single target language is conceptually the simplest setup, and the need for such translation is possibly the most widespread, there are many situations in which multilingual translation is called for. Translation from many languages into a single language will be required by large information-gathering and processing organizations. Translations from a single language into many languages will be required in the context of foreign trade, for instance, when operation and other manuals for industrial equipment need to be translated from the language in which they were originally written into the languages of the countries where the equipment is to be marketed. The most striking example of the need for translation from many languages into many languages is simultaneous translation at an international meeting—diplomatic, cultural or scientific.

1.3.4   Text and Speech Translation

The viability of simultaneous translation depends on advances in integrating machine translation with speech recognition and synthesis. With the progress in speech-related technologies, research in the subfield of speech-to-speech automatic translation has become more realistic; see, for instance, Tomita et al. 1988a. In order to translate spoken language, the following issues must be addressed, in addition to the traditional ones:

- *Speech recognition:* The acoustic signal must be converted into internal symbols representing phonemes, which are then grouped into syllables and words.

- *Discourse translation:* MT must be applied to spontaneous discourse, which is inherently different from well-written text. To wit, spoken utterances are often ungrammatical or incomplete. Moreover acoustical recognition errors (e.g., in the presence of homophones or nearphones) must be taken into account. These problems complicate the language-analysis phase of MT. Conversely, the syntactic complexity of spoken language is somewhat less than that of written text.

- *Speech generation:* After the text is translated it must be spoken in the target language. Present technology provides near-acceptable speech-synthesis devices for the most common languages. Therefore, the greatest technological challenges lie in the first two steps.

In addition to developing the component steps outlined above, a high degree of integration is desirable. This need is most evident in the propagation of syntactic and semantic expectations from the language analysis module back to the acoustic recognition one. Such expectations constrain the recognition process to a smaller number of viable alternatives and improve overall performance in terms of both speed and accuracy. We discuss speech-to-speech translation in greater detail in chapter 7.

1.3.5 Evaluating the Quality of Translation

As a routine part of its development, every field of science and technology must develop procedures for evaluating the quality of its results. In machine translation there have been several contributions centrally devoted to this topic. First, the ALPAC report itself suggested procedures for evaluating MT systems and results (see ALPAC 1966, Appendix 10). Van Slype 1979 contains a set of procedures used by the EEC for evaluating machine translation. Lehrberger 1988 is a cumulative account of the translation-evaluation methodologies, both translation results and machine translation *systems*, as discussed below.

The criteria for translation quality first suggested in ALPAC and then carried through a number of other evaluation methodologies are *fidelity* ("the extent to which the translated text contains the same information as the original," Lehrberger 1988, 208; see also Carroll 1966), *intelligibility* ("the degree of clarity and comprehensibility of each sentence," Gervais 1980) and *stylistic appropriateness*. All three can be established only through human judgment, since no automatic procedure can be envisaged and no purely quantitative measure has been provided. Human judgments must also be sensitive to the specifics of the intended use of the translation being evaluated; see Slocum 1985 and King 1989.

1.3.6 Quality and Utility of MT Systems

To discuss questions of quality and utility of machine translation systems, King 1989, extending Lehrberger 1988, distinguishes nine categories of target language texts. The first criterion for text classification is the potential impact of the translated text (or, in other terms, the potential cost of erroneous translation). The scale of text types for this measure ranges from translations of legal texts which will, similarly to the source texts, "serve as the definitive reference for law" (p. 5), to texts intended for a quick scan by a specialist who needs only to select and classify texts according to preselected topics. King also suggests the combined criterion of *accuracy* and *style* of the translation, with the range from "absolute accuracy and good style are required for the translation" to "a rough translation will suffice" (p. 5). In King's report, the ALPAC measures of fidelity and intelligibility are conflated into a single measure of accuracy. But, as we discussed earlier, semantic errors can be far more serious than intelligibility degradations and hence should be measured separately and weighed more heavily in the overall evaluation.

A system producing high-quality translations of texts of all degrees of importance is, according to this measure, the ideal system. In fact, a number of other quality measures should be added to the description of an ideal system. Using an extended measure of quality, an ideal system would be defined as one that (i) works for every text in every language required by a customer, (ii) is completely automatic, and (iii) produces high-quality translations.

Many other types of MT systems, though falling short of ideal performance, can still be useful. The utility of MT systems should be measured in terms of their cost-efficiency compared to human translations of comparable quality. A translation cycle that includes MT usually also includes human involvement (see chapter 8 for details). In most cases, therefore, the calculation of cost-efficiency should take into account both the automatic and the manual components of the translation cycle.

1.3.7   A More Comprehensive Set of MT Performance Metrics

Instead of relying on the rather limited quality and performance measures available in the days of ALPAC, or their more recent derivatives outlined above, we would like to offer a more comprehensive set of criteria that encompass generality, quality of translation, utility, and extensibility, as follows:

- *Linguistic generality:* the number of source and target languages covered by the system and the *extent of coverage* in the grammar and the general vocabulary (including such "closed-class" lexical items as prepositions, conjunctions, parentheticals, etc.). Grammatical coverage can be calculated as (i) a percentage of complete sentences totally parsed (or generated) by the system for a given source (or target) language; (ii) a percentage of grammatical and standard ungrammatical phenomena (e.g., ill-formed inputs) from a specially prepared list that are parsed correctly. In systems that feature bilingual dictionaries, mappings should be available between the general vocabulary items in every source language and their correlates in every target language. In systems that feature language-independent domain models, mappings should be available between entities in the latter and lexical units in dictionaries of every source and target language.

- *Application-domain generality:* the number of subject domains covered by the system and the *extent of coverage* of each domain. The greater the inventory of the subject domains that a system can cover, the higher the general utility of the system.

- *Degree of automation:* the extent to which the human must intervene in the translation cycle. The less there remains to do for a human user, the better the system, if translation quality remains invariant. As discussed earlier, human intervention can take on many forms: pre- and postediting of text, interactive disambiguation, and so on. If we add the amount of time required for human intervention and divide it by the total time required to translate the same text manually (and gather a statistically representative sample of texts over which to take our measurements) then we establish the degree of automation as the efficiency enhancement ratio of an MT system. A refinement of this measure would include weighing the human time by the cost of the skills required. For instance, a posteditor is usually a skilled translator, whereas a pre-editor or a disambiguator need not know the target language, and may therefore be a less costly human resource.

- *Semantic accuracy:* the degree to which the translated target text expresses the same meaning as the source text. Measurements can be weighed to penalize subtle semantic shifts less than gross errors. Usually, this is the central criterion establishing a baseline for quality of technical translations. Translations of operating manuals, weather forecasts, legal documents and so on must be, above all, accurate renditions of their source texts. Semantic accuracy depends most of all on the depth of analysis and the richness of the semantic-domain model.

- *Intelligibility:* the degree to which the translated text is easily understandable by readers of the target language without access to the source text. This measure is the same one discussed in the previous section, which, when combined with semantic accuracy, is sometimes labeled "overall accuracy" or "quality" of the translation.

- *Appropriateness:* the degree to which the target text is stylistically appropriate for its intended audience. For instance, a translation of English into Japanese might result in an inappropriate level of familiarity in the language—perfectly intelligible and semantically accurate, as all readers will know exactly what it says, but socially inappropriate, and therefore unusable without postediting. A different example would be the selection of lexical items in the target language that presuppose a higher level of education on the part of the reader than will actually be the case—again intelligible to a sophisticated reader and semantically accurate, but inappropriate. This measure is a bit harder to quantify, and perhaps not as central as the others in the early stages of system development.

- *Domain and language portability:* the ease with which additional subject domains and languages can be added. This can be measured in total human developer time to add grammar rules (for new languages), semantic concepts (for new domains) and dictionary entries for new terminology (for both new languages and new domains). In systems with bilingual dictionaries (Type I), every term in every source language must be mapped into a corresponding term in all of the target languages. In systems without bilingual dictionaries (Type II), a language-independent description of the domain must be produced, and mappings must then be developed into it from every source language and from it into every target language. Thus, systems of Type II require an extra step—building a language-independent domain model. Type I systems, however, require that *all* bilingual dictionaries between each language pair be updated (not just the language-concept mapping) when a new term is added.

- *Extensibility:* the degree to which an MT system provides for seamless and incremental extensions to the grammatical and lexical coverage of the languages and subject domains already in the system. A convenient means of effecting these extensions must be provided. This is typically best accomplished by producing perspicuous and declarative representations of the grammar and dictionary entries and by providing knowledge acquisition and maintenance tools. The time to extend a system can be measured in terms of how long it takes to encode, test and verify a new grammatical construction or a dictionary entry, and whether or not the new knowledge exhibits unforeseen and undesirable repercussions elsewhere in the system.

- *Improvability:* the degree to which a system permits changes and enhancements to the level of automation as domain or lexical knowledge improves, without significantly compromising the quality of translation. In some systems this functionality is facilitated by the general design (*open-ended systems*). Some MT system designs do not support improvability and cannot be expected to improve their quality without a major redesign effort.

- *Ergonomics:* the extent to which the user interface provides maximum communication bandwith, maximal clarity and minimal opportunity for errors. In a machine translation cycle with human involvement, convenient means of interaction between the human and the machine must be provided to facilitate and speed up the overall process of translation. Advanced high-quality interfaces must also include various decision aids for the human users, including machine-readable human-oriented dictionaries and encyclopedias, hypertext-type indices into the text of translation, a translation archive and so on.

- *Integrability:* the extent to which an MT system can be an integral component of a complete authoring and document-production facility. It is advantageous for an MT system to be integrable with other information-processing applications, such as retrieval systems, optical character readers, authoring systems, message-processing systems, text production and publishing and so forth.

- *Software portability:* the ease with which the MT software can be ported to other hardware platforms, other operating systems and so on. It is best to implement at the virtual machine level (such as UNIX or OS/2) in a standard language (such as C or COMMONLISP) in order to maintain maximal flexibility and portability across multiple platforms, including those that are not yet on the market.

1.4 Problems in MT, as Viewed by System Developers

The questions in the previous section were posed from the point of view of a consumer of MT. From the point of view of an MT developer, the crucial design-related questions concern the internal workings of the computer programs that carry out the translation, the linguistic basis of the programs and the encoding and use of various knowledge sources. In this section we discuss MT from that perspective.

All modern machine translation systems involve a measure of linguistic analysis of the source language text. The purpose of this analysis is to facilitate finding target language correlates for the various meanings expressed in the source language through its lexical units, syntactic constructions and word and sentence order. The major differences among the machine translation systems relate to the differences of opinion with respect to the depth of the source language analysis. Some researchers maintain that a relatively shallow, usually syntactic, analysis is sufficient. Others believe that deep understanding is essential.

We believe that the single most important strategic decision that must be made by MT developers early in their work concerns the depth of understanding of the source language text. In actual machine translation systems, the depth of understanding is effectively determined by the nature of the results of the analysis stage. Thus, for instance, when the analysis stage was first identified as a separate component of a machine translation system, a syntactic parse of an input sentence was usually deemed a sufficiently deep representation (cf. the nature of internal representation in such seminal systems as CETA (Vauquois 1975)). Much deeper and more detailed text-meaning representations have been suggested since then, especially in the artificial intelligence tradition.

Research and development efforts tend to grow significantly with the depth of source language analysis desired in a system. Therefore, some projects perform a relatively shallow analysis in the hope that it will actually prove sufficient for providing posteditable translations. In other projects, one of the central tasks is to determine the meaning of the source language text, that is, to analyze the input texts very deeply. The adherents of shallow analysis sometimes justify their choice not only by the constraints on the current technology but also by claiming that deep understanding is *not necessary* (Pericliev 1984; Ben Ari et al. 1988) and/or *infeasible* in principle (e.g., Arnold and Sadler 1990; Amano 1989). The first claim is partially supported by evidence that in some cases disambiguation of source language texts is unnecessary, since the ambiguity can be carried over into the target language. In the general case, however one must bite the proverbial bullet and resolve the difficult problems. The infeasibility claim is usually based on general philosophical grounds, which are usually variations of the well-known nominalist-realist or behaviorist-mentalist debates. The long history of successful human translation supports the belief in the analyzability in principle of source text meaning. We discuss the first claim later in this section and the second one in chapter 2.

In reality, in a field such as machine translation, the necessary level of understanding must be defined as that level at which all the kinds of ambiguous expressions can be resolved. In other words, this is the level at which a correct target language realization can be found for every component of the input text, be it the meaning of a lexical unit, a syntactic structure, or a particular word, phrase or sentence order configuration. Often this level is discussed in terms of finding correlates for source language syntactic structures themselves, not their meanings. This approach seems to be predicated on the erroneous assumption that similar syntactic structures always carry similar meanings in various languages. In fact, for instance, the meaning of a relative clause in one language can be equivalent to that of, say, a participial construction in another language. In what follows, we illustrate the depth of source language analysis necessary to attain adequate understanding for MT.

Understanding source language text involves a number of different levels, the main stages of analysis being (in ascending order of complexity) morphological, syntactic, semantic (relating to meanings of lexical units and relations among these meanings) and pragmatic (relating to linguistic meanings in textual as well as speech-situation context). Detailed discussions of problem types in natural language processing in general, and machine translation in particular, can be found

in Carbonell et al. 1981, Waltz 1982, Weischedel 1987 and Nirenburg 1987b. In
what follows we give a very brief overview of problems in understanding.

1.4.1   Selected Problems in Text Understanding

Morphological analysis is used for obtaining uninflected stem forms of source
language words, given any word form that can be used in a text. This type of
morphology is called *inflectional morphology*. English is a very simple language
morphologically. For instance, the maximum number of distinct morphological
verb forms in it is only five (e.g., *give, gives, gave, given, giving*). In some
languages, however, a word can have dozens of forms. It is clear that with
morphological analysis the number of the dictionary entries becomes significantly
smaller, since there is a need for only one entry for all the inflectional variants of
each word. In some cases, morphological analysis can, in fact, help disambiguate
the meaning of the source language text. For instance, even though *work* can be
either a noun or a verb, the form *worked* is clearly a verb form. Conversely, *works*
can be either the plural form of the nominal sense of *work* or the third person
singular of the verbal sense. To eliminate this ambiguity it is necessary to perform
determination of the part of speech of *work* in an input context. And this is already
a part of syntactic analysis.

A more sophisticated version of morphological analysis involves word-formation, not form-formation as in inflectional morphology. Derivational morphological
analysis will, for instance, understand the word *worker* as a noun with the meaning
of *actor*, derived from the basic verb *to work* with the help of the word-formation
suffix *-er*. The use of derivational morphology will reduce the size of a root-form
lexicon still further. However, a problem arises due to polysemy of certain suffixes.
And while *-er* in *larger* can be distinguished from the same suffix in *worker* as a
result of syntactic analysis, the difference in meaning of *-er* in *worker* and *locker*
can be explained only semantically.

The results of syntactic analysis partially disambiguate the SL text and facilitate finding target language correlates for the source language lexical units and
syntactic structures. The main repositories of knowledge that support the search
for lexical correlates after syntactic analysis are bilingual dictionaries. The search
for grammatical correlates relies on special "transfer" grammars that contain data
about correspondences of syntactic structures in a particular SL-TL pair. It should
be clear at this point that systems relying largely on syntactic analysis are the Type
I systems (see above). The TL synthesis stage in such systems is responsible essentially for *linearizing*, that is, typing out, left-to-right, the leaves of the TL trees,

obtained as a result of transfer, according to the rules of a TL grammar.

The first useful result of syntactic analysis is the determination of correct lexical categories ("parts of speech") of input lexical units. Consider the sentence

(1.2)   If the display is not bright, change the batteries.

In the *Longman Dictionary of Contemporary English* (Procter et al. 1978), *display* has 3 nominal senses, *bright* has 7 senses, *change* has 14 verbal senses, and *battery* has 6 senses as a countable noun. The combination of these possibilities leads to a 1,764-way ambiguity. This is a very large number. But without syntactic category assignment we would have had also to consider *display* as a verb, the 7 nominal meanings of *change* and the numerous meanings of *battery*—which would have led to a 6,116-way ambiguity.

Syntactic analysis also helps establish phrase boundaries within each sentence of the input text and dependency structure within every phrase. In most cases (such as the above) syntactic knowledge is not sufficient for disambiguation. Types of ambiguities that cannot in the general case be resolved by syntactic knowledge include lexical-semantic word-sense ambiguities, as well as prepositional phrase attachment and decomposition of noun-noun compounds in English.

The commonplace lexical-semantic ambiguity of natural language has been singled out by Bar-Hillel as the major obstacle for MT. To illustrate the point further, consider the following example.

(1.3)   Print your *paper* on heavy bond white *paper*. Do not fold or crease your *paper*.

In this example the three instances of the word *paper* refer to three different senses of this word, the first of them synonymous with *article*, the second denoting a material and the third denoting a quantity and topological configuration of material. In Spanish, for example, the preferred lexical selections are *artículo, papel* and *hoja*, respectively. Semantic analysis for disambiguation is therefore required to translate this sentence correctly.

With noun-noun compounds there are two main problems: syntactic and semantic attachment. The hypotheses for syntactic attachment are (i) to combine the two rightmost nouns together first, and then attach each previous one, in order, to this combination (right-associativity; see figure 1.2); (ii) perform left-associative analysis as in figure 1.3. (The principles of left- and right-associativity are discussed in Hausser 1988, 1989.)

No determination of syntactic attachment can be performed based on purely syntactic knowledge. For instance, one will need to know that napkins are usually

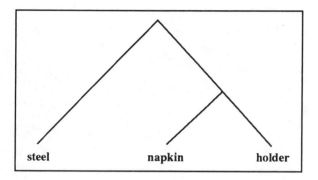

Figure 1.2: **A right-associative structure.**

not made of steel. In fact, in a more general case even the above hypotheses appear to be too simplistic, as demonstrated by the example in figure 1.4.

The problems of *semantic* attachment in general deal with establishing the exact relationship between a phrase head and each of its modifiers. At the level of noun phrases, for instance, we need to understand *big black wooden spoon* as follows:

```
[spoon
    size: big
    material: wood
    color: black]
```

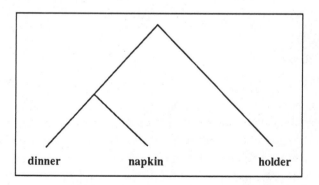

Figure 1.3: **A left-associative structure.**

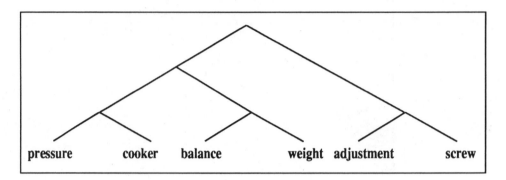

Figure 1.4: **A hybrid compound-noun structure.**

On the other hand, *black Monday* will be analyzed as:

```
[day
    day-of-the-week: Monday
    speaker-attitude: negative]
```

and *wooden face* as:

```
[face
    expression: none]
```

Translation correlates for lexical units in the above examples cannot be determined without taking into account the context (that is, in this case, the results of semantic attachment). At the level of sentences, the semantic attachment process for *Supplies were airlifted* must yield the following:

```
[deliver
  agent: <unknown>
  theme: supplies
  instrument: airplane]
```

The same analysis will be produced for the input sentence *An airlift delivered supplies* and other possible paraphrases. Thus, semantic analysis does not directly follow from syntactic analysis of the surface form of an utterance.

Generally, of course, mapping from syntactic dependency structures into semantic ones involves ambiguous cases like, for example, *the IBM lecture*, which cannot be treated without pragmatic knowledge, that is, knowledge of trans-sentential as well as extralinguistic context.[4] This mapping problem ranks with the lexical disambiguation problem as a major task of semantic analysis. A number of semantic interpreters have been developed to address large subsets of these problems (see, e.g., Lytinen 1987; Hirst 1987; Fass 1988; Kee et al. 1991; etc.). If these problems are not solved, determination of translation correlates cannot be accomplished automatically.

Another problem in source language analysis is referential ambiguity resolution. Consider the translation of the following from English into French.

(1.4)   He took the book from the table and read it.

It is imperative to apply the semantic case-role constraint that books and not tables are legitimate fillers of the "patient" case of the verb *to read*. In this way the pronoun *it* will be translated in the masculine *le* as opposed to the feminine *la* (for table).

Other important problems for analysis include the following:

- *Metaphor and metonymy understanding* (cf. Carbonell 1982; Fass and Wilks 1983). Metaphors are not reserved for poetic texts; they are prevalent in all styles of writing and in all domains (see, for instance, Lakoff and Johnson 1980, for a survey). A machine translation system must know whether the systems of metaphorical comparisons among languages are similar and whether they can, therefore, be translated directly. For instance, the Spanish metaphor *de golpe* must be translated into English as *suddenly* and not rendered literally as *of a hit*.

- *Problems due to ill-formed input* (cf. Carbonell and Hayes 1983; Weischedel and Ramshaw 1987).

- *Ellipsis*. The fragment (due to Carberry 1985) in (1.5a) cannot be translated into, say, Russian without understanding that the second (elliptical) sentence actually means something like *Can you please give me this money in bills of large denomination?* In Russian the noun phrase for *large denominations* should be put in the instrumental case, and without resolving the ellipsis there is no way of achieving this result. The appropriate Russian for the second sentence is given in (1.5b), with the noun phrase underscored.

---

[4] *IBM lecture* can mean "lecture given by IBM people," "lecture given at IBM," "lecture sponsored by IBM" and so forth.

(1.5) a. I would like to withdraw $300. Large denominations only, please.

   b. (Ne mogli by vy dat' mne den'gi) bol'shimi kupjurami, pozhalujsta.
      [(Could you give me the money in) large denominations, please]

This sampling of problems in machine translation-oriented analysis is far from complete. Its purpose is simply to demonstrate that in the general case, it is impossible to achieve high-quality, fully automatic translation without relatively deep understanding of the source text. To hope otherwise is a delusion.

1.4.2 Does an MT Program Really Need to Understand the Source Text Fully?

Of course, a trivial answer to this question is negative—let the program understand as much as it can, and human help will then be requested in producing the necessary level of understanding. In general, however, the entire burden of understanding cannot be assigned to a human helper, as it merely transforms the translation task into an interpretation one requiring just as much human invention. Instead, we need minimal human intervention for those aspects of semantic analysis that are most difficult to automate but still may be necessary for accurate translation.

In many current MT systems dedicated to a small domain, most if not all ambiguities are treated by a combination of syntactic and semantic restrictions that simplify the analysis. However, as the machine translation systems become larger, and especially with the success of the recently popular research in (semi-) automatic transformation of on-line human-oriented dictionaries into machine-oriented dictionaries, one cannot expect to avoid ambiguity forever.

Some MT developers hope that machine translation systems would be able in some cases to preserve the input ambiguities in the target language text, for instance, by translating prepositional phrases separately and ordering them in the same order as in the original sentence or by translating a personal pronoun with a direct correlate without looking for an antecedent.

(1.6) a. I saw a man on the hill with a telescope.

   b. J'ai vu un homme sur la colline avec un telescope.

   c. Ja uvidel čeloveka na xolme s teleskopom.

   d. Ja uvidel čeloveka na xolme v teleskop.

In this well-known example, translation in French will work, because both the "possession" and "instrument" prepositional meanings can be rendered by the same preposition in English and French. In the case of Russian, however, if the attachment is not resolved, there will be no way of deciding which of the two variant translations to choose. (Note that without the use of a suprasentential context it is impossible to disambiguate the sentence.) Example (1.4) demonstrated the need to resolve pronominal reference for accurate translation.

In limited-scope MT systems, which perform translations for a single language pair in a single direction and within a small domain, there is indeed a possibility of enumerating most of the cases in which disambiguation will actually be redundant. This is most emphatically not the case in larger, multilingual, multidomain, wide-scope systems. The only way steadily to produce adequate-quality results is to account for the input text ambiguities in a regular, general way. In fact, the task of comparing phenomena in a single pair of languages with the view of determining possibilities of retaining ambiguities is in itself a complex, time-consuming task. Indeed, an entire scientific field, contrastive linguistics, is devoted to such types of questions, albeit its results and objectives are not restricted to machine translation. It seems logical to consider spending this research time not on finding ways of bypassing the central research issues in the field, but rather on tackling them head on and continuing work on semantic and pragmatic analysis of natural language texts. This latter type of work will be useful in multiple domains and languages, and will not have to be repeated for each new language pair and each new domain.

1.5 Knowledge-Based Machine Translation

The machine translation paradigm we describe in this book has come to be known as *knowledge-based machine translation*. The central principle underlying this approach is the stress on functionally complete understanding of the meaning of the source text as a prerequisite to successful translation. The term *functionally* means that the meaning representation should be (merely) sufficient for translation to a number of languages, rather than sufficient for *total understanding*, which entails a more complete, human-like inferential process for understanding all implicit and explicit information.

Architecturally, knowledge-based machine translation systems belong to the class of interlingua- (or pivot-) based systems, in which translation is basically a two-step process (analysis and generation). (This is in contrast to the class of systems that involve three steps—analysis, source-to-target language transfer and generation—and are therefore called transfer systems.) Example of interlingua systems that are not knowledge-based are CETA (Vauquois and Boitet 1985), DLT (Witkam 1983) and Rosetta (Landsbergen 1989). The main difference between such systems and knowledge-based machine translation ones is the expected depth of source language analysis and the reliance of KBMT systems on explicit representation of world knowledge.

The knowledge-based machine translation tradition in which we work is relatively recent. The first system of this kind was developed by Yorick Wilks at Stanford University (Wilks 1973). Further experiments were conducted by Jaime Carbonell, Rich Cullingford and Anatole Gershman at Yale University (Carbonell et al. 1981) and Sergei Nirenburg, Victor Raskin and Allen Tucker at Colgate University (Nirenburg et al. 1985). Larger-scale development work followed, and a number of pilot knowledge-based machine translation systems have been implemented. The major efforts included ATLAS-II (Uchida 1989 a and b), PIVOT (Muraki 1989), ULTRA (Farwell and Wilks 1991), the KBMT system for doctor-patient communication (Tomita et al. 1987), KBMT-89 (Goodman and Nirenburg 1991) and DIONYSUS (e.g., Nirenburg and Defrise in press, a and b; Meyer et al. 1990; Carlson and Nirenburg 1990). Some other systems (e.g., HICATS/JE, Kaji 1989) are using some features of the knowledge-based approach (such as semantic primitives for organizing the dictionary structure) while still maintaining the overall transfer architecture.

Most of the material in this book relies on our own experience in knowledge-based machine translation and therefore the examples of particular knowledge structures and processing components are drawn from the three knowledge-based machine translation systems developed at the Center for Machine Translation at Carnegie Mellon University.

Traditionally, the types of meanings represented in knowledge-based natural language processing systems have been almost entirely propositional. A large number of nonpropositional—pragmatic and discourse—meanings, such as thematic structure, speech act, modality, discourse cohesion, speaker attitudes and so on, were not overtly represented. In knowledge-based machine translation such information traditionally has been left for future research. In transfer systems they are not addressed either, but there is an implicit hope that the nonpropositional information will be transferred. This hope is based on the observation that often no special processing need be done other than simple transfer of lexical clues or, sometimes, a structural transformation. Such an approach, however, is prone to error and does not support any paraphrasing capability necessary when text-level stylistic decisions are treated. We have argued elsewhere (Nirenburg and Carbonell 1987) for the necessity of incorporating nonpropositional knowledge into

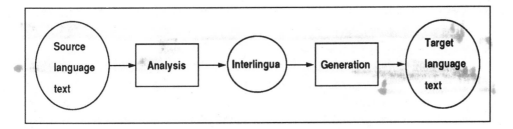

Figure 1.5: **The flow of control in KBMT systems.**

the representation of the results of text analysis. We give a detailed description of our approach to representation of text meaning in chapter 2.

Recent experience in knowledge-based machine translation suggests that systems adhering to this paradigm can be useful beyond limited sublanguages and without a heavy postediting burden. This can be seen in the ULTRA (Farwell and Wilks 1991) and ATLAS-II (Uchida 1989 a and b) systems. With special attention paid to acquisition of large knowledge bases and with the advent of new tools (including representation languages, human-computer interfaces, database and knowledge-base management systems, etc.) the practicality of the knowledge-based approach is growing steadily. Since a totally comprehensive automatic analysis of meaning is not yet feasible, and the attainment of this goal will remain the central objective of computational linguistics for years to come, a practical knowledge-based machine translation system will be necessarily of a hybrid nature—it will attain a lesser depth of understanding and often include a measure of human involvement. However, while in transfer systems human involvement invariably means post-editing, human-aided knowledge-based systems may use human help *during* the process of translation, to finalize the representations of the meanings in a source language text. It is expected that the target language texts produced from such improved meaning representations will be of comparable quality with translations produced by human translators knowledgeable in the subject domain.

The flow of control in KBMT systems is illustrated in figure 1.5. In brief, the input or source language text is processed by a battery of text analysis programs. Using the knowledge recorded in the source language grammar and lexicon, these programs (after several stages of processing) produce an expression (usually called *interlingua text* or ILT) in a specially defined unambiguous textual-meaning representation language. Elements of ILTs are produced based on lexical, grammatical and pragmatic meanings extracted from the source text. Some ILT elements are instances of concepts in a domain model. Some others are values of various semantic and pragmatic properties suggested as necessary components of ILT. Very generally, ILTs are hierarchical structures of clause-level representation units connected through domain and textual relations from a predefined set.

At present, complete ILT cannot be produced fully automatically, except in restricted domains. Systems therefore use an interactive "augmentor" (the concept of such a program was first demonstrated by Kay 1973). As knowledge about language processing grows, the role of the augmentor will be expected to diminish.

A complete ILT produced jointly by the analyzer and the augmentor is passed on to the generator suite of programs, which includes a text planner, a lexical selection module and a syntactic realizer. The generator uses a TL lexicon and grammar and other heuristic knowledge sources necessary for generation.

The purpose of the above discussion of our view of meaning-based machine translation is not to give a complete or adequate account of its workings. As such, it certainly fails. Our intent is to illustrate the complexity of system organization, which cannot be readily summarized in the triangular icon of the interlingua approach. In a narrow sense, the "interlingua" in our systems is the set of all well-formed expressions (ILTs) in the textual-meaning representation language. In a broader sense, it should also include the domain model underlying (most entries in) the lexicons.

1.5.1   Transfer or Interlingua?

Three major types of MT systems have been traditionally recognized—direct, transfer and interlingua. Historically, the knowledge-based machine translation approach is a descendant of interlingua-oriented machine translation of old. Indeed, the emphasis on multilingual translation, and the resultant insistence on separating the source and target languages in the translation process, remains an important methodological precept in knowledge-based machine translation, just as it was in earlier interlingua approaches. However, there are important differences between our view of MT and the interlingua projects that are the precursors of our efforts (such as CETA, e.g., Vauquois and Boitet 1985). The central point of difference is our position on the depth of source language analysis. The knowledge-based machine translation approach requires a much deeper level of source language analysis. In fact, depth of analysis leading to increasingly superior semantic disambiguation is the hallmark of knowledge-based machine translation, regardless of whether it is purely interlingua or fully automated.

Direct MT systems relied on finding direct correspondences between source and target lexical units, and have been justly criticized for their *ad hoc* quality; they have, therefore, lost their scientific standing.[5] So at present the choice of architectures for machine translation systems is reduced to the transfer and knowledge-based/interlingua approaches.

In this section we will comment on the essential differences between transfer-based and knowledge-based machine translation. We suggest that the traditional paradigmatic distinctions are possibly less important methodologically than the differences in attitude to meaning analysis and linguistic coverage. A more detailed methodological analysis of the meaning-oriented approach to machine translation is given in the next chapter.

Transfer systems involve a measure of target language–independent analysis of the source language. This analysis is usually syntactic, and its result allows substituting source language lexical units with target language lexical units *in context*. That is, it permits taking into account the types of syntactic sentence constituents in which lexical units appear.

In interlingua systems the source language and the target language are never in direct contact. The processing in such systems has traditionally been understood to involve two major stages: (i) representing the meaning of a source language text in an artificial unambiguous formal language, *interlingua*, and then (ii) expressing this meaning using the lexical units and syntactic constructions of the target language. Few interlingua systems have been fully implemented because of the very significant complexity (both theoretical and empirical) of extracting a "deep" meaning from a natural language text.

The major distinction between the interlingua- and transfer-based systems is, in fact, not so much the presence or absence of a bilingual lexicon but rather the attitude toward comprehensive analysis of meaning. In practice, those machine translation researchers who believe in translating without deep understanding (or perhaps who believe in the unattainability of deep understanding) of the source language text, tend to prefer the transfer paradigm. The price they must pay for avoiding meaning analysis is the need for an extra step in the translation process, namely intensive postediting.

Inherently, a transfer system can involve many levels of meaning analysis. This becomes clear when one considers that different transfer-based systems have widely varying levels at which transfer occurs—from simple phrase-structure trees to detailed representations that use subcategorization patterns and even selectional restrictions. There is a new trend in transfer-based machine translation to downplay

---

[5]Some of the current commercial MT systems, notably SYSTRAN, were built using the direct MT technology and are currently being converted to have separate analysis, transfer and generation components.

the need for structural transfer, that is, the stage of transforming standard syntactic structures of the source language into the corresponding target language structures. This is in part due to the prevalence of grammatical theories that eschew transformations and seek universally applicable representations of grammatical structures and relations. This trend is essentially interlingua in nature. Transfer-based systems can also deal with lexical semantics; the language in which the meanings of source language lexical units are expressed is often the target language itself. This can be implemented through a bilingual lexicon featuring disambiguation information. The recent movement toward "deep transfer" (see, e.g., work on Eurotra (Arnold and Sadler 1991); Tsujii and Fujita, 1990) is, in essence, a movement toward an interlingua architecture.

In interlingua systems, the meanings are represented in a formal language (such as that of frames or first-order logic). This is because such a language is better suited for the formulation of disambiguation rules necessary for producing an adequate meaning of a source language text, in part because it was specifically designed for this purpose.[6]

Distinctions between the transfer and the interlingua approaches are best drawn at a theoretical level. In reality, when practical systems are built, much of the work will be the same for both approaches (notably, the grammars and programs for syntactic analysis and synthesis). For some other types of work the very nature of the material dictates the necessity of methodological compromises—for instance, some source language lexical units for which the interlingua does not, at the moment, have an adequate representation can be treated in a transfer-like manner in a practical knowledge-based machine translation system. At the same time, for those (very frequent) cases when there is no possibility of direct transfer of a lexical unit or a syntactic structure between two languages, a transfer system would benefit by trying to express the meaning of such lexical units and syntactic structures in an internal unambiguous form and construct a target language correlate from this more detailed and transparent representation. The requirements of practical use, indeed, pose similar difficulties for both approaches—consider such universal problems as ill-formed input, special symbols and codes, document layout preservation, translatable material in figures and so on. ATLAS-II (Uchida 1989 a and b) is an example of a hybrid system that displays features from both major approaches, though philosophically it is an interlingua system.

---

[6]A very good example of what happens when an interlingua system chooses a human-oriented language as the interlingua is the DLT project (Witkam 1989). This project's researchers selected Esperanto as the interlingua and subsequently had to undertake a significant overhaul of the language in order to support the types of processing that an interlingua must support.

1.5.2 Nature and Size of Knowledge Bases

Knowledge-based machine translation must be supported by world knowledge and by linguistic semantic knowledge about meanings of lexical units and their combinations. A KBMT knowledge base must be able to represent not only a general, taxonomic domain of object types such as "a car is a kind of a vehicle," "a door handle is a part of a door," "artifacts are characterized by (among other properties) the property *made-by*"; it must also represent knowledge about particular instances of object types (e.g., "IBM" can be included into the domain model as a marked instance of the object type "corporation") as well as instances of (potentially complex) event types (e.g., the election of George Bush as president of the United States is a marked instance of the complex action "to-elect"). The ontological part of the knowledge base takes the form of a multihierarchy of concepts connected through taxonomy-building links, such as *is-a, part-of* and some others. We call the resulting structure a multihierarchy because concepts are allowed to have multiple parents on each link type.

In a world model, the ontological concepts can be first subdivided into objects, events, forces (introduced to account for intentionless agents) and properties. Properties can be further subdivided into relations and attributes. Relations will be defined as mappings among concepts (e.g., "belongs-to" is a relation, since it maps an object into the set {*human *organization}), while attributes will be defined as mappings of concepts into specially defined value sets (e.g., "temperature" is an attribute that maps physical objects into values on the semiopen scale [0,*], with the granularity of degrees on the Kelvin scale). Concepts are typically represented as frames whose slots are properties fully defined in the system.

Special interactive tools are required for the acquisition and maintenance of domain models. An example of one such system of tools is Ontos (see, e.g., Nirenburg et al. 1988b; Monarch and Nirenburg 1988), used in KBMT projects at Carnegie Mellon University.

Domain models are a necessary part of any knowledge-based system, not only a knowledge-based machine translation one. Indeed, a typical configuration of an advanced knowledge-based natural language processing application is as shown in figure 1.5. This is a generalization of the structure of a knowledge-based machine translation system (which will be seen in figure 5.4 (p. 130)). In figure 1.6, the double arrows on the left represent the flow of data from the input text through various internal representations to an output text, and the flow of control in the system. The thin arrows represent the flow of reference data between the various data repositories ("static knowledge sources") and the various processing modules. Among the static knowledge sources are natural language grammars, machine-tractable dictionaries and the system's domain model(s) on which the semantic components of these dictionaries are based. The processing modules are, in order of application, the analysis module, the reasoning module and the generation module. The analysis module has the task of obtaining a natural language input (which could be a text or a dialogue) and producing a representation of its meaning (an interlingua text, such as that discussed in chapter 3); this representation should be sufficiently detailed for a particular reasoning module (e.g., a question-answering system, an information retrieval system, a machine translation system, etc.) to function successfully. Depending on the purpose of a particular system, the analyzer must perform some or all of the following tasks on any given input: morphological analysis, syntactic analysis, lexical-semantic analysis, semantic dependency determination, treatment of reference and determination of pragmatic parameters (such as speech-act information, discourse cohesion, speaker attitudes and knowledge about speech situation).

The task of the generation module is to take an internal representation of the text produced by the reasoning component and realize its meaning in the chosen target language. Depending on the type of input and the type of application, the generation component can be as basic and primitive as a selector of prefabricated "canned" messages or it can involve a variety of interrelated component tasks such as target text sentence boundary and configuration determination; lexical selection of the target language's open- and closed-class lexical items; determination of the syntactic structure of target language clauses; introduction of anaphoric, deictic and elliptical ways of rendering input meanings; ordering target language elements (e.g., ordering adjectives in a noun phrase); realization of the various pragmatic factors (e.g., politeness levels, verbosity/lapidarity, discourse cohesion clues, speech acts, etc.); and syntactic and morphological decisions.

The reasoning component of knowledge-based natural language processing systems differs dramatically from application to application. For instance, if the system is an advanced spelling checker, the analyzer will be constrained to dealing with inflectional and possibly derivational morphology, will operate with a single word at a time, and the result of the analysis will be either an "OK" message or an error flag, optionally, with suggestions for correction. The reasoning system in this case will obtain an incorrectly spelled word and will attempt to analyze it with the help of its internal knowledge about typical misspellings. This knowledge will constitute the ontology or the domain model for this particular application. The results of this operation will be passed on to the generator, which will produce appropriate messages for the user, possibly through a set of canned messages, together with possible orthographic corrections.

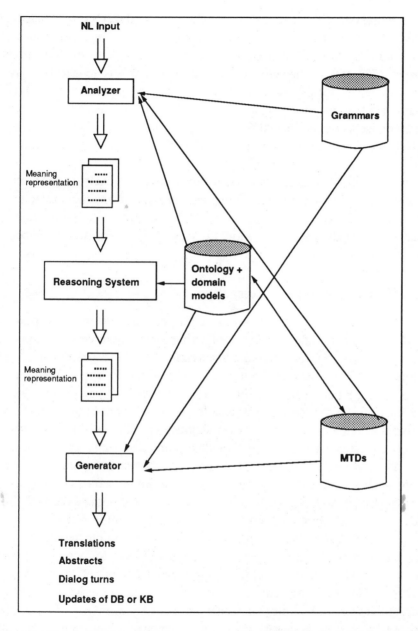

Figure 1.6: **The role of knowledge sources, including machine-tractable dictionaries, in a comprehensive NLP system. Except for the link between the ontology and the lexicons, single arrows represent data flow from static knowledge sources to processing modules.**

In a natural language interface to a database, the analyzer's task is translating a natural language input into a query in a data manipulation language, such as QUEL. The reasoning system picks up this query and performs its instructions, returning an answer. The task of the generator in such a system is to render the answer in a form convenient for the user. In some systems the output is produced using a standard data manipulation language, so that the generator becomes spurious. In some other such systems canned responses (filled templates of answers) are used. Finally, some of the interfaces perform actual generation of responses in a natural language.

In a knowledge-based machine translation system, the analyzer performs morphological, syntactic, semantic and pragmatic analysis of the input text, and produces an internal representation from which the generator later produces a target language text. In such a configuration, the reasoning system is a component of a source text disambiguation process.

1.5.3   Human-Computer Interaction

The idea of human-aided machine translation occurred to machine translation researchers very early on. As mentioned earlier, human intervention can occur in a number of ways, see, for instance a discussion in Nirenburg 1987a or Carbonell and Tomita 1987. In the KBMT approach the use of human help is typically in the form of having a human user verify, improve and finalize the system's decisions during analysis. The system may be unable (due to a lack of knowledge) to prefer one candidate reading of the input over another. Or, alternatively, its knowledge might be too restrictive, ruling out all of the candidate readings. In such situations, human intervention may become necessary. The human-computer interface that supports such a clarification interaction has been implemented on a small scale in the MIND machine translation project at the RAND Corporation (Kay 1973; the module was called "disambiguator"). A device of this sort was also discussed by Tomita (1986c). A slightly larger interactive module was implemented in KBMT-89 where it was known as the "augmentor" (Brown 1991). In fact, the augmentor serves as more than an interface, providing a general filter between analysis and generation. The interactive component of the augmentor queries the user about the residual lexical ambiguities—residual problems in attachment of prepositional phrases and subordinate clauses, properties on which nominal modifiers are linked to the heads in noun-noun compounds and so on—but only in the case when domain knowledge proves insufficient for automated disambiguation.

1.5.4 MT as an Experimental Testbed for Computational Linguistics

In addition to its utility as a machine translation shell, knowledge-based machine translation systems can be very profitably used as research tools and testbeds in computational linguistics and artificial intelligence. To illustrate briefly:

- Knowledge-based machine translation provides an excellent tool for devising and testing new and more powerful specialized semantic-interpretation algorithms, such as noun-noun compound resolution or prepositional phrase attachment. With more types of semantic and pragmatic knowledge appearing in the knowledge representation, more specialized *microtheories* (Nirenburg and Defrise forthcoming, b; Nirenburg and Pustejovsky 1988) will be devised and/or incorporated into the process in order to deal with each phenomenon in a computationally tractable manner.

- An additional advantage of using knowledge-based machine translation as a research vehicle is that, being a *comprehensive* system, it allows immediate testing of new components, such as a new parser or a generator, in the context where actual output can be obtained and evaluated.

- The interface component of a KBMT system can serve as a medium for building other interfaces, notably for the purpose of computer-aided instruction and, in particular, for teaching foreign languages (see, e.g., Levin et al. forthcoming). The interface can be also very useful in machine learning systems, especially those studying learning from text or learning by being told, or in systems that investigate hybrid learning processes that involve natural language.

- Components of a KBMT system can be individually recycled. The analysis module, for instance, can be useful for natural language interfaces to complex applications such as expert systems. More comprehensive understanding-and-generation systems can also be used as components of a system modeling a cognitive agent—alongside other modules, such as planning and problem solving, perception and action-simulation components.

- The ontological and domain knowledge in a knowledge-based machine translation system can serve as a tool for research in the area of acquisition and maintenance of large knowledge bases. In fact, the Ontos acquisition and maintenance system developed for KBMT-89 (Goodman and Nirenburg 1991) is already being used to build domain models in the fields of molecular biology, law, financial transactions and computer software in the framework of projects in the areas of diagnostic expert systems, qualitative process theory and computer-aided instruction. The domain models can also serve as the underlying substrate for a hypertext-type index to a large corpus of human-readable information.

- The computing technology embodied by a knowledge-based machine translation system can be used in other applications. One of the areas in which knowledge-based machine translation can yield immediate practical results is design and development of high-quality translator's workstations. The interaction environment can be extended to include additional types of human-computer interaction. Additional knowledge sources can be connected to the system (for instance, human-readable dictionaries and encyclopedias). And the presence of working analyzer and generator modules will allow the system to suggest acceptable solutions (or informed choices) to the human translator; this is a feature not present in any current translator's workstation.

- Outside of machine translation proper, the technology developed for a knowledge-based machine translation system is readily usable in applications that require different types of inputs and/or outputs to a natural language processor. Thus, instead of forwarding an interlingua text to the generator, one can pass it on to a special reasoning program that will produce an abstract of the input text, or answer questions based on it, or categorize the input text into one of a number of taxonomic classes (see, e.g., Hayes and Weinstein 1990). Knowledge-based machine translation systems can also be reconfigured for supporting natural language interfaces to database systems. Indeed, if a data manipulation (query) language is substituted for the interlingua, the task of query formulation can become quite similar to that of analyzing a natural language input for translation.

1.6   Reader's Guide

The rest of this book is laid out according to the following plan:

Chapter 2, "Treatment of Meaning in MT Systems," locates our approach to semantic phenomena in terms of a discussion of the differences between the transfer and the interlingua approaches. We discuss a number of criticisms of the interlingua approach.

Next, in chapter 3, we describe the knowledge-representation language used in our KBMT research. The description largely uses the example of the TAMERLAN meaning-representation language.

In chapter 4 we discuss the structure and function of the lexicons in knowledge-based machine translation. Of course, KBMT lexicons require much more information than do lexicons for other systems because of the more extensive requirements on the availability of large amounts of diversified knowledge for decision-making.

The process of mapping between a natural language text and its representation is the topic of chapter 5. Here we discuss the key roles of morphological, syntactic, semantic and pragmatic or discourse analysis.

Chapter 6 offers an introduction to natural language generation in light of the requirements imposed by knowledge-based machine translation. We give particular attention to the issue of text planning in generation for machine translation.

Speech translation constitutes a significant part of modern MT research. In chapter 7 we review work in speech recognition and its use in systems that translate between spoken languages in real time. Efforts to integrate speech and natural language analysis in such systems are assessed, including the complexity and benefits of such enterprises.

While fully automatic translation is of course the central goal of MT research, there has been a great deal of progress and interest in using the methods, techniques and tools developed in that research to assist human translators. A development program aimed at creating a knowledge-based language processing environment for machine-aided translation is the topic of chapter 8.

Finally, in chapter 9, we note and evaluate some major trends in machine translation and offer thoughts about where these might lead. The goal here is not to make definitive predictions, but rather to present a meditation on the future of an exciting discipline—a discipline that despite its youth offers extraordinary potential and human interest.

Chapter 2

Treatment of Meaning in MT Systems

2.1   Transfer versus Interlingua

Fully automated, high-quality MT systems can be developed only if a realistic way to treat meaning in natural languages is found. This chapter analyzes a set of positions on the treatment of meaning in machine translation, which we consider the crucial point of difference among MT approaches. We suggest that the methodological debate between the interlingua and the transfer approaches to MT is, in fact, misplaced. The meaning-based approach to MT can, in principle, be explored using either of these architectures or—perhaps more promisingly—a combination thereof.

At the methodological level, polemics about the state of the art in MT are most often couched in terms of the differences and tensions between the transfer and the interlingua approaches. Over the years, a great deal of folklore has accumulated about the pros and cons of each of these MT paradigms. We believe that the discourse on this topic is not as organized as it should be. A number of public claims and opinions on the subject have been expressed, but they have not been thoroughly analyzed. Unfortunately, most such discussions have appeared only in prefaces and introductions to books and articles on machine translation. After mentioning the predominant methodological issue on the first page and briefly identifying their own positions, MT authors typically plunge into descriptions of their own systems or models without further analysis of the methodological issues. Under these circumstances, it is not surprising that the methodological argument is not conducted at an adequate level of detail.

Even in discussions devoted specifically to the "transfer versus interlingua" issue (such as, for instance, the panels on this topic at MT Summit I in Japan or the 1989 MT workshop in Manchester) many of the arguments remain too general and iconic. As a result, a discrepancy can be detected between the methodological beliefs held by MT practitioners and the actual (theoretical and practical) preferences and results in the field. Even at the methodological level, criticisms are often directed at opinions that are not, in fact, held or defended by one's opponents.

Judgments about paradigms may differ depending on the specific profile of a system. MT is simultaneously an empirical discipline and a technological pursuit. Depending on the primary direction of research and development in a project, different criteria should be used to evaluate the utility and quality of systems developed in it. There are (i) MT systems in regular use, (ii) MT system prototypes, (iii) proof-of-concept systems which demonstrate the utility of a theoretical or descriptive approach to MT or a component process in machine translation (e.g., syntactic analysis, treatment of referential meaning, etc.) and (iv) technological testbeds for producing MT systems (including specialized knowledge acquisition interfaces, debugging tools, control environments, etc.).

One must also distinguish between evaluations of particular projects and evaluations of entire approaches. If it is claimed that Project A used Approach X and failed, it does not necessarily follow that Approach X is bad. Similarly, the claim that Project B used Approach Y and succeeded in a very limited prototype does not in itself mean that Approach Y is superior. One reason for this caution is that large MT projects tend to feature elements from several MT paradigms. Therefore, it is often a gross generalization to call a particular project purely interlingua or purely transfer or, for that matter, purely syntactic or lexical. A finer-grained taxonomy of MT approaches is needed. This is a central methodological point of this section.

Actually, the components of an interlingua text are produced by and informed by several interconnecting subsystems. In our knowledge-based MT system, KBMT-89 (Goodman and Nirenburg 1991), the interlingua is created by an analyzer that consists of a set of programs and knowledge sources, including source-language lexicons and grammars, mapping rules for syntactic features and structures, and an ontology or domain model. The generation side of the triangle is equally complex.

We would like to argue that the ultimate point of contention in methodological debates among MT researchers is not so much the differences between the transfer and interlingua approaches but rather the attitude to treatment of meaning. It so happens that, as a rule, those MT workers who de-emphasize the importance of meaning extraction tend to favor transfer-oriented systems, while those who insist on understanding as a prerequisite of translation tend to prefer interlingua-oriented ones.

In what follows, we discuss several opinions that are frequently put forward in arguments against meaning-oriented MT. The following list summarizes these opinions and puts them in a logical chain of arguments which goes from extremely strong and general criticisms toward more specific and limited ones. The list is by no means complete, but it is representative. After presenting the list of criticisms, we evaluate each in turn and in greater or lesser detail. Of course, the discussion is primarily in terms of knowledge-based machine translation, and so this approach will enjoy the most attention.

1. Translation is *not possible*. If it is, then

2. Meaning is *not required* for translation. If it is, then

3. Meaning is *not definable*. If it is, then

4. Meaning in different languages is different and *not compatible*. If it is compatible, then

5. One *cannot represent* this meaning in a language-independent way because

   - the language of representation will be heavily slanted toward one particular natural language;
   - it is difficult to come up with the necessary set of language-independent primitives and to ensure completeness of meaning representation.

   Furthermore,

6. It is not possible to base meaning representations on a complete logical calculus. Therefore, one can never *prove* the correctness of any representation, particularly that it is free of contradiction, or that the same meanings will be always represented similarly. If constraints of this sort are demonstrated to be manageable or unnecessary, then

7. It is impossible to ensure that the meaning can *actually be extracted* from the source-language text and rendered in the representation language; at least, it is not possible to extract meaning *completely automatically*.

8. Even if meaning-based translation systems can be built, they will produce not translations but rather paraphrases of source language texts.

2.2   On the Possibility of Translation

A rich history attaches to philosophical arguments against the possibility of translation as a re-representation of meaning. Of course, the *locus classicus* is Willard Van Orman Quine's *Word and Object* and his theory of radical translation. The point of radical translation was that "manuals for translating one language into another can be set up in divergent ways, all compatible with the totality of speech dispositions, yet incompatible with one another. In countless places they will diverge in giving, as their respective translations of a sentence of the one language, sentences of the other language which stand to each other in no plausible sort of equivalence however loose ..." (Quine 1960, 27). In other words, there is no single uniquely true translation manual.

Quine's behavioristic translation manuals may be understood loosely as analogues of the grammars, lexicons and programs of machine translation. The idea of radical translation was not that it is impossible to translate natural languages—humans do it all the time—but that what is translated is not the "same meaning." In other words, there are no meanings *qua* meanings to translate: The alleged absence of independent identity conditions for meanings entails that there are no language-neutral semantic entities. Put still differently, a single, independent "meaning" cannot be a shared attribute or property of two sentences, even if they "mean" the same thing.

There are at least two responses to this:

First, it is mistaken.[1] As Katz (1988, 252) puts it, "Quine cannot be among those who, like Kurt Gödel, terminated an entire philosophical program." At center and in brief, Quine is concerned about the purported absence of controls or constaints on the matching of expressions as synonymous. Katz suggests that we receive from *Word and Object* no argument at all against the possibility of such independent controls but, rather, a tacit pointer back to "Two Dogmas of Empiricism" (Quine 1953) and the argument there against synonymy. But *that* argument rests on the assumption that "substitution criteria are the proper way to clarify concepts in linguistics" (p. 240) and these criteria are not defended independently of Bloomfieldian linguistics. In any case, as defenders of interlingua representations, we can provisionally offer a solid constraint on interlingua meaning

---

[1]The following is adapted from the longer discussion in Goodman and Nirenburg, forthcoming.

representations—the judgments of bilingual or multilingual humans. To be sure, this raises additional issues, but they are not directly to the point of Quine's critique.

Second, it is just not clear how to apply Quine's arguments to machine translation as such. The goal of Quine and some of his followers was mainly to demonstrate that scientific theories are underdetermined by evidence, and it would be specious to transport the issues and arguments too quickly to our domain. If the problem of machine translation is understood as an empirical problem, then we should be loathe to presume on philosophical grounds the result of an inchoate inquiry. As Quine so clearly recognized elsewhere, we can err by citing a philosophical or logical "truth" and forswearing that the world can be otherwise. Even if an interlingua as an empirical posit were underdetermined it would do no damage to our underlying thesis, or at least do no more damage than underdetermination does to other scientific posits. This point could be quite congenial to Quine, at least more recently:

> The critique of meaning leveled by my thesis of indeterminacy of translation is meant to clear away misconceptions, but the result is not nihilism. Translation remains and is indispensable. Indeterminacy means not that there is no acceptable translation, but that there are many. A good manual of translation fits all checkpoints of verbal behavior, and what does not surface at any checkpoint can do no harm (Quine 1987, 9).

2.3 Understanding and Translation

It has been suggested that meaning is not required for machine translation. The idea is that a source language sentence might be translated automatically into a target language sentence by *statistical* means. The idea is as old as MT itself and attracted Warren Weaver in the 1940s, motivating the early approaches at the RAND Corporation and the National Bureau of Standards through the early 1960s (see de Roeck 1987 and references cited therein).

More recently, Peter Brown et al. (1988, 1990) report on experiments with a statistical approach to machine translation which " ...eschews the use of an intermediate mechanism (language) that would encode the 'meaning' of the source text." This renewal of interest in a statistical approach is difficult to evaluate fully—it is too recent, and important work is still under way. The following remarks are therefore offered solely as preliminary thoughts.

The contention that underlies the approach is that " ... translation ought to be based on a complex glossary of correspondence of fixed locutions" and, more fully,

> Translation can be somewhat naïvely regarded as a three stage process:
>
> (1) Partition the source text into a set of fixed locutions.
>
> (2) Use the glossary plus contextual information to select the corresponding set of fixed locutions in the target language.
>
> (3) Arrange the words of the target fixed locutions into a sequence that forms the target sentence (Brown et al. 1988, 2).

In other words, language in this approach is treated not as a productive system but as a fixed and unproductive set of canned locutions, a view rejected by all schools of modern linguistics. To be sure, such an *ad populum* cannot count as an argument: the statistical approach, though strikingly outside the MT canon, is not *a priori* wrong. However, adopting it, at least in a pure form, entails moving machine translation out of applied science and into pure engineering. But in that event, the criteria for evaluating success and failure are different.

The applicability of an MT system built according to this approach is restricted to the cases where there are vast textual corpora of translation equivalents. But even when such materials are available, completely uninterpreted comparison will lead to errors simply because the human translators who produced the translations in the corpus in the first place do not translate word-for-word or even sentence-for-sentence. The meaning expressed by a lexical unit in the source language can be rendered as an affix or as a syntactic construction in the target language. Nagao (1989a, 6f) writes: " ... although they are infrequently used in European languages, in Japanese there are many words of respect and politeness which reflect the social positions of the speakers, as well as distinctly male or female expressions which lie at the heart of Japanese culture. These are factors which must be considered when translating between Japanese and European languages ... Even if those factors are not explicitly expressed in the target language, they should be inferable from the context, from the psychological state of the speaker, or from the cultural background of the language." It will be virtually impossible for a purely statistical system to detect such phenomena because the correlate is not in the meaning of the words or in syntactic form, but rather is spread over the text.

While it does not seem that a purely statistical approach is adequate to the task of MT, we believe that a statistical component can be very useful in a practical MT system, both as an aid in knowledge acquisition and as a way of testing meaning preferences.

That meaning understanding is not necessary is also maintained by another group of researchers who observe that, for instance, the polysemous Spanish noun *centro* is translated into German as *zentrum* no matter which of the senses of *centro* was used in the SL text (see below). The question then is, why waste time detecting and representing the meaning of the input string when the target language correlate is always the same? Similar claims have been made about syntactic ambiguities (e.g., Pericliev 1984) and ambiguities of prepositional phrase attachment (e.g., Kay 1989).

A typical formulation of this position is given by Ben Ari et al. (1988, 2): "It must be kept in mind that the translation process does not necessarily require full understanding of the text. Many ambiguities may be preserved during translation . . . , and thus should not be presented to the user (human translator) for resolution."

Similarly, Isabelle and Bourbeau (1985, 21) contend that, "Sometimes, it is possible to ignore certain ambiguities, in the hope that the same ambiguities will carry over in translation. This is particularly true in systems like TAUM-AVIATION that deal with only one pair of closely related languages within a severely restricted subdomain. The difficult problem of prepositional phrase attachment, for example, is frequently bypassed in this way. Generally speaking, however, analysis is aimed at producing an unambiguous intermediate representation."

This position is, in fact, a system-completeness argument. It claims that, for a given SL–TL pair and (i) a given set of dictionary senses of each SL word and (ii) recognized SL syntactic patterns, there will be cases in which all the senses of a SL lexical unit will be realized by a single lexical unit in the TL, or an SL syntactic construction can be re-created without change in the TL.

The set of arguments about preserving ambiguity has serious limitations. It is clear, for instance, that *centro ciudad* is best translated in colloquial English not as "city center" but as "downtown." The argument by Pericliev (1984) is supported by a manual analysis of 200 short English phrases and their translations into Bulgarian. No syntactic ambiguity was found in about 150 of these phrases. In about 25 cases ambiguity could be preserved by simple substitution. And the remaining 25 could not be treated this way. Therefore, Pericliev's claims lack generality. Indeed, what does one do with the other 25? Deciding automatically when an ambiguity can be preserved and when it must be resolved is as difficult as resolving the ambiguity and, therefore, the entire paradigm of selective ambiguity resolution is questionable.

Considering the amount of work required to put together a non-trivial MT system, it is quite reasonable to strive to constrain the size of the knowledge acquisition task. At the same time, one must remember that a system strongly relying on the "ambiguity preservation" method, in addition to offering no computational advantage when ambiguity-preserving situations must be identified dynamically, is extremely vulnerable in situations where (i) the lexicon is growing while the system is in use or (ii) when additional languages must be introduced. Every new word sense added to the lexicon carries the potential of ruining the possibility of retaining ambiguity in translation for all previous entries. And this means that extra attention must be paid to the maintenance of the lexicons.

The problem of working with increasingly large dictionaries and grammars remains to be solved for all MT systems, irrespective of the theoretical approaches they follow. There are also cases (especially when very concrete technological terminology is concerned) when knowledge about the field of translation and the authoring style of a particular type of text will lead to the possibility of rendering certain elements of SL through unconditional (and, possibly, multilingual) substitution by TL counterparts. However, actual MT systems will be judged by their "maximum" capabilities in treating complex, not simple, problems.

Some of the MT literature is devoted mostly to design and metalevel (not to say MT-theoretical) issues (King 1981; Arnold and des Tombe 1987; Warwick 1987). Typically, such contributions suggest or discuss an abstract theory of translation as a series of transformations among representations. A typical series of definitions follows:

> The following diagram forms a good basis for the study of representations in a transfer-based translation system:

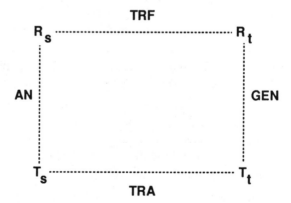

> In [the above figure], Ts and Tt are texts, where a language is regarded as a set of texts. TRA is a binary relation, consisting of pairs of texts

[Ts, Tt] where Tt is a translation of Ts. So, given two languages, SL and TL, TRA $\leq$ SL $\times$ TL. We introduce, furthermore, ρ which is a set of representations of some kind. Rs and Rt are both members of this set. We will write R when it is unimportant whether we are dealing with Rs or Rt, or when the context makes it clear which is intended (Johnson et al. 1985, 158).

In other abstract definitions of the translation process the number of transformations is larger, but in none of them is the question of semantic ambiguity dealt with centrally. Thus, for instance, having sketched an abstract view of the translation relation, Whitelock (1989, 6) characteristically adds: "One question I have not touched on here is the question of ambiguity. What I have been talking about is a many-many relation 'possible translation' which may be computed monotonically from the axioms of the grammar and lexicon of the languages concerned. Optimally, this is viewed as a totally different question from determining the best translation, given an unbounded amount of real world knowledge, discourse context, etc. Computing this relation requires inference which is presumably defeasible."

Intrinsic in this statement is the opinion that what the understanding of meaning adds to the quality of translation is the possibility of getting to the "best" translation, as opposed, presumably, to an "adequate" though not best one. We believe that the translation relation suggested by Whitelock has no way of guaranteeing even an adequate, let alone the best, translation. It has been amply and repeatedly demonstrated through multiple examples in the MT and natural language processing literature, starting with Bar Hillel (1960), that no adequate translation of realistic-sized texts can be obtained if semantic issues are not addressed. A great deal of ingenuity and *ad hoc* knowledge acquisition is needed to avoid ambiguity resolution in MT. And, in fact, translation using this approach can be successfully achieved only for carefully selected subsets of texts, served by dictionaries in which single-sense entries predominate. This is one reason why postediting is such a necessary stage in typical direct-approach and transfer-oriented MT environments. It is evident that even when discussing general design issues in machine translation, considerations of ambiguity resolution cannot be excluded.

2.4   Meaning Across Languages

Some MT researchers adopt the position that different languages employ different concepts, or employ concepts differently, and this short-circuits attempts at meaning extraction. Thus Amano (1989, 2) writes that "Natural languages have their own articulation of concepts according to their culture. Interlingua must naturally take account of this." To illustrate this point, Amano reports that where the English word *moustache* is customarily defined in English dictionaries as comprising hair on the upper lip, the Japanese *kuchi-hige* is defined in one (unspecified) Japanese dictionary as a "beard under the nose." (Actually, the kanji ideographs for *kuchi-hige* stand for "lip" or "mouth," plus "whiskers.") From this we are urged to infer that what Japanese speakers *mean* by *kuchi-hige* is somehow different than what English speakers mean by *moustache*. Of course, this opinion is simply a particularly hirsute version of Sapir-Whorfism that depends crucially on the vagaries of dictionary entries. In addition, Amano's statement displays a common misunderstanding of the concept of interlingua. What differs among languages is not the meaning representation but rather the lexical and syntactic means of realizing this meaning. The meaning of *kuchi-hige* and *moustache* will be represented in the same way in an interlingua text. The realizations of this meaning in the two languages will be different. It is in the interlingua–TL dictionary that a connection is established between an interlingua meaning representation and the language-particular linguistic expression.

This is not the place to argue against linguistic and cognitive relativism. The idea of linguistic relativity is, in fact, neutral with respect to the tasks of computational linguistics. It should be sufficient to point out that however efficient dictionaries might be as explicators of meaning for humans, it is a mistake to appeal to them as formal indices of a culture's conceptual structure. That is to say, even within a language, many terms may be rendered in different and apparently incompatible ways. To contend that meaning exists within a language but not across languages is to subscribe to an extreme sort of relativism usually associated with treating language as a mass of individual dialects or even idiolects. In practice, of course, indigenous *realia* can be described encyclopedically and then assigned a linguistic sign (possibly a direct calque from the original language).

2.5   Feasibility of General Meaning Representation

One argument against language-independent meaning representation, usually referred to as interlingua, is known as "cultural-imperialist." To wit, the way the interlingua is built reflects the world view behind one dominant language. Examples of phenomena with respect to which "cultural imperialism" can be established include the cross-linguistic difference in subcategorization behavior of verbs, the grain size of concept description and the difference in attitude similar to the above *moustache* case. For instance, a single interlingua concept can be suggested to represent the main sense of the English *put* (as in *Put a book/glass on the table*). This might be considered a case of English cultural imperialism because in Russian this meaning can be expressed either as *položit'* or *postavit'* depending on some properties of the object of *put*.[2] Additional examples abound in the MT literature.

The granularity of a large-scale meaning representation is always influenced by linguistic data, since the acquisition of knowledge necessary to support such a representation is done by humans who are, naturally, influenced by the languages they speak and the textual corpora and human-oriented dictionaries they use to determine meaning unit boundaries. It seems that the "cultural imperialism" argument is directed at the wrong target.

The simple view of the interlingua as a representation capturing all meanings in all languages is certainly simplistic because it talks about an ideal approachable only asymptotically. Compare, for instance, the following statement by Nagao (1989a, 6): " ... when the pivot language method [i.e, interlingua] is used, the results of the analytic stage must be in a form which can be utilized by all of the different languages into which translation is to take place ... This level of subtlety is a practical impossibility." On a more technological level, Schneider (1989, 128) justifies the choice of paradigm in the METAL project as follows: "METAL employs a modified transfer approach rather than an interlingua. If a meta-language [an interlingua] were to be used for translation purposes it would need to incorporate all possible features of many languages. That would not only be an endless task but probably a fruitless one as well. Such a system would soon become unmanageable and perhaps collapse under its own weight."

This "maximalist" view of interlingua is so popular probably because it is conceptually the simplest. In operational terms, however, it is as useful to talk about such a conception of the interlingua as about a set of bilingual dictionaries among all the language pairs in the world. A practical interlingua should be viewed both as an object and as a process. Viewed as an object, developed in a concrete project, an interlingua should be judged by the quality of the translations that it supports between all the languages for which the corresponding SL–interlingua and interlingua–TL dictionaries have been built. As a process, its success should be judged in terms of the ease with which new concepts can be added to it and existing concepts modified in view of new textual evidence (either from new languages or from those already treated in the system). In practice, all interlingua systems start with the description of the semantic (sub)realms of a small set of languages and

---

[2]The difference can be glossed as that between *put flat* and *put upright*. A book can be "put" either way; a glass will be usually "put upright."

expand only when it becomes necessary and feasible from the standpoint of project resources. This is true about such different interlingua systems as ATLAS-II (Uchida 1989 a and b), Rosetta (Landsbergen 1989) and KBMT-89 (Goodman and Nirenburg 1991).

It is characteristic, though, that even interlingua-oriented workers find it necessary to offer qualifying explanations of their paradigmatic choices. Thus, Landsbergen (1989, 85) writes:

1. From the point of view of the system's architecture Rosetta is clearly an interlingua system. It consists of an analysis component that translates from the source language into an intermediate language, of which the expressions are semantic representations, and a generation component that translates from this intermediate language into the target language.

2. On the other hand, the intermediate language of Rosetta is not a universal interlingua, but is defined for a specific set of languages. So Rosetta is not interlingua in this strict sense.

3. In an ideal interlingua system the analysis and generation component for each language can be developed independent of the other languages. We will not discuss here to what extent this is desirable or possible, but it is clearly not the case in Rosetta.

A system (such as Rosetta) based on the principles of meaning analysis and absence of direct correspondences between the elements of SL and TL must have the right to be called "interlingua" unapologetically. It does not seem appropriate (in fact, it looks like a double standard) to require completeness as proof of feasibility for interlinguae, while allowing barely adequate behavior, typically in a limited domain for a limited set of language pairs (usually, a single language pair) to be the criterion of success of a transfer system.

Often, the argument about infeasibility of interlingua MT is presented as a "basic assumption" and not argued for, as done, for instance, by Arnold and des Tombe (1987, 117): " ... the translation relation is fundamentally and irreducibly a relation between *linguistic* objects. The representation languages must be linguistic in nature, and cannot therefore be completely neutral with respect to different natural languages, in the way that a genuine interlingua would be." It is not clear what is meant by "linguistic." Is the formalism Arnold and des Tombe suggest (or formalisms based on similar principles, presented, e.g., in Johnson et al. 1985 or Arnold et al. 1988) in any sense a more linguistic notation than an artificial language designed to capture textual meaning? If "linguistic" is equated with "stemming only from a syntactic theory" then we strongly disagree, because, in our understanding, translation is based on mapping meanings, not syntactic structures.

The maximalist view of the interlingua sometimes constitutes the main reason for not selecting this approach for a particular project. This is sometimes the case even in the presence of task specifications (such as multilinguality) which suggest an interlingua approach. Thus, the reasons for not selecting this approach for the original Eurotra project are given by King (1981) as follows: "Eurotra tries, at its deepest level of representation, to characterize the semantic relations between constituents in the text via a set of relations based on an expanded form of case grammar ... However, since the set of relations are defined as those useful for translation and are only 'universal' within the project, there is no attempt to reach a [sic] ideal, genuinely universal semantic representation."

In reality, the Eurotra approach evolved in such a way that many of the elements usually associated with the interlingua approach (first and foremost, analysis of meaning) are undeniably present (cf. Durand et al. 1991). Therefore, the traditional arguments against interlingua and for transfer approaches should perhaps be presented today as arguments against the use of meaning in translation. If meaning is not considered essential for translation, then a version of a transfer approach should be the choice, since interlingua approaches crucially depend on meaning representation. We still believe that it would be more convenient and general to couch the meaning analysis in language-independent form rather than analyze the meaning of a source language in terms of lexical units of a target language (and this is what bilingual transfer dictionaries, in fact, do). But this argument is of a secondary nature. The main point established by this convergence in approaches is that treatment of meaning is central to the task of MT. We are in reality arguing mostly about the method and perhaps about the depth of analysis required.

We want at this point to discuss several well-known opinions about and criticisms of interlingua MT. It seems that most of them, indeed, refer to treatment of meaning rather than to interlingua as such.

The most well-known and large-scale early experiment with interlingua representations ended in self-admitted failure: " ... we have tried an approximation of the interlingua ('pivot') approach and found it wanting. In the ... CETA system, the pivot representation was of a hybrid sort, using as vocabulary the lexical units of a given natural language, and as relations the so-called 'universals' corresponding to our current logical and semantic relations, plus abstract features such as semantic markers, abstract time and aspect and so on" (Vauquois and Boitet 1985, 35).

Design characteristics of the CETA "interlingua" were, in fact, drastically different from those usually associated with modern interlingua systems. Hutchins (1986, 190f) summarizes the characteristics of the CETA pivot language as follows: "The formalism was designed primarily as an interlingua for syntactic features, i.e., as the common 'deep syntactic' base of the languages in the system ... Its lexicon, however, did not represent a common base; instead the pivot language conjoined the lexical units of whichever two languages were being processed ... In other words, while the CETA pivot language was a true interlingua in syntax, it was a bilingual 'transfer' mechanism in lexicon. Further, it was not intended that all sentences with the same meaning would be analyzed as ... one unique pivot language representation. Nevertheless, although there were thus as many 'pivot languages' as there were SL–TL pairs analysed, all shared the same syntax and in this respect CETA considered their formalism as a first step in the direction of a 'universal language.'" As described above, the design of CETA is interlingua only in name. In fact, it is practically identical to that of a standard modern transfer-based MT system!

Still, the fact that this was labeled by its designers as interlingua, and by their admission failed, has been used to justify objections to interlingua MT, for instance, in the METAL project: "It is frequently argued that translation should be a process of analyzing the source language into a 'deep representation' of some sort, then directly synthesizing the target language ... We and others (King 1981) contest this claim ... One objection is based on large-scale, long-term trials of the 'deep representation' approach by the CETA group at Grenoble ... After an enormous investment in time and energy, including experiments with massive amounts (400,000 words) of text, it was decided that the development of a suitable pivot language (for use in Russian-French translation) was not yet possible" (Bennett and Slocum 1985, 112). Comparing this opinion to the above discussion of the CETA project, one has to conclude that the self-admitted failure of CETA should have raised doubts about the feasibility of the *transfer* approach rather than the interlingua one.

It is sometimes claimed that a meaning representation that does not use elements of natural language is difficult to design: "It is very difficult to design [a meaning representation] in the first place, and ever more so if the vocabulary must also be independent of any particular natural language" (Vauquois and Boitet 1985, 35).

In the years since CETA was designed and tested, a large body of knowledge has been acquired in the area of representing models of real-world entities in the computer. And even though the task still remains difficult it is more feasible using the modern knowledge representation languages, advanced knowledge acquisition interfaces with built-in consistency and validity checks, suites of programs for processing machine-readable human-oriented dictionaries and encyclopedias and so on. With respect to the choice of names for primitives (the "vocabulary" of Vauquois and Boitet), different knowledge-based systems choose different approaches (e.g., in KBMT-89 the primitives have the status of elements in an artificial language, while in the PREMO system (Slator and Wilks 1991) English word senses are used).

Another typical criticism of meaning-based MT, expressed as a criticism of the interlingua approach, concerns the process of TL text generation. Vauquois and Boitet (1985, 35) write: "The absence of surface-level information makes it impossible to use contrastive knowledge of two languages to guide the choice between several possible paraphrases at generation time." This opinion is seconded by Warwick (1987, 28): "One major difficulty with the interlingua approach—aside from the complexity of defining such an abstract model—was that language-specific attributes necessary for defining translation equivalents on the lexical and structural level were neutralized in the interlingua representation, thereby complicating the task of generation considerably."

In a typical transfer system, TL generation usually is concerned only with the syntactic part of the process. Text planning and lexical selection are both avoided, the former by uniformly translating every SL sentence by a sentence in the TL,[3] the latter by substituting TL lexical units through bilingual dictionaries. In fact, in early versions of transfer systems, generation was little more than a left-to-right scanning and writing out of the terminal elements in a transfer phrase structure tree.

As long as lexical ambiguity is not treated in an MT system, the traditional absence of a real lexical selection mechanism is justified simply because there isn't any choice—a single translation variant is suggested for every SL lexical unit. If a more sophisticated variety of the transfer approach can incorporate lexical ambiguity resolution while continuing to use TL as the language for representing the meaning of SL lexical units, then lexical selection in generation may continue to be a simple task for approaches that use contrastive lexical knowledge. The focus, however, is still on the analysis side. By using a metalanguage with a higher expressive power than a natural language (we are talking only about expressive power for computer programs that must treat lexical units as uninterpreted black boxes, rather than humans who have greater interpretive power), a meaning-oriented MT

---

[3]This rule is a fairly good default approximation, but still constrains the expressive power of a generator. The ability and license to break SL sentences into several TL sentences or combine several of them into one is, as above, a powerful tool in the hands of a human translator.

system can allow lexical selection in generation to be performed at the level of sufficiently fine-grain semantic features, not at that of monolithic lexical units.

This deeper interpretation allows one to smooth out many cross-linguistic incompatibilities, such as problems of inexpressibility of certain concepts in single-word lexical units in some languages. Multiple examples of such phenomena can be found in MT and general linguistic literature, many of them dealing with translation of kinship terms. One of the latest contributions is by Amano (1989), who states that Japanese has two lexical units corresponding to the English word *aunt*, one referring to an older sister of a parent and another referring to a younger sister. (In fact, the two words are phonetically the same, though different kanji characters are used to represent them.) Note that Amano uses this example to support his opinion that direct correspondences between languages alleviate the problem of lexical gaps of this sort. Indeed, his criticism of the interlingua approach includes the statement that, in the cases like the above, use of a descriptive phrase like "father's younger sister" constitutes explanation rather than translation. Following this questionable logic, real translation, then, will necessarily involve either a meaning loss or a potential error in translation. Indeed, for translation from Japanese into English, if the "explanation" mode is to be avoided, both the Japanese lexical items will have to be rendered as "aunt" in English. This is meaning loss. Establishing correct correspondence in the opposite direction will be utterly impossible without extra knowledge (the relative age of the person in question and one of her brothers or sisters)—either using bilingual correlations or using the interlingua method. The difference is that a typical transfer MT system does not have a mechanism to support such an inference even if this knowledge is in principle available, whereas interlingua systems are in principle designed to address such problems. Thus, only a knowledge-based interlingua approach could correctly translate "the aunt who is eldest in her family" into a single Japanese lexical unit by inferring the information needed for correct Japanese lexical selection. Thus, while attempting to do the opposite, Amano's example provides powerful motivation for an intermediate semantic representation.

Yet another objection to the interlingua approach to MT is based on "practical" considerations. Bennett and Slocum (1985) contend that "since it is not likely that any natural language processing system will in the foreseeable future become capable of handling unrestricted input—even in the technical area(s) for which it might be designed—it is clear that a 'fail-soft' technique is necessary. It is not obvious that such is possible in a system based solely on a pivot language."

"Fail-softness" is a worthy goal for a software system. However, this concept is invoked in the MT literature usually, and only, to stress a theoretical point, as in the passage quoted just above. In practice, neither transfer-based nor interlingua-based systems have at present a good means of dealing with unexpected or ill-formed input. Nothing in knowledge-based MT *per se* precludes the design and implementation of architectures and algorithms facilitating fail-softness. Just as in transfer systems, a target lexical unit can be picked at random (or based on probabilistic judgments) when no principled semantic disambiguation is possible. So in interlingua systems some decisions could be made based on similarly weak and universally applicable heuristics upon failure of more definitive knowledge-based selection procedures. The name of the game, however, is to translate correctly, without guessing. The above criticism is, thus, a nonstarter. It probably stems from the observation that such weak heuristics are seldom used or discussed in meaning-oriented projects because these projects are typically research-oriented rather than devoted to building application-system prototypes. However, if such a system is built using a meaning-oriented approach the objective of fail-softness can be achieved equally well, if not better. In essence, fail-soft heuristics would be used as a backup to more accurate knowledge-based processes, rather than at all times, as is the case in direct and transfer methods without semantic analysis.

2.6 How Formal Must Meaning Representation Be?

It is widely supposed that knowledge-based machine translation requires grounding in a fully interpreted logical calculus, that a meaning-based approach cannot be presented with such formal rigor and hence that meaning-based MT cannot succeed. This argument may be understood as demanding formal proofs of the correctness of translated meaning representations. Without such proofs, it is supposed, there is no guarantee that a translation will be free of contradiction or that the same meanings will be always represented similarly.

The formalist approach to machine translation is heir to Richard Montague's view that there is or should be no distinction in principle between natural and formal languages. But even if Montague, thus glossed, were correct, it would not follow that uniquely *formal* representations are necessary for the task of machine translation. That is to say, with Wilks (1990, 330),

> [...] we do need representations (as opposed to the current trend
> of connectionism) [...], but their form, if interpretable, is largely
> arbitrary, and we may be confident it has little relation to logic. I
> shall restate the view that the key contribution of AI in unraveling
> how such complex tasks as "understanding" might be simulated by

a machine lies not in representations at all but in particular kinds of procedures [...]. It would be the most extraordinary coincidence, cultural, evolutionary, and intellectual, if what was needed for the computational task should turn out to be formal logic, a structure derived for something else entirely. Although, it must be admitted, strange coincidences have been known in the history of science.

The demand for proofs that a target language text will contain no contradiction is of course a demand that cannot be met. But, fortunately, the problem of avoiding contradiction—in machine translation in particular and natural language processing in general—is an empirical issue and not clearly delimited by formalist claims and purported requirements. That is to say, while it might be nice to be able to offer such proofs, it would be a grievous error to abandon any enterprise unable to provide a formal proof of its future success. Indeed, the formalist gambit has been tried against any number of sciences, including physics, and has come up short. Human translations are not "provably correct." Moreover, very few computer programs actually can be proved correct—and then only with respect to formal specifications and not to real-world implementations.

It is perhaps worthwhile to point to Quine's admission that some things can be radically translated, and explicitly to recall that his thesis was not that all radical translation is necessarily indeterminate. Quine recognized that elements from a "decidedly different domain"—that of truth functions—could be translated no matter whether a native was proffered occasion or standing sentences (1960, 57ff).[4] It is not clear how one would press the point, but one might confront formalist demands by suggesting that if truth functions can be deterministically translated, then the (formal) avoidance of contradiction will not be quite so difficult as proposed. At any rate, the intuitions underlying "not," "and," "or" and so forth are indisputably common and accessible to natural-language users in the absence of any sort of formalism. If they can be formalized, so much the better for logic; but on what grounds is this formalization required for natural language *understanding*?

The formalist claim is sometimes made by criticizing uninterpreted formalisms. The elements from which our representations are built are "interpreted" in terms

---

[4]Note, though, the following point, made by Yorick Wilks (personal communication): $(A \supset B)$ and $\neg (A \text{ and } \neg B)$ are obviously truth-functionally equivalent, but a native who assented to both in the same context could not be said to hold them equivalent by virtue of "sameness of meaning." This is quite right, but it suggests a goal broader than the one sought at this point. If for example, reading with Quine, "The semantic criterion of negation is that it turns any short sentence to which one will assent into a sentence from which one will dissent, and vice versa" (1960, 57), then the upshot is that the negative particle is what goes through deterministically, not the entire sentence it negates.

of an empirically constructed domain model rather than through an axiomatically defined set of possible worlds or well-formed formulae in a logical system. To be sure, one must avoid over-facile appeals to future research and empirical criteria as a hedge against formalist strictures. Nonetheless, such a line can be productively deployed against the claim that meaning-based MT cannot ensure that same meanings will get the same translations. If sameness of intralingua meaning is in fact preserved in translation—as corroborated by the judgments of bi- or multilingual humans, say—then this should be regarded as *evidence* in favor of the meaning-based approach. It would be folly indeed to disregard such evidence in the absence of a formal proof of the possibility of attaining such evidence!

Now some MT researchers maintain that there is no need to use an artificial language for representing meanings, that a natural language, such as Aymara, Sanskrit or Hebrew, will do. Others maintain that instead of inventing new artificial languages, MT can use some of the available artificial languages, such as Esperanto.[5] The crucial difference between languages—either naturally evolved or invented—used by humans and languages designed for the use of a computer program is the set of assumptions about the agent of understanding. Natural languages are used by humans. Artificial languages have computer programs as understanding agents. For humans (powerful understanding machines, though endowed with a less reliable memory), brevity is at a premium, even at the expense of ambiguity and having to render some parts of the information only implicitly, expecting the understander to be able to recover this information. For computer programs (at present, still rather low-performance understanding machines) lack of ambiguity and explicitness of representation is at a premium, even at the expense of verbosity.

The key to an effective interlingua format is that it be unambiguous, explicit and compositional in its semantics. Otherwise, ambiguities resolved in source language analysis are needlessly reintroduced prior to target language generation. This burdens the system with the need for a second analysis and creates an unnecessary source of potential error.

Furthermore, the characteristics of the communication channel suggest that the texts in languages spoken by humans be single-dimensional strings. With computers, knowledge can have a much more complex topology—of hierarchies or even multidimensional lattices. The only way in which one can say, loosely, that a natural language is used as interlingua is when lexical units of this language are used to tag ontological concepts. However, there is ample additional representational apparatus which is entailed in designing an interlingua.

---

[5]Among artificial languages designed for human use there is even one called "Interlingua"!

It is not impossible to use lexical units from certain natural languages or human-oriented artificial languages like Esperanto as markers for ontological concepts. In fact, in our own work we use combinations of English lexemes to tag concepts. However, in order to turn such a language into an efficient text-meaning representation for MT, (at least some of) these meanings will have to be explicated in terms of their properties and typical connections with other concepts.

2.7 Extractability of Meaning

It is argued that it is impossible to ensure that the meaning can *actually be extracted* from the source language text and rendered in the representation language. As stated above, the present state of the art does not allow a completely automatic disambiguation and representation of all the semantic and pragmatic phenomena. This is especially true for systems like those coming out of the KBMT-89 project at the Center for Machine Translation, in which the expected results of analysis are very detailed.

Hutchins summarizes the scene as follows (1987, 49): "In semantic analysis there has been successful treatment of homography and syntactic ambiguity; and there have been successful implementations of case frames, of semantic features, of distributional semantic information, and recently of Montague semantics; but, nevertheless, the profounder problems of interlingua semantic analysis have proved elusive." These "profounder" problems presumably include treatment of reference (including ellipsis), abductive inference-making on the basis of world knowledge, speaker attitudes, indirect speech acts, stylistic factors, and so forth. We are making inroads into these and other difficult areas. In the meantime, meaning-based systems can become practical through reliance on the concept of microtheories for separately motivated but coordinated treatment of these phenomena, through continued work on the acquisition of domain models and through use of an interactive augmentor (a program that supports interactive disambiguation and knowledge acquisition to address those semantic phenomena that cannot be treated automatically within the current state of the art). This has already been demonstrated at the research level. The long-term objective, of course, is to reduce interactive augmentation to the point where it is required only for an occasional consultation, and thus make accurate KBMT systems practical.

Thus, the role of the augmentor will progressively diminish as our research on meaning extraction progresses. But it is strange to doubt that monotonically increasing automation in quality machine translation is not real progress.

2.8 Translation and Paraphrasing

Hutchins (1987, 49) claims that in meaning-oriented MT systems " ... the abstract-ness of 'content' representations result[s] in losses of information about 'surface' structures of texts," and from this he concludes that "versions produced by AI methods are not translations but rather paraphrases."

This opinion relies too much on the formulation of translation as a relation among texts, not among textual meanings (cf. the similar definitions in Johnson et al. 1985 and Arnold and des Tombe 1987, as quoted above). If we agree that the invariant in translation is meaning, then translation becomes a paraphrase, only a special one; in this type of paraphrase the lexical, grammatical and prosodic means of a different language are used (see, e.g., Whitelock 1989 for a similar argument).

In fact, the "paraphrasing as translation" argument is a facet of a more general question: Does one need to treat the *form* of the input text during translation? This question naturally arises because the dichotomy of substance and form has been a central point of discussion in such fields as semiotics and art theory and history. By "form of text" we refer to a number of diverse phenomena: the syntactic structure of the input sentences; its phonetic and prosodic properties, such as alliteration, meter, rhyme and so on; and the layout of a printed page, which can include diagrams, formulas, pictures, examples and other highlighted material, special fonts and so forth.

The layout of the text on a page is a feature independent of text meaning, but influences the overall impact of the text. It can be called on to carry an aesthetic message (as, for instance, in Apollinaire's poems or Lewis Carroll's tale written in the *form* of a tail in *Alice in Wonderland*). In expository, aesthetically neutral text, which is the type of text best suited for machine translation, it is sometimes desirable to preserve page layouts in translation (especially for pages with diagrams, illustrations, etc.), as, for instance, in the case of multilingual equipment manuals.

It is clearly difficult to preserve phonetic characteristics of the source text in the target text. We will therefore not expect to deal with these issues. However, the use of special fonts (e.g., italics) carries a meaning which should be recreated in the target text. Sometimes lexical units from languages other than the main language of the text are highlighted. These should be recognized as material not to be translated but rather reproduced "as is" in the target text. However, in some cases italics are used for purposes of marking sentential stress (e.g., "I do not want to see *any* of them"), and in such cases this meaning should be represented and later re-created in the target language using its own means of expressing sentential stress.

Outside the field of artistic texts—poetry and fiction—preservation of the *syntactic form* of the source text in translation is truly unnecessary and, in fact, superfluous because the meaning and use of, say, passive voice constructions in a source and a target language should not necessarily be identical. Direct structural correspondences between certain pairs of languages can be exploited in MT systems of a particular type, but they should be treated as idiosyncratic occasions rather than phenomena that occur as a rule. From the point of view of quality of expository text translation, it is immaterial whether the syntax of the target sentences is similar to that of the source sentences, so long as emphasis, topic-comment and other nonpropositional information is preserved. Interlingua MT systems are typically geared to capture such information, in addition to semantic content, in order to generate better-quality target text.

To summarize, there is no reason to aspire to translate the form of the input text. However, if an MT system does not possess sufficient knowledge to analyze SL texts deeply enough to allow understanding sufficient for realization of corresponding TL texts, it may rely on preserving the syntax of the source text in the target text as a very crude default heuristic, regularly violated in a large number of cases.

2.9   Conclusion

While we have emphasized the key points of difference between the two main MT paradigms, transfer and interlingua, it is also productive to conclude with mention of the positions which seem to be held jointly by *all* MT system developers. These platforms for agreement seem to include the following:

- Translation is a relation between texts in the source and target languages, such that the invariant between them is meaning. In other words, translation is rendering a set of meanings realized in a source language using the realization means of a target language. (Some researchers also believe that syntactic form should be preserved; others argue that form-preservation is secondary or beside the point.)

- Machine translation deals primarily with expository texts, where artistic considerations do not play an important role.

- Meanings in such texts are, in practical terms, completely expressible in all relevant source and target languages. Of course, not all concepts lexicalized in one language can be directly lexicalized in others—descriptive phrases may be required to cover lexical holes. But this is exactly what we do *intra-*lingually when a language lacks the lexical means to express a (sometimes new) concept.

- Fully automated, completely accurate, general purpose MT is not feasible at present, but

- The main research direction is toward full automation or, in systems that are already fully automated, toward increased accuracy in translation.

Additionally, here are some positions held by researchers in meaning-oriented MT that are not emphasized by other MT workers:

- SL ambiguity resolution is a primary goal in MT research, as it is the only way to achieve fully accurate machine translation.

- Design considerations must crucially take into account the preceding requirement.

Interlingua MT systems tend to favor the meaning-based approach, while transfer systems hope to render meaning without the added requirement of representing it. Theoretically, meaning-oriented MT is not restricted to the interlingua paradigm. One can, in principle, incorporate meaning analysis into the transfer approach, as is the case in most advanced transfer systems in Japan and Europe. However, in practice, as such attempts proliferate, it will become clear that the interlingua paradigm is more convenient for the support of the analysis of meaning, and is far more practical for the construction of multilingual MT systems according to well-defined software engineering principles. We also believe that the amount and complexity of knowledge acquisition for interlingua MT systems is at worst roughly equal to that which would have to be mastered for meaning-oriented transfer MT. At best, the acquisition component of an interlingua approach will be more compact, well-organized and more readily reusable as new languages are added to the system.

Chapter 3

The Concept of Interlingua

3.1 Requirements

In building a knowledge-based machine translation system, one of the basic tasks is developing a knowledge representation language, an interlingua, which would allow the representation of a wide variety of domain and discourse meanings unambiguously and in a canonical way. This language is preferably open-ended and extensible. Its well-formed expressions will represent meanings of actual natural language texts. An important property of such a representation scheme should be its capacity to express the complex interrelations among all the types of knowledge relevant for treatment of text.

It is important to stress at this point that designing an interlingua involves not only the formulation of the syntax of the knowledge representation scheme. The well-formed constructs of this language must be given semantic interpretation. Indeed the knowledge representation language one develops will certainly be usable for tasks beyond representing text meaning. The meaning of a natural language text, as represented in an interlingua notation, is subject to operational-semantic interpretation in terms of an underlying world model, a model of the speech situation and a model of the participants in this situation. In order to carry out this interpretation, the set of knowledge sources required for meaning extraction (and hence for interlingua MT) must include instances of all such models and of regular mappings between linguistic signs and elements of these models. These mappings are recorded in the lexicon and used during system operation.

To treat text meaning in the context of translation, a knowledge representation scheme will have to address issues connected with the meaning-related activities in both natural language understanding and generation. While the semantic processing in these two tasks is different in nature (in lexical semantics, for instance, understanding centrally involves resolution of ambiguity, while generation deals with resolution of synonymy for lexical selection), the knowledge bases, knowledge representation approaches and the underlying system architecture and control structures should be shared. For instance, in the DIONYSUS natural language processing project at Carnegie Mellon University's Center for Machine Translation (see Nirenburg and Defrise, forthcoming, a) many of the static knowledge sources and the basic control architecture are, indeed, shared, while the type of processing is quite different.[1]

In our understanding, the complex of knowledge sources for an interlingua MT system includes the following:

1. A world model, including knowledge about types of things in the world, relationships among them and "remembered instances" (the latter comprise the episodic memory); this model consists of

   - An ontology: a general model of the physical world which describes the basic types of objects and events; ontologies are assumed to be shared among all intelligent agents;

   - Domain models: models of particular fields of knowledge, such as chemistry, corporate law or baseball; the presence or absence of a domain model underlies the delineation of the *sublanguage* for which a natural language processing system has been developed;

   - A discourse model, the producer's knowledge about mental and verbal objects, actions and states allowing him to create coherent text of a chosen style (e.g., a textbook, a scientific article, etc.); this model embodies a computational theory of rhetoric and stylistics;

   - A knowledge base of remembered instances of the various ontological and domain model objects, events and properties (e.g., "IBM," "Luciano Pavarotti" or "unsuccessful Soviet military coup");

---

[1]In fact, our general attitude to computational processing of natural language extends to other projects, such as Xcalibur (Carbonell et al. 1983, 1985), TRANSLATOR (Nirenburg et al. 1987), POPLAR (Nirenburg et al. 1985; see also Nirenburg and Lesser 1986), KBMT-89 (Goodman and Nirenburg 1991), Ontos (Monarch and Nirenburg 1989), and others.

- A text understanding/creation record,[2] the attentional context, needed for determining the boundaries of inference propagation in such tasks as, for example, treatment of pronominal anaphora; the text-creation record includes a representation of those portions of text that have already been planned, as well as an indication of which background knowledge (from the domain and discourse models) was activated during text planning.

2. A lexicon for each of the natural languages in the system. The lexicon contains the union of types of information required for analysis and generation.[3] The information in entries for polysemic lexical items includes knowledge supporting lexical disambiguation. The same type of information is used to resolve synonymy in lexical selection during generation.

3. A formalism for representing textual meaning, including semantic, discourse and pragmatic features.

4. Knowledge about semantic processing, including

- Structural mappings relating syntactic and semantic dependency structures;
- Reference treatment rules (anaphora, deixis, ellipsis);
- Unexpected input treatment rules (including metaphor and metonymy, but also orthographic and grammatical deviations);
- Text structure planning rules;
- Representation (in analysis) and realization (in generation) of discourse and pragmatic phenomena as defined in the *general* discourse model (examples include cohesion, textual relations and producer attitudes).

---

[2]This term is a modification of Thomason's (1990) term "conversational record" and denotes the publicly available information created by the text producer (author or speaker) and the text consumer (reader or hearer) in the process of an instance of verbal communication.

[3]In our earlier systems (see, e.g., Nirenburg and Raskin 1987b) we maintained that different lexicons have to be produced for analysis and generation. It seems now that this decision was in a large part induced by the logistics of knowledge acquisition in a large application project. In fact, the overlap of the knowledge in the two lexicons is quite considerable — even the collocation information that we once considered useful mostly in the lexical selection process of natural language generation appears to be valuable in certain situations in analysis.

Components of a general meaning-oriented natural language understanding and generation system can be viewed as evolving modules in a comprehensive computational model. Indeed, our theoretical position eschews the generalization that absolute meaning exists externally in the world. For us, meaning is relative to particular ontologies, episodic memories, lexicons and so on. Since these knowledge repositories can contain errors, our meaning representations can be imperfect at any given time. The crucial point here is that all these knowledge sources, as well as all the processing components, can (and in practice are) constantly improved and corrected, so that the quality of a system improves over time. When such an approach to building interlingua-oriented MT systems is taken, it becomes clear that expecting the interlingua to be a perfect representation system from the outset (as some of the critics of this approach suggest) is uncalled for.

Text understanding consists in representing, using a specially designed notation, the semantic and pragmatic (discourse, attitude, intention) information encoded in each clause of a natural language input, augmented by the representation of domain-related and text-related connections (relations) among natural language clauses or sets thereof.

The final result of the process of text understanding may include some information not overtly present in the source text. For instance, it may include results of reasoning by the consumer, aimed at filling in elements required in the representation but not directly obtainable from the source text. It may also involve reconstructing the agenda of rhetorical goals and plans of the producer active at the time of text production and connecting its elements to chunks of meaning representation.

Early AI-related natural language understanding approaches were criticized for not paying attention to the halting condition of meaning representation. They were open to criticism because they did not make a very clear distinction between the information relayed in the text and information retrieved from the understander's background knowledge about the entities mentioned in the text. This criticism is only valid when the program must apply all possible inferences to the results of the initial representation of text meaning and not when a clear objective is present (such as resolution of ambiguity) beyond which no more processing is required.

This philosophy describes our general approach to the treatment of meaning in natural language texts. In what follows we illustrate some concrete features of our method of meaning representation. We concentrate on the ontology, on the lexicon and on the actual formal language for representing text meaning (the interlingua proper). The versions of the ontology and the meaning representation language discussed here have been developed in the framework of the DIONYSUS project

(Nirenburg and Defrise, forthcoming, a). The meaning representation language in DIONYSUS is called TAMERLAN.

Our approach to the treatment of meaning in natural language has among its origins the conceptual dependency approach of the Yale school of artificial intelligence (e.g., Schank 1975; Schank and Abelson 1977; and Carbonell et al. 1981), the work of Yorick Wilks (e.g., Wilks 1973) and, more recently, approaches described in Nirenburg and Carbonell 1987; Carbonell and Tomita 1987; Nirenburg et al. 1987; and Nirenburg and Levin 1989. Additional detail on text-meaning representation issues is provided in Nirenburg and Defrise, forthcoming, a and b.

3.2 Ontology

A theoretically sound model of the world, an *ontology*, provides uniform definitions of basic semantic categories (such as objects, event-types, relations, properties, episodes and many more) that become the building blocks for descriptions of particular domains and the creation of machine-tractable lexicons for comprehensive natural language processing. We believe that an optimum way of organizing this world model is as an extensive, multiply interconnected network of ontological units, for which theoretically sound storage, access and update procedures are available.

The underlying representational apparatus on which the ontology, TAMERLAN and other higher-level representation strata are build is the FRAMEKIT knowledge representation system (Carbonell and Joseph 1985; Nyberg 1988). The basic unit of representation is a frame, which has a unique name and a set of property-value pairs, called slots and fillers, respectively. "Filler" either refers to frame names or contains literals (numerals, reserved words or character strings). There are additional means of expression in the language, such as facets, which allow different kinds of fillers, including meta-level ones to be represented in a frame; and views, which permit selective but shared access to the knowledge base by different processes. Finally, a multi-parent, extensible inheritance mechanism provides a general facility for default reasoning and localization of knowledge at the highest valid generalization level.

The requirements of knowledge representation extend above and beyond providing an adequate formalism in which to record knowledge and adequate means of storage and retrieval. One has to specify the *contents*, the semantics of the knowledge units. And, if the goal is to build a semantic processing model, an actual large model of the world must be produced (whereas for theoretical purposes a general mechanism for creating such a world view is usually deemed sufficient, especially if supported by several examples). The task of creating an actual ontology is less formalizable than the syntactic aspects of knowledge representation, and this is one reason why relatively less progress has been made in AI with respect to ontological world modeling. Even today this area of scientific research remains, to a large degree, as it has been for over 2,500 years, within the purview of philosophy. While a number of important theories have been propounded in philosophical ontology, we believe that it is necessary to reformulate the goals and methodology of this inquiry, similarly to the way the finite time/space constraints of practical computation changed the style and attitudes of certain areas of discrete mathematics, giving birth to the modern theory of computation.

An ontological model must define a large set of generally applicable categories for world description. Among the types of such categories are the following:

- Perceptual and physical categories

- Categories for encoding actions, intentions, plans and beliefs

- Categories that help describe meta-knowledge (i.e., knowledge about knowledge and its manipulation, including rules of behavior and heuristics for constraining search spaces in various processor components).

The choice of categories is not a straightforward task, as anyone who has tried realistic-scale world description knows all too well. Following are some examples of the issues encountered in such an undertaking (taken from Gates et al. 1989).

Which of the set of attributes pertinent to a certain concept should be singled out as *concept-forming* and thus have named nodes in the conceptual network corresponding to them, and which other ones should be accessible only through the concept of which they are properties? As an example, consider whether you would further subdivide the class *vehicle* into *water-vehicle, land-vehicle, air-vehicle* or rather into *engine-propelled-vehicle, animal-propelled-vehicle, gravity-propelled-vehicle*; or maybe into *cargo-vehicle, passenger-vehicle, toy-vehicle, mixed-cargo-and-passenger-vehicle*? Or maybe it is preferable to have a large number of small classes, such as, for instance, *water-passenger-animal-propelled-vehicle*, of which, for instance, a rowboat will be a member?

Which entities should be considered *objects* and which ones *relations*? Should we interpret a cable connecting a computer and a terminal as a *relation*? Or should we rather define it as a *physical-object* and then specify its typical *role* in the static episode or "scene" involving the above three objects? Should one differentiate between *relations* (links between ontological concepts) and *attributes* (mappings from ontological concepts into symbolic or numerical value sets)? Or rather define attributes as one-place relations? Is it a good idea to introduce the ontological category of *attribute-value-set* with its members being primitive unstructured meanings (such as the various scalars and other, unordered, sets of properties)? Or is it better to define them as full-fledged ontological concepts, even though a vast majority of relations defined in the ontology would not be applicable to them (such a list will include case relations, ownership, causals, etc.)? As an example, should we represent colors *symbolically*, as, say *red, blue* and so on, or should we rather define them in terms of their spectrum wavelengths, positions on the white/black scale and brightness?

How should we treat *sets* of values? Should we represent *The Three Stooges* as one concept or a set of three? What about *The Pittsburgh Pirates*? What's an acceptable way of representing *complex causal chains*? How does one represent a concept like *toy gun*? Is it a gun? Or a toy? Or none of the above? Or is it maybe the influence of natural language and a peculiar choice of meaning realization on the part of the text producer that poses this problem—maybe we don't *need* to represent this concept at all?

In designing and implementing an actual world model, we must, for any given level of detail, provide concrete answers to these questions. We have used the knowledge acquisition and maintenance system Ontos (see Nirenburg et al. 1988b) to produce several prototype ontological models. Figure 3.1 shows the content of the "event" node, as well as several subnetworks in one of the ontologies developed using this system. Such displays already illustrate answers to some of the preceding questions. The Ontos graphics browser facilitates fast overview and navigation in the ontological model. But this model is, in fact, much more than a set of symbols (frame names) connected through *is-a* and *part-of* links.

In addition to an ontological world model, as sketched above, it is often useful to encode past experiences, both actually perceived and reported. The *lingua mentalis* equivalent of a text is an *episode*, a unit of knowledge that encapsulates a particular experience of an intelligent agent, and which is typically represented as a temporally and causally ordered network of object and event instances.

The ontology and the episodes are sometimes discussed in terms of the contents of two different types of memory: semantic and episodic (e.g., Tulving 1985). This distinction seems useful in computational modeling as well. In our knowledge base, we represent, with varying degrees of specificity, both ontological concepts and remembered instances of events and objects, which comprise the episodic memory.

Episodes are indexed through the type they correspond to and can be interrelated on temporal, causal and other links. The participant roles in the episodes can be either instantiations of object and event types in the semantic memory or

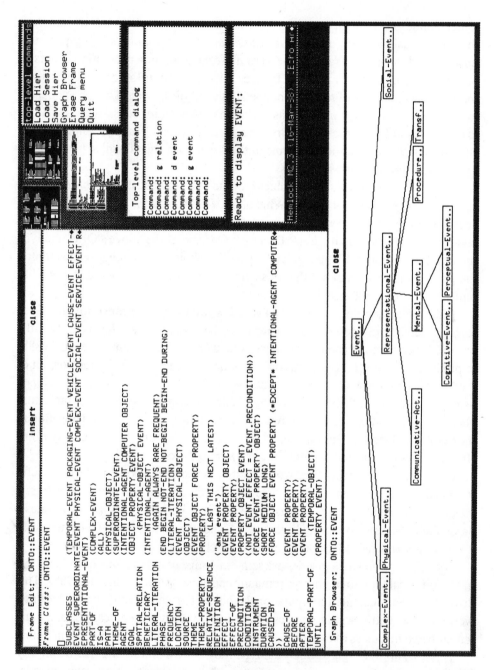

Figure 3.1: **Screen display of contents of the** `event` **concept node, and representations and names of some subnetworks. The graphics browser permits rapid navigation around the ontological model.**

references to existing named instances, stored outside semantic memory but having links to their corresponding types (see figure 3.2; cf. Nirenburg et al. 1991). The figure illustrates the typology of structures comprising a world model. The basic ontological world model is augmented (for the purposes of specific processing types, such as analogical reasoning) with a repository of experiential knowledge. Our system must satisfy the knowledge representation needs of such a repository and abundantly cross index it with the resident ontology. The presence of a systematic representation and indexing method for episodic knowledge is not only necessary for processing natural language, but is also an enablement condition for case-based reasoning (see, e.g., the contributions in Kolodner and Riesbeck 1986) and analogical inference (Carbonell 1983).

3.3   Representation of Meaning

In this section we present the "top-of-the-line" version of our interlingua, TAMER-LAN. For practical KBMT systems we have used selected subsets of the full representational power of this language. Since it is always easier to select the relevant subsets of a powerful representation language than to augment a limited one, we designed TAMERLAN for maximum expressive power. Detailed causal relationships and some discourse relations are among the features that will not be used in all KBMT applications. The structure of the rest of this chapter is roughly organized according to a BNF (Backus-Naur Form) decomposition of the elements of the TAMERLAN language.

All communication, including written text, occurs between agents who have well-defined goals, rhetorical or otherwise, for producing and consuming text. TAMERLAN addresses these issues by representing such agent-oriented knowledge explicitly.

Producers and consumers of text communicate successfully by manipulating knowledge that includes representations of various meanings of language elements, knowledge about the speech situation, including the knowledge about the interlocutor(s), knowledge about analysis and generation of the various language elements, and knowledge about the world in general. The last is permanently stored in the ontology, while the former, including knowledge about habitual speech situations and their participants, is stored in episodic memory; knowledge about treatment of language elements is stored declaratively in the various types of analysis and generation knowledge bases. When the actual processing occurs, structures are instantiated in working memory that capture the actual knowledge necessary to "understand" a text or to produce a text or a turn in a dialogue. We believe there is

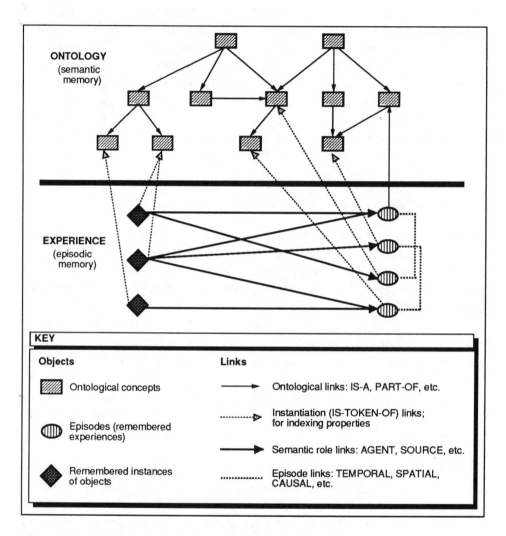

Figure 3.2: **A knowledge base's semantic and episodic memory, along with the kinds of links among concepts and remembered episodes and objects. With varying degrees of specificity, ontological concepts and remembered instances of events and objects can be represented.**

a well-defined set of knowledge elements whose existence constitutes a necessary and sufficient condition for a text to be considered understood. In our theory the same elements are required to ensure successful generation of a text.

These knowledge elements belong to one of the three dimensions that our theory distinguishes for the treatment of communicative activity — the linguistic, the psychological or the sociological one. The linguistic dimension deals with text meaning and relates exclusively to language behavior. The psychological dimension has to do with goal-directed activity of the agent, of which linguistic behavior is a subset. The sociological dimension has to do with the agent's knowledge about the set of communication-situation components, such as places, times and social relationships among interlocutors.

Let us call the collection of knowledge elements sufficient for understanding or production of a text the *text supermeaning*. The supermeaning is a triad,

$$(3.1) \qquad SM = \{T, G, S\}$$

where T stands for textual meaning, G represents an agent's active set of goals and plans and S the setting of the communication situation, including pragmatic factors, such as forcefulness of expression and parameters of the speech situation (e.g., the spatiotemporal context and the properties of the participants and their relative social status, etc.) In what follows we discuss each of these elements in turn. An extended example is offered in section 3.4.

3.3.1 Textual Meaning

The meaning of a text is a quadruple,

$$(3.2) \qquad T = \{C, R, A, I\}$$

where $C = \{clause_1, clause_2, \ldots, clause_n\}$ is a set of propositional representations of the meaning of natural language clauses and $R = \{relation_1, relation_2, \ldots, relation_k\}$ is a set of connections among elements of the representation (clause components, clauses, sets of clauses). $A = \{attitude_1, attitude_2, \ldots, attitude_l\}$ is the set of attitudes to the various components of the meaning representation on the part of a text consumer or producer or another intelligent agent ("reported attitudes"). $I = \{producer\text{-}intention_1, producer\text{-}intention_2, \ldots, producer\text{-}intention_m\}$ represents the speech act meanings in the text.

The meaning of a clause is a quadruple,

$$(3.3) \qquad clause_i = \{onto_i, tr_i^j, aspect_i, time_i\}$$

where $onto_i$ is an instance of a concept in the ontology, possibly with additional constraints added to its ontological properties due to contextual influences in the input text. The features of the representation language for representing semantic content of natural language clauses are an augmented and modified version of the interlingua knowledge representation language used in the KBMT-89 machine translation system (Goodman and Nirenburg 1991). Basically, we represent the semantic content of natural language utterances by instantiating ontological entities or reasserting remembered instances of such entities that are found (with the help of a lexicon) to be the most closely semantically related to lexical units in the input. The tasks of (i) lexical disambiguation of candidate readings of the input lexical items and (ii) construction of a semantic dependency structure are performed by the semantic analyzer. The creation of the *onto* structures in clause-meaning representations and in producer-intention representations is the only process in our theory where the ontology and the text meaning interact. tr_i^j is a pair $\{role\text{-}name_i^j, onto_i^j\}$ where $role\text{-}name_i^j$ is the name of a thematic role (case role, semantic actant—their inventory is listed among the relation-type properties in the ontology) and where $onto_i^j$ is, again, an instance of an ontological concept, possibly with property values modified due to contextual influences. $aspect_i$ represents the aspectual properties of $clause_i$ through three dimensions—its phase (beginning, continuation, end), duration (momentary or prolonged) and iteration (single or multiple). The $time_i$ component of $clause_i$ is used for representing absolute time references (relative times are represented through relations; see below).

TAMERLAN relations are represented as a triad,

$$(3.4) \qquad relation_i = \{relation\text{-}type_i, \ arguments_i, \ relation\text{-}value_i\}$$

where $relation\text{-}type_i$ is taken from a predefined set of relation types (see section 3.3.4); $arguments_i$ can hold either a set of TAMERLAN components or the set $\{first_i, \ second_i, \ third_i\}$. Members of this set refer to a TAMERLAN component, $third_i$ being an optional member (we don't directly represent relation with more than three arguments); $relation\text{-}value_i$ is an optional member; but when it is present, it refers to a point or a range on a $\{0,1\}$ scale.

The attitudes are represented as a quintuple,

$$(3.5) \qquad attitude_i = \{type_i, \ value_i, \ attributed\text{-}to_i, \ scope_i, \ time_i\}$$

where $type_i$ is the type of the attitude; $value_i$ is the value of the attitude, represented as a point or a region on a $\{0,1\}$ scale; $attributed\text{-}to_i$ points at the intelligent agent this attitude is attributed to; $scope_i$ takes as its value that part of the meaning representation to which the attitude is held; and finally $time_i$ represents the absolute time at which this attitude is held.

A producer-intention is a pair,

$$(3.6) \qquad producer\text{-}intention_i = \{onto_i,\ scope_i\}$$

where $onto_i$ refers to an ontological concept which is a descendant of verbal-action, and $scope_i$ refers to a meaning-representation component. This feature is needed because natural language clauses do not always have an illocutionary force. For instance, in the promise *If you drop by, you'll be able to see my pictures* the first clause (the antecedent to the conditional relation) has no illocutionary force. Rather, the scope of the promise is the whole sentence which, in TAMERLAN, is represented by two clauses. A complete set of producer goals and plans is stored in the G component of the text supermeaning. The producer intention is used to connect those with other meaning components.

3.3.2 The Goal and Plan Component

The G component of the text supermeaning is a collection of structures of goal and plan instances which, the text consumer believes, are active in the text producer memory during the production of this text. Since we are interested in language communication, we describe only the goals and plans that (i) presuppose the situation with at least two cognitive agents (minimally, the text producer and the text consumer) and (ii) relate to rhetorical realizations of goals. These pointers are not directly realized, but serve as background knowledge during the realization process of other elements of input. Reasoning about goals and plans of the producer during the planning stage of natural language generation is a widely accepted approach (cf. Moore and Paris 1989; Hovy 1988 a,b,c). The stored plans are realized in the text only when a direct speech act is produced, in which case the realization usually involves generating a separate target language clause. In the framework of natural language understanding, the representations of producer goals and plans are constructed by the consumer. The success of this process serves as a major halting condition on the process of semantic (and pragmatic) interpretation. That is, when the purpose or intent of a clause or action is discerned, no further processing is required. This attributive reconstruction process subsumes lexical and grammatical disambiguation, which is a shallower halting criterion often used in practical KBMT applications.

Depending on the context and other parameters, the producer may decide, for instance, to produce *I will return at 10* or *I promise to return at 10*. In the latter case the decision is made to realize the the speech act overtly. The mechanism for this is as follows: traversing the goal-and-plan hierarchy, the producer gets to the relevant point in the agenda, which is the (primitive) plan PROMISE (or THREAT, etc., as the case may be). Since the realization rules for speech acts prescribe their realization as first-person-singular clauses with the lexical realizations of the names of appropriate speech plans (acts), the natural language clause *I promise X* gets produced, and eventually X is expanded into the subordinate natural language clause *to return at 10*.

3.3.3   Speech Situation

The speech situation S is represented as the pair

(3.7) $S = \{deictic\text{-}indices,\ pragmatic\text{-}factors\}$

Deictic indices include the time and the place of the utterance of a text and the speaker and hearer. The pragmatic factors describe stylistic parameters of the speech situation.

The microtheory of pragmatic factors used in our approach is largely inspired by Hovy (1988d). The set of pragmatic factors in our model includes *formality, simplicity, color, force, directness* and *respect*. Values of these factors are represented as points or ranges on the scale from 0 (low) to 1 (high). The default value of pragmatic factors is 0.5.

The various knowledge representation systems in artificial intelligence have traditionally stressed representation of propositional meaning (see, e.g., Schank 1975; Sowa 1984; Creary and Pollard 1985; Brachman and Schmolze 1985; and many others). We describe our approach to propositional meaning representation in detail in Nirenburg and Defrise forthcoming, a and b.

3.3.4   Relations

We distinguish domain relations, text relations and relations between intentions and domain-related text components. In what follows, we further develop this taxonomy, taking into account semantic and pragmatic phenomena. For some of them we provide an example of lexical realization.[4]

---

[4]A full study and description of all the possible realizations of each subtype is needed. At this point, we have only partial results, which will be extended in the future.

3.3.4.1   Domain Relations

Domain relations connect events, states and objects. We further subdivide domain relations into six main subtypes: causal, conjunction, alternation, coreference, temporal and spatial. Discussion of these groups and their further sudivision follows.

Causal   Causal relations describe a type of *dependence* among events, states and objects. We distinguish the following subtypes:

- *Volitional* causal relations hold between a deliberate, intentional action of an intelligent agent and its consequence. ("John turned the ignition key and the engine started.")

- *Nonvolitional* causal relations hold between a nonintential action or a state of an intelligent agent and its consequence. ("I fell and broke my leg.")

- Relations of *reason* hold among an event or state and a deliberate, intentional action by an agent. Often (but not always) they are lexically realized in English through *because, since* or *for the reason that*. ("I am prepared to help him because he helped you.")

- An event *enables* another event or a state when it removes the obstacles that were preventing the latter from occurring. ("Because the weather has improved, we can go on a walk." "The plug developed a leak, so the water escaped.")

- Event A is a *purpose* for event or state B if A describes a goal that an intelligent agent tries to achieve by performing B. ("He will leave early to catch the plane.")

- Event or state A is a *condition* for event or state B if A is a cause, reason, enablement or purpose of A, and A is an event or a state that has not actually happened and is, thus, hypothetical. ("If I win in the lottery, I'll travel to Java.")

Conjunction   The relation of conjunction holds among adjacent elements in a text that can be seen as components of a larger textual element. We distinguish the following subgroups:

- *Addition* is a type of conjunction in which one (or more) of the conjuncts are set apart from others, sometimes for rhetorical purposes. ("Playing this piece involves real musical talent as well as technique.")

- *Enumeration* is a type of conjunction in which all of the conjuncts have equal status. ("Athos went to Paris, bought a horse, visited his cousin, and strolled along the Seine.")[5]

- *Adversative* relations connect conjuncts whose differences are stressed in the utterance. ("Playing this piece involves real musical talent, not only technique.")

- Event or state A stands in a *concessive* relation to event or state B if A is typically not believed to be a result of A. Often introduced in English by *(even) though*. ("Even though the brick hit the window, the glass didn't break.")[6]

- Entity A stands in the relation of *comparison* to entity B if the speaker believes that A and B are in some sense similar. ("Peter walked around the kitchen table like a hungry wolf.")[7]

Alternation   Relations of alternation are used in situations of choice, parallel to the logical connector *or*.

- *Inclusive 'or'*. ("If you are an ex-prisoner of war or handicapped, you are entitled to state benefits.")

- *Exclusive 'or'*. ("I'll either go to the seaside or visit Florence.")[8]

Coreference   The relation of coreference is established among textual references to an object, an event or a state. Thus, in the following,

---

[5]In Quirk et al. 1985, enumeration and addition are subtypes of the *and* relation.

[6]The distinction between adversatives and concessives was found in Rudolph 1988.

[7]This relation is adapted from Warner 1979, where, however, it is not considered to belong to the conjunction class.

[8]This relation is adapted from Warner 1979.

(3.8)   [George Bush]₁ hosted [Gorbachev]₂ at the White House; then [he]₁ invited [him]₂ to Camp David; the next day [the Soviet president]₂ left for Minnesota.

coreference relations hold among similarly bracketed entities. This relation is similar to *designation* in Quirk et al. 1985, 630.

Temporal   Our current theory of temporal relations is deliberately simplified. In our application work we do not seem to require a finer grain size of description of temporal relations. If such a necessity occurs, we would of course further develop the microtheory of time. We believe that complex representations of time (such as the interval-based theory suggested by Allen (1984)) practically always constitute overkill for the purposes of machine translation. We use three relations:

- The *at* relation. Two events happen at the same time (the events can be either momentary or prolonged). ("When the war began she was in Vienna.")

- The *after* relation. One event succeeds another. ("The king abdicated. Later, he was reinstated.")

- The *during* relation. One event takes place after the beginning and before the end of another event. ("While the war was raging, they exchanged letters about bird-watching.")

Spatial   We distinguish the following spatial relations: *in-front-of, left-of, above, in, on* and *around.* Just as in the case of temporal relations, we do not at this point have a fine-grained microtheory of spatial relations. The development of such a theory is among the directions of future research, if and when they prove necessary.

3.3.4.2   Text Relations

Text relations are relations among elements of text—sentences, enumeration items, paragraphs and so on—rather than among events and/or objects described in the text. We distinguish three types of text relations, as follows:

1. The *particular* relation connects two textual elements (sentences, paragraphs, etc.) one of which is an example or a special case of the other. ("It is important that young children should see things and not merely read about them. For example, it is a valuable educational experience to take them on a trip to a farm" (Quirk et al. 1985, 668)).

2. The two textual elements connected by the relation of *reformulation* have a similar speaker meaning expressed in different ways. ("Peter works too much. That is to say, he neglects his family.")

3. In the relation of *conclusion,* a text element serves as a marker of end of discourse (including summary) for the other. ("In short, ...")

In an earlier version of this taxonomy (see, e.g., Nirenburg and Defrise forthcoming, a), we included additional text "pointer" relations, as well as relations delineating discourse structure boundaries. We believe now that such relations (for instance, meanings like the one which is typically realized in English by *in the previous chapter*) are devices for maintaining text cohesion and readability and that they representationally belong in the *text plan*, the structure that is produced from text meaning representation during the first stage of the generation process. In the text planning rules for DIOGENES, for example, we have used *textual-before* as a relation that connects text plan elements. In general, we offer the following taxonomy of these text plan relations:

1. Text pointers

   • *textual-before* ("In the previous chapter, we dealt with the question of anaphora.")

   • *textual-at* ("We give a further example on page 6.")

2. Discourse structure boundaries

   • *now:* ("We will now turn to the next point.")

   • *pop:* ("Anyway, let's return to the main point.")

   • *end:* ("And that's the end of the story.")

3.3.4.3   Intention-Domain Relations

The following relations connect the events described in the text with the intentions of the speaker, as made manifest in speech acts:

1. *Temporal intention-domain* relations connect the time of speech with the time of the action or event expressed by the utterance. There are two subtypes of such relations:

- *intention-domain-during:* ("It is raining [*at the time of the utterance*]." "John is a teacher [*at the time of the utterance*].")

- *intention-domain-after:* ("Paul went to Paris [*before the time of the utterance*].")

2. *Motivation* relations connect a speech act to a clause expressing an event or an attitude. The content of the clause motivates the reason to perform the speech act (that is, the reason to utter the clause whose illocutionary force corresponds to the speech act). ("Your mother didn't come back last night. [*I know this*] Because the mail is still in the mailbox." "Can you meet me at the office before three? [*I need this because*] I have a meeting at four.") The causal link expressed by *because* in the first example above does not express a causal link between two domain-related facts, that is, between (i) the mother not coming back and (ii) the mail being left out. It rather means that the producer can perform the speech act of *informing* the consumer of fact (i) having made an inference based on the fact that the mail is out. In the second example above, the domain fact *I have a meeting at four* is the reason for the speech act of *request-information*.

3.3.5 Discussion

Domain structure and text structure discovery procedures interact. That is why a cooperative text producer can afford not to make all available relations explicit in the text—there is no need to mention every fact explicitly since the author can depend on the reader's ability to make inferences to fill in gaps.

The interlingua language TAMERLAN, as presented above, is far from complete. We must, however, treat an interlingua not only as a complete set of statements about meaning in a sublanguage of a given application, but also as a sequence of consecutive versions of such a language, which come progressively closer to an ideal all-encompassing language. This progression of interlingua versions is at the core of the research and development methodology in knowledge-based machine translation.

In our work, we adopt the methodological attitude of developing the natural language processing functionalities in a breadth-first fashion. That is to say that, unlike many other projects, we do not tend to describe exhaustively a specific linguistic phenomenon (e.g., negation, anaphora, aspect, scope of quantifiers) or type of processing (e.g., text planning, lexical selection, syntactic realization) before proceeding to the next one (this approach can be considered depth-first). We prefer to go for a complete functioning system that contains all (or, in practice, most) of the above components and covers all (or most) of the above phenomena. It is clear that, at the beginning, the treatment of each (or most) of these components is incomplete, and not every phenomenon is described in sufficient detail. However, this methodology allows us to benefit from a complete experimentation environment and an open-ended architecture that facilitates the addition of knowledge to the system and its testing and debugging. In addition, the breadth-first methodology coupled with a working system enforces consistency of treatment for each phenomenon and focuses attention where it is most needed—on the phenomena whose treatment most needs to be improved from the standpoint of the overall system performance.

3.4   An Extended Example

We illustrate the actual format of TAMERLAN text through the representation of a sample text. The natural language text we use in this illustration is a fragment of an advertisement published in *The Daily Hampshire Gazette*, Northampton, Massachusetts, on April 26, 1985.

> Drop by your old favorite Dunkin' Donuts shop and you'll not only
> find fresh donuts made by hand, fresh Munchkins donut hole treats,
> the delicious smell of fresh-brewed coffee, and more. You'll also find
> a fresh new Dunkin' Donuts shop.

In the FRAMEKIT intepretation, a TAMERLAN text is a directed graph rooted at the *text* frame, whose nodes are frame identifiers or terminal symbols (slot values), and whose arcs are slot names.

Prefixes on symbols in the TAMERLAN representation have the meanings given in table 3.1.

```
(make-frame text_1
        (clauses (value clause_1 clause_2
                        clause_3 clause_4
                        clause_5 clause_6 clause_7 ))
        (relations (value relation_1 relation_2
                        relation_3 relation_4
                        relation_5 relation_6
                        relation_7 relation_8))
        (attitudes (value attitude_1 attitude_2 attitude_3))
        (producer-intentions (value producer-intention_1)))
```

PREFIX	MEANING
&	A symbolic constant, a member of a value set defined in the ontology as the range of an attribute.
%	An instantiated ontological concept. Note that the TAMERLAN syntactic structure identifier tokens (*text, clause, relation, attitude*) are not prefixed with '%' since they are not part of the ontology.
%%	A *generic* instance of an ontological concept, used to represent set elements and other similar entities to which one doesn't individually refer.
$	A "remembered" instance, e.g., *John F. Kennedy*.
*	A concept from the ontology.
<symbol>	A special variable.

Table 3.1: TAMERLAN **symbol prefixes and their meanings.**

The text frame serves as the index for all the clauses and relations in it. This particular text has 7 clauses and 13 relations. `clause_1` represents the meaning of "Visit your favorite Dunkin' Donuts shop!"

```
(make-frame clause_1
        (head (value %visit_1))
        (aspect (duration prolonged)
                (phase begin)
                (iteration 1))
        (time (value time_2)))

(make-frame %visit_1
        (is-token-of (value *visit))
        (agent (value *consumer*))
        (destination (value %shop_1)))
```

The special variables `*producer*` and `*consumer*` represent models of the speaker/writer/author and hearer/reader, respectively. Aspectual properties are represented as values on three properties—*duration, phase* (that is, beginning, continuation or end) and *iteration*. A detailed description of our microtheory of aspect is presented in Nirenburg and Pustejovsky 1988. In this example, we stress the fact that a visit is not an instantaneous event and that the phasal meaning is inchoative (beginning). The properties *agent, experiencer, destination* and *theme* are case roles.

```
(make-frame %shop_1
            (is-token-of (value *shop))
            (part-of (value $dunkin-donuts))))

(make-frame %shop_1_1
    (time-token-of (value %shop_1))
    (time (value (until time_4))))

(make-frame %shop_1_2
    (time-token-of (value %shop_1))
    (time (value (since time_4))))
```

Object instances in TAMERLAN are represented as trees of time-stamped frames. This is required to be able to refer (i) to an object instance when some of its properties change over time and (ii) to previously held beliefs about some properties of this instance. In our example, shop_1 is the root of the tree, the timeless reference to a particular object instance. Its timed subinstances, shop_1_1 and shop_1_2 represent the shop before and after remodeling. However, if after another visit it will appear that the shop was, in fact, *not* remodeled after all, then the representation of the instance will consist of the following subinstances:

- shop_1_1_1 —the consumer's remembered belief, after the first visit, about the state of the shop before the first visit

- shop_1_2_1 —the remembered belief, after the first visit, about the state of the shop after the first visit

- shop_1_1_2 —the belief, after the second visit, about the current state of the shop

In this example, the subinstance shop_1_1_1 is identical to shop_1_1_2. At the moment, for the sake of simplicity, we disregard the representations of producer beliefs about object instance property changes. In future implementations, however, we expect to introduce not only producer beliefs but also an indication of the strength of these beliefs, which would help in processing heuristic preference rules in both analysis and generation.

In the current example, both the time-stamped instances (shop_1_1, see relation_7, and shop_1_2, see %involuntary-visual-event _1 and relation_8) have a *relative* time constraint, specified in relation_7 and relation_8.

The meaning of *find* will be understood as a perceptual-event. Since the consumer will not deliberately look for the things that he will perceive, it will be classified as an `involuntary-perceptual-event`. **In fact, in the underlying ontology, the perceptual action subnetwork has the following form:**

```
perceptual-event
   voluntary-perceptual-event
         voluntary-visual-event        (look)
         voluntary-auditory-event      (listen)
         voluntary-tactile-event       (touch-1, run fingers across)
         voluntary-gustatory-event     (taste-1)
         voluntary-olfactory-event     (sniff, smell-1)
   involuntary-perceptual-event
         involuntary-visual-event      (see)
         involuntary-auditory-event    (hear)
         involuntary-tactile-event     (touch-2)
         involuntary-gustatory-event   (taste-2)
         involuntary-olfactory-event   (smell-2)
```

The meaning of "the consumer will perceive (i) donuts, (ii) Munchkins, (iii) the smell of coffee, (iv) a new shop and (v) additional things" is represented in TAMERLAN using as many clauses as there are instances of perception involved. Thus, the doughnuts, the Munchkins and the new shop are understood as having been involuntary perceived *visually* (this is, in fact, the default mode of perception), coffee as involuntary perceived *olfactorily*, and the meaning of "other things," which is a gloss of the meaning of *more* in the input, is realized as an instance of `involuntary-perceptual-event` because it is not specified what type of perception may be involved.

`clause_2` represents the meaning of "the consumer will perceive donuts."

```
(make-frame clause_2
    (head (value %involuntary-perceptual-event_1))
    (aspect
      (phase begin)
      (duration prolonged)
      (iteration 1))
      (time (value time_3)))

  (make-frame %involuntary-perceptual-event_1
    (is-token-of (value *involuntary-perceptual-event))
    (experiencer (value *consumer*))
    (theme (value %set_1)))

(make-frame %set_1
    (is-token-of (value *set))
    (type (value conjunctive))
    (element (value %%doughnut-1)))
```

```
(make-frame %%doughnut-1
    (is-token-of (value *doughnut))
    (age (value (< 0.1))))
```

The age of doughnuts is a range of values on a scale. The 'age < 0.1' slot expresses the fact that the doughnuts are fresh. Note that it is necessary to mark an instance of %%doughnut, %%doughnut-1, because of the constraint (the age) which is true only of this group of doughnuts. (See below the similar treatment of %%munchkin.)

Multiple fillers of the value facet of a FRAMEKIT frame are interpreted as conjoined elements. Sets in TAMERLAN are of two kinds—single element-type sets, as in the text about doughnuts, or enumerated sets, in which elements are overtly listed, as in the following example.

```
(make-frame %set_x
    (is-token-of (value *enumerated-set))
    (elements (value %element_1 %element_2 ...)))
```

Note that elements in the representation above can, naturally, be sets in their own right.

In this example, one representational property of *set, its cardinality, is not shown. The reason for this is that the cardinality of none of the sets used in our example is known.

clause_3 represents the meaning of "the consumer will perceive Munchkins."

```
(make-frame clause_3
    (head (value %involuntary-perceptual-event_2))
    (aspect
      (phase begin)
      (duration prolonged)
      (iteration 1))
    (time (value time_3)))

 (make-frame %involuntary-perceptual-event_2
    (is-token-of (value *involuntary-perceptual-event))
    (experiencer (value *consumer*))
    (theme (value %set_2 )))

(make-frame %set_2
    (is-token-of (value *set))
    (type (value conjunctive))
    (element (value %%munchkin-1)))
```

```
(make-frame %%munchkin_1
    (is-token-of (value *munchkin))
    (age (value (< 0.1))))
```

clause_4 represents the meaning of "The consumer will find a new shop."

```
(make-frame clause_4
    (head (value %involuntary-perceptual-event_3))
    (aspect
     (phase begin)
     (duration prolonged)
     (iteration 1))
     (time (value time_3)))
```

```
(make-frame %involuntary-perceptual-event_3
    (is-token-of (value *involuntary-perceptual-event))
    (experiencer (value *consumer*))
    (theme (value %shop_1_2 )))
```

clause_5 represents the meaning of "the consumer will perceive aroma of coffee."

```
(make-frame clause_5
    (head (value %involuntary-olfactory-event_1))
    (aspect
     (phase begin)
     (duration prolonged)
     (iteration 1))
      (time (value time_3)))
```

```
(make-frame %involuntary-olfactory-event_1
    (is-token-of (value *involuntary-olfactory-event))
    (experiencer (value *consumer*))
    (theme (value %coffee_1)))
```

```
(make-frame %coffee_1
    (is-token-of (value *coffee))
    (age (value (< 0.1))))
```

clause_6 represents the meaning of "the consumer will perceive things." At this point the representation does not specify that these "things" do not include those mentioned earlier in the text. This information may not be needed in some applications, such as, for instance, machine translation, where no reasoning is expected that would involve the determination of what these "things" actually are. An extension of the TAMERLAN text will be needed for such applications where this information may be essential, such as, for instance, question answering systems.

```
(make-frame clause_6
    (head (value %involuntary-perceptual-event_4))
    (aspect
     (phase begin)
     (duration prolonged)
     (iteration 1))
     (time (value time_3)))

(make-frame %involuntary-perceptual-event_4
    (is-token-of (value *involuntary-perceptual-event))
    (experiencer (value *consumer*))
    (theme (value %set_3 )))

(make-frame %set_3
    (is-token-of (value *set))
    (type (value conjunctive))
    (element (value (set-difference ontosubtree(physical-object)
                        (*doughnut *munchkin *coffee *shop)))))
```

Now, ontosubtree is a function that returns a list of all concepts in the subtree(s) of its argument(s), which should be ontological concepts. All elements of the set %set_3 are therefore the ontological descendents of physical-object, with the exception of the concepts *doughnut, *munchkin, *coffee and *shop. Intuitively, this means that additional things that one can see in the shop are all kinds of objects other than those mentioned in the text.

clause_7 represents the meaning of "Doughnuts at Dunkin' Donuts are made by hand."

```
(make-frame clause_7
    (head (value %produce_1))
    (aspect
     (phase continue)
     (duration prolonged)
     (iteration 1))
    (time (value *always*)))

(make-frame %produce_1
    (is-token-of (value *produce))
    (theme (value %set_1))
    (production-mode (value &manual)))
```

clause_8 represents the sense of "The shop has been recently remodeled."

```
(make-frame clause_8
    (head (value %remodel_1))
    (aspect
        (phase end)
        (duration prolonged)
        (iteration 1))
    (time (value time_4)))

(make-frame %remodel_1
    (is-token-of (value *remodel))
    (theme (value %shop_1_1)))

(make-frame relation_1
    (type (value domain-conditional))
    (first (value %visit_1))
    (second (value  %involuntary-perceptual-event_1)))

(make-frame relation_2
    (type (value domain-conditional))
    (first (value  %visit_1))
    (second (value  %involuntary-perceptual-event_2)))

(make-frame relation_3
    (type (value domain-conditional))
    (first (value %visit_1))
    (second  (value %involuntary-perceptual-event_3)))

(make-frame relation_4
    (type (value domain-conditional))
    (first (value  %visit_1))
    (second (value %involuntary-olfactory-event_1)))

(make-frame relation_5
    (type (value domain-conditional))
    (first (value  %visit_1))
    (second (value %involuntary-perceptual-event_4)))
```

These five relations represent the idea that it is possible to perceive all the things in the new shop (including the new shop itself!) if one visits it.

```
(make-frame relation_6
    (type (value domain-temporal-during))
    (first (value  time_3))
    (second (value  time_2)))
```

The perception of doughnuts, Munchkins, coffee, "other things" and the re-modelled shop (time_3) occurs during the visit (time_2).

```
(make-frame relation_7
    (type (value domain-temporal-after))
    (relation-value (value 0.8))
    (first (value time_2))
    (second (value time_5)))
```

The positive attitude toward the shop existed long before the visit was made. (This is the realization of "*old* favorite.") The relation value is an estimate of the distance of the two events (making the visit and holding the attitude). The value 0.8 corresponds roughly to "large." (The value 1 means "infinite" distance.)

```
(make-frame relation_8
    (type (value intention-domain-temporal-after))
    (relation-value (value 0.2))
    (first (value time_1))
    (second (value time_4)))
```

The shop was remodeled not long before the statement was made. "Not long ago" is realized through `relation-value`.

```
(make-frame relation_9
    (type (value domain-conjunction-enumeration))
    (arguments (value %involuntary-perceptual-event_1
                      %involuntary-perceptual-event_2
                      %involuntary-perceptual-event_3
                      %involuntary-olfactory-event_1
                      %involuntary-perceptual-event_4))
```

```
(make-frame relation_10
   (type (value intention-domain-temporal-after))
   (relation-value (value 0.2))
   (first (value  time_2))
   (second (value time_3)))
```

`relation_10` represents the fact that visiting should start before the perception.

```
(make-frame attitude_1
    (type (value &evaluative))
    (attitude-value (value 0.9))
    (scope (value %shop_1))
    (attributed-to (value *consumer*))
          (time (value (since time_5)))))
```

The presence of `attitude_1` is the TAMERLAN way of realizing the meaning of "favorite." The value of the `attributed-to` slot realizes the meaning of "your." Epistemic attitudes to events, objects or properties are not overtly listed if their values are 1.

```
(make-frame attitude_2
    (type (value &saliency))
    (attitude-value (value 0.7))
    (scope (value %involuntary-perceptual-event_1
                  %involuntary-perceptual-event_2
                  %involuntary-perceptual-event_4
                  %involuntary-olfactory-event_1))
    (attributed-to (value *producer*)))

(make-frame attitude_3
    (type (value &saliency))
    (attitude-value (value 1))
    (scope (value %involuntary-perceptual-event_3 ))
    (attributed-to (value *producer*)))
```

The hearer will expect to find fresh douhgnuts, fresh Munchkins and fresh coffee in a Dunkin' Donuts shop. A redecorated shop will be unexpected.

```
(make-frame producer-intention_1
    (is-token-of (value *commissive-act*))
    (scope (value relation_1 relation_2 relation_3 relation_4)))
```

The speech act performed by uttering the above text is a conditional request.

As one can see from the above example, the TAMERLAN representation of the text is detailed, unambiguous and explicit, reflecting the difference mentioned early between text (concise but ambiguous and partially implicit) and computer-manipulable text (verbose but unambiguous and completely explicit). Some details, of course, need not to be represented in TAMERLAN for certain types of practical tasks (such as limited-domain translation).

Chapter 4

Lexicography and Knowledge Acquisition

In knowledge-based machine translation systems, lexicons play as central a role as in any other approach to machine translation. However, the amount of information included in KBMT lexicon entries is typically much larger than that in other systems. This is because KBMT lexicons must support deeper levels of natural language processing—not just morphological and syntactic but also semantic and pragmatic. All knowledge-based machine translation lexicons rely on the existence of an ontology (as described in chapter 3) and a sufficient number of domain models to provide the internal vocabulary for describing the meanings of various lexical units.

In some knowledge-based machine translation systems there can be two lexicons, one for analysis and one for generation. This approach was advocated by Nirenburg and Raskin (1987 a and b). In some other systems the information needed for both types of processing is incorporated in a single lexicon, although the *processes* of analysis and synthesis may be quite different. Lexicons for knowledge-based machine translation can take a large number of shapes and forms. However, all of them must support all of the morphological, syntactic, semantic and pragmatic analysis, as well as text planning, including lexical selection and realization in generation.

4.1   The Lexicon Structure

In this section we illustrate the lexicon structure appropriate for knowledge-based machine translation using the lexicon of the DIONYSUS project. We will do so through a set of annotated examples.[1] The examples show only those senses of the corresponding lexemes that are used in the sample text of chapter 3. So, the following is the lexical entry for one nominal sense of the English word *doughnut*.

```
(donut
    (make-frame
        +doughnut-n1
        (CAT (value n))
        (STUFF
              (DEFN "pastry cooked in fat, usually in the shape of
                   a ring or ball")
              (EXAMPLES "Dunkin' Donuts produces more donuts than
                   all other fast food outlets put together"))
        (ORTH (variants doughnut))
        (SYN
             (count +) (proper -))
        (SEM
             (LEX-MAP
                   (%doughnut))))))
```

The `stuff` zone in the definition contains human-oriented information and is not used by the system itself. Examples come from text corpora, and definitions from machine-readable dictionaries (MRDs). The `orth` zone lists spelling variants. The `syn` zone lists paradigmatic syntactic features, in this case, the fact that the English noun *doughnut* is countable and common. The `sem` zone in the above example is a simple lexical mapping of the meaning of this sense of *doughnut* into a corresponding ontological concept, which happens to have the same name due to a decision by the domain model builder. Detailed semantic information is contained only in the ontology and referenced in the lexicon via the `lex-map` field.

The following entry demonstrates our way of recording inflectional irregularities:

```
(find
 (make-frame
  +find-v1
  (CAT (value v))
  (STUFF
```

---

[1]A more detailed description of this is given in Meyer et al. 1990.

```
(DEFN "to discover by chance, to come across")
(EXAMPLES "drop by your old favorite Dunkin Donuts
           shop and you'll not only find fresh donuts made
           by hand"
           "when I arrived home last night, I found a drunk
           sleeping on the porch/that a drunk was sleeping
           on the porch"))
(MORPH
 (IRREG (*v+past* found) (*v+past-part* found)))
(SYN-STRUC
           (*OR* ((root $var0)
                  (subj (root $var1) (cat N))
                  (obj  (root $var2) (cat N)))
                 ((root $var0)
                  (subj (root $var1) (cat N))
                  (xcomp (root $var2)(cat V) (form pres-part)))
                 ((root $var0)
                  (subj (root $var1) (cat N))
                  (comp (root $var2) (cat V) (form fin)))))))
(SEM
    (LEX-MAP
          (%involuntary-perceptual-event
                (experiencer (value ^$var1))
                (theme (value ^$var2))))))
```

Here, the `syn-struc` zone describes the subcategorization classes of the entry
head. In the entry above there are three subcategorization variants, all with different
types of direct objects that *find* may take. The variables in the specifications are
used for binding the values of arguments. In the `lex-map` slot of the `sem` zone
these bindings help to determine which syntactic entities the arguments' intensions
(semantic interpretations) correspond to. (The '`^`' prefix marks the intensions.) The
lexical mapping above says that the given sense of *find* is mapped in TAMERLAN as
an instance of the `%involuntary-perceptual-event` ontological concept.
Moreover, the semantic interpretation of whatever occupied the `subj` position in
the f-structure should be assigned as the value of the `experiencer` thematic role
in the above concept instance; the meaning of whatever occupied the `obj`, `xcomp`
or `comp` position in the f-structure should be assigned as the value of the `theme`
thematic role in the concept instance.

Now consider the following:

```
(drop
    (make-frame
        +drop-v1
        (CAT (value v))
```

```
(STUFF
        (DEFN "to visit a place")
        (EXAMPLES "drop by your old favorite Dunkin'
                  Donuts shop"))
(SYN-STRUC
            ((root $var0)
             (subj ((root $var1) (cat n)))
             (obliques ((root $var2) (prep by)))))
(SEM
      (LEX-MAP
              (%visit
                      (AGENT (value ^$var1))
                      (THEME (value ^$var2)
                             (sem *location)
                             (relaxable-to *object)))))))
```

As can be seen from this example, verbs with particles are treated through the same mechanism as particle-less verbs. The `lex-map` slot above says two things. First, the meaning of the head of the structure that fills the `obliques` f-structure slot carries a semantic constraint; it must be an instance of a concept in the ontological subnetwork rooted at `*location`. The slot also says that this constraint can be relaxed in real text to the subnetwork rooted at `*object`. The relaxation statement is used to process metonymy, as in the sentence *Drop by the committee meeting*.

Next, consider the frame for *delicious*:

```
(delicious
    (make-frame
        +delicious-adj1
        (CAT (value adj))
        (STUFF
            (DEFN "very pleasing to sense of taste or smell
                  or sight")
            (EXAMPLES "delicious meal" "delicious smell"
                      "the meal looks delicious"))
        (SYN
            (attributive + -))
        (SYN-STRUC
                ((root $var1)
                 (cat n)
                 (mods ((root $var0)))))

                ; pattern shown for attributive use only
```

```
(SEM
    (LEX-MAP
      (^$var1
        (instance-of (sem (*OR* *ingestible
                                *olfactory-attribute
                                *gustatory-attribute
                                *visual-attribute))))
                (ATTITUDE
                    (type (value evaluative))
                    (attitude-value (value 0.8))
                    (scope (value ^$var1))
                    (attributed-to (value *producer*)))))))
```

The meaning of *delicious* is a speaker attitude of type evaluative, with a high value on the zero-to-unity scale. The attitude can be toward a perception attribute, as specified in the constraint on the meaning of the noun that *delicious* modifies.

Now, the preposition *by*:

```
(by
    (make-frame
      +by-prep1
      (CAT (value prep))
            (DEFN "using the instrument of")
            (STUFF "made by hand" "designed by computer"
                   "produced by machine"))
      (SYN-STRUC
                ((root $var1)
                 (cat n)
                 (pp-adjunct ((root $var0)
                              (obj (root $var2)
                                   (cat n)))))
      (SEM
          (LEX-MAP
                (^$var1
                    (instance-of (sem *physical-event))
                    (instrument (value ^$var2)
                                (sem
                                  (*OR* *hand *artifact)))))))))
```

Here, the sense of the preposition *by* is specified in terms of constraints on the head of the NP inside the PP introduced by *by* and the head of the phrase to which the prepositional phrase is attached. The latter is constrained to an instance of physical-event (which can be realized by a verb or a noun). The former must be an instance of an entity in the ontological subnetwork of either *hand or

*artifact. Moreover, the latter should play the thematic role of instrument in the latter.

Now note the (neg +) marker in the following:

```
(only
    (make-frame
        +only-adv1
        (CAT (value adv))
        (STUFF
                (DEFN "=merely, simply")
                (EXAMPLES "you'll not only find fresh donuts made
                        by hand ... you'll also find a fresh
                        new Dunkin' Donuts shop"))
        (SYN
            (neg +))
        (SYN-STRUC
            ((root $var1)
            (cat v)
            (adjuncts ((root $var0)))
            (obj ((root $var2)))))

        (SEM
            (LEX-MAP
                    (ATTITUDE
                        (type (value saliency))
                        (attitude-value (value 0.3))
                        (scope (value ^$var3))
                        (attributed-to (value *producer*)))))))))
```

The (neg +) marker is used to show that *only* in this sense is preceded by *not* and is a part of the correlative *not only...but also*. The meaning of *only* is represented through a relatively low-saliency attitude value. Intuitively this means that the content of the clause introduced by *only* in this sense is considered less salient by the text producer than the content of the clause introduced by *but also*.

Let's take a look at the final two frames:

```
(your
    (make-frame
        +your-poss1
        (CAT (value poss))
        (STUFF
                (DEFN "very general sense of association with
                    a service institution")
                (EXAMPLES "drop by your old favorite Dunkin Donuts
                        shop"
```

```
                        "your local post office should be able
                           to help"
                        "your friendly neighborhood gas station"))
        (SYN
            (number s2 p2))
        (SYN-STRUC
                ((root $var1)
                 (cat n)
                 (poss ((root $var0)))))
        (SEM
            (LEX-MAP
                  (^$var1
                         (instance-of (sem *service-corporation))
                         (has-customer (sem *human)))))
        (PRAGM
            (ANALYSIS-TRIGGER
                (coreferential ^$var1.has-customer *consumer*))))

(make-frame
    +your-poss2
    (CAT (value poss))
    (STUFF
        (DEFN "owned by/belonging to you")
        (EXAMPLES "can I borrow your book" "if you
        sell your store, you'll have lots of money"))
    (SYN
        (number s2 p2))
    (SYN-STRUC
            ((root $var1)
             (cat n)
             (poss ((root $var0)))))
    (SEM
        (LEX-MAP
            (^$var1
                (instance-of (sem *all))
                (owned-by (sem *human)))))
    (PRAGM
        (ANALYSIS-TRIGGER
            (coreferential ^$var1.owned-by *consumer*))))))
```

The salient point of the above definitions is the presence of the analysis-trigger slot in the pragmatics zone. The meaning of *your* includes the information that its referent is coreferential with the text consumer. The semantics of the second sense above also includes the indication that the relation between the object modified by *your* and the text consumer is that of ownership. The first sense above is constrained to modifying property meanings; these are typically realized in natural language through adjectives.

4.2   Lexicon Acquisition

Current research in computer lexicology and lexicography has three somewhat interrelated but generally distinct aims:

- Enhancing existing lexical resources and creating new ones for human users of dictionaries;

- Using human-oriented machine-readable dictionaries to perform computational tasks traditionally supported by hand-crafted specialized dictionaries;

- Developing methods for automatic transformation of information in human-oriented dictionaries into a form suitable for a variety of computational applications. For instance, most of the fields in the lexical entries illustrated above are not contained overtly in a dictionary for humans and must be extracted from dictionary definitions (see Wilks et al. 1990) or added from other sources, such as text corpora.

The third direction is the most relevant one from the standpoint of natural language processing (NLP) applications. In fact, when dictionaries are treated as source texts for automatic program-oriented dictionary creation, the entire enterprise falls well within the familiar paradigm of subworld/sublanguage-oriented natural language processing. The task at hand is, therefore, intrinsically no less (and no more) difficult than automatic language processing in other well-defined specialized domains. If developers of other computational linguistics applications, such as machine translation or dialog systems, are to rely on (become *consumers* of) the results of this research to provide the lexicons to support their systems, they will have to postpone development of their applications until the lexicon acquisition problem is solved. While this strategy may in the long run prove to be the wisest, in the short run it may be quite impractical. A compromise solution seems more appropriate—to acquire lexicons in a hybrid environment in which automatic analysis of on-line resources coexists with tools for manual knowledge extraction.

Scaling up the dictionaries and other knowledge bases of a knowledge-based machine translation system is essential for the overall success of the field of machine translation. There are several ways in which the indispensable and massive knowledge acquisition task can in principle be conducted. One can envisage developing a machine learning system for automatic acquisition of vast quantities of knowledge through corpus analysis in a subworld. Such a system can in principle delimit concepts and thus build an ontology and/or the model of a specific domain. Connecting elements of a natural language with elements of this ontology will, of course, be an additional and nontrivial task. Alternatively, one can design a natural language processing system whose task would be to read natural language texts and understand them. As the next step, these programs would compile facts learned about entities in the world, as well as elements of language and its usage, into on-line encyclopedias and dictionaries suitable for use in computational-linguistic and general artificial intelligence applications. It is doubtful whether these approaches can succeed, at least in the short run, because in order to build a machine-learning or a natural language processing system with the above-mentioned capabilities, we first need to supply it with knowledge bases and dictionaries of a size and sophistication comparable to those which these systems would be supposed to produce; compare the discussion in Lenat and Guha 1988, 19. We arrive at the bootstrapping problem, which seems to be central in many approaches to (at least semi-) automated knowledge acquisition. The Japan Electronic Dictionary Research Institute (EDR) has arrived at a similar position, as one can infer from their decision to rely on totally hand-coded monolingual and bilingual MT-oriented dictionaries of a significant size (Uchida 1990).

It is very time consuming to handcraft lexicons of the kind that most knowledge-based language processing systems require. But until recently the prevalent attitude was that it is impossible to finesse the knowledge acquisition problem, and that one must therefore be prepared to bite the bullet even though it might take several person-centuries to be completed. Let us call this the pessimistic position.

It is natural, however, to look for ways to simplify the acquisition task. The recent availability of on-line human-oriented dictionaries has raised hopes for the success of a large-scale automatic dictionary acquisition task. Significant results have been obtained in extracting information supporting morphological (e.g., Byrd et al. 1986) and syntactic (e.g., Boguraev and Briscoe 1987) analysis. Researchers working in this paradigm are optimistic—they believe that the amount of effort to produce a large, computer-oriented lexicon through processing human-oriented dictionaries will be significantly smaller than that required for hand-coding it. However, relatively few practical results have been so far obtained in extracting meaning from machine-readable dictionaries and in representing it in a format suitable for the use of application programs (natural language analyzers and generators). Considering the complexity of automatic conversion of human-oriented dictionaries into computer-oriented ones, it is not surprising that initial efforts have proved only partially successful.[2] Often research of this type leads not directly to creation of a program-oriented lexicon, but rather to a prerequisite, such as, for instance, large hierarchies of genus terms (Amsler 1980; Chodorow et al. 1985).

Developers of comprehensive natural language applications such as machine translation systems or human-computer interfaces can already use some of the results of MRD processing, especially with respect to syntactic information. Recent results and ongoing projects promise significant practical reverberations in the not too distant future. Instances of this work include Knight's (1989) research on lexicon acquisition in the framework of the CYC project (Lenat and Guha 1988); Boguraev's new work on extracting semantic information from MRDs (personal communication); and especially the results of the New Mexico State University group (e.g., Wilks et al. 1988, 1990). Of course, it does not seem realistic to expect *all* the problems of lexicon acquisition for computational applications to be solved through research in transforming MRDs that serve humans into "machine-tractable dictionaries" (MTDs) in Wilks's terminology) built specifically to serve natural language analysis and generation. But, as the size of the knowledge acquisition task for MT is formidable, the use of the results of the research on automatic MRD-to-MTD conversion may well hold the key to creating large application-oriented dictionaries.

At present no natural language system employs an automatic means of dictionary acquisition. In part this is because many such systems are of the "demonstration" kind and don't require sizable lexicons. In contrast, most large-scale transfer-oriented MT systems started with bilingual dictionaries that are little more than word-level transfer tables. Although gradually enriched through subsequent development, such lexical resources are inherently simpler and do not feature knowledge necessary for deeper analysis of source text, especially the knowledge required for lexical disambiguation. The MTDs described in this chapter centrally include such information. The direct use of machine-readable dictionaries as resources for NLP does not seem to be a viable option, since the size of the knowledge base of specialized heuristics and techniques for extracting the various types of information from such dictionaries will, for any realistic system, be of the same order of magnitude as a specially handcrafted lexicon. (For a more detailed justification of this position, with respect to machine translation applications, see Slocum and Morgan, forthcoming.) Work on automatic compilation of MTDs from MRDs has

---

[2]Of course, it is not easy to construct even a purely syntactic "polytheoretical" lexicon—as shown by Ingria (forthcoming)—in which a large set of information items for syntactic lexicons is sketched, and many existing program-oriented syntactic dictionaries are compared.

become by now a well-defined research area whose results will be immediately useful for acquiring knowledge in NLP systems. However, this point will not be reached overnight, and the potential consumers of the automatic knowledge extraction technology should not (and could not) put their own work on hold until such results are obtained. A reasonable strategy is to develop a methodology of gradual enhancement for automation in lexicon acquisition, preferably in the framework of a hybrid, computer- *and* human-initiative knowledge acquisition environment.

Some such hybrid work can already be done today, especially in simpler, transfer-oriented MT systems. Extensive semantic analysis is seldom used in such systems, even though their lexicons sometimes list semantic and pragmatic information. Thus, for example, in an early version of the the METAL machine translation system (Bennett and Slocum 1985) monolingual lexicon entries include the TAG feature, which lists subject domain information; the TY feature, which stands for the semantic type (presumably from an independently derived semantic type list); and the ARGS feature, which specifies, albeit in syntactic terms, the valency information about the entry head. In the current METAL system the subject-domain information is used for partial lexical disambiguation (Geert Adriaens, personal communication) during the transfer stage:

Fehler $\rightarrow$ bug   when   TAG: DP   (data processing)
Fehler $\rightarrow$ mistake   when   TAG: GV   (general vocabulary)

It seems quite conceivable that a significant portion of such a dictionary could be produced automatically using current dictionary processing techniques. The extraction of the above semantic features can be achieved using a program like Slator's lexicon-provider (Wilks et al. 1988). Thus, the TAG feature in METAL is similar to Slator's "pragmatic" slot; the TY and ARGS features could be derived from Slator's "type" slot. Of course, additional research should be performed to allow for automatic extraction of other semantic, syntactic and morphological information from human-oriented bilingual dictionaries as well as dictionaries of proper names, abbreviations and specialized subject-domain terminology.

Knowledge of specialized terminology, including abbreviations and proper names (see a discussion in Amsler 1987 and forthcoming) is also needed for the support of knowledge-based machine translation systems. Dictionaries for knowledge-based machine translation systems are typically required to contain significantly more semantic and pragmatic information than transfer-oriented MT systems.[3] In addition, KBMT MTDs rely on a language-independent knowledge base

---

[3]Although the content of the KBMT dictionaries is much richer than in transfer-oriented systems, the number of dictionaries has to be smaller since in KBMT systems there is no need for bilingual and

describing the subworld of translation, as well as some very general ontological statements about the world, about speakers and hearers and about the structure of texts and dialogs. These features are needed to support semantic and pragmatic disambiguation during the analysis stage. Knowledge requirements for knowledge-based MT systems are discussed in some detail in earlier chapters, as well as in Nirenburg 1987a. In principle, such systems must possess most of the types of inference-making capabilities of natural language processing systems in AI (cf., e.g., Waltz 1982 for a survey of relevant phenomena).

Dictionaries supporting target language generation in knowledge-based MT must include information about synonyms, antonyms and hyperonyms, which is needed to enhance the expressive power of the lexical selection module, notably, to support the ability to generate definite descriptions (cf. Sondheimer et al. 1990). Another generation-related requirement is providing information about syntagmatic collocation constraints on target language lexical units to ensure that the target text is colloquially adequate. Thus, while *wide* and *broad* are synonyms, the former collocates with *variety* and the latter does not. Collocation constraints, unlike selectional restrictions, are highly idiosyncratic and do not lend themselves easily to generalizations. If a degree of automation in the acquisition of this information is desired, special dictionaries must be used (e.g., the BBI dictionary, Benson et al. 1986) or specialized routines working on very large text corpora must be developed.

Descriptions of interactive knowledge acquisition systems can be found in Goodman and Nirenburg 1991 and in Nirenburg et al. 1988). Knowledge acquisition has been performed manually, with the help of specially designed tools, briefly described below. Having gone through relatively large-scale knowledge acquisition, we can clearly see the advantages of at least partial automation of this process. We present below a preliminary design for a knowledge acquisition environment. Such an environment would include some functionalities from the MRD-to-MTD research, as well as enhance human-directed acquisition. Developing a "knowledge acquisition workstation" of this sort can be accomplished without waiting for the the MRD-to-MTD research to reach a high level of practicality.

The MRD-to-MTD research operates at present under several methodological constraints which, while making certain results feasible, somewhat limit the kinds of semantic and lexical knowledge that can be included in the outputs of current systems. Wilks et al. (1988, 5) articulate some such constraints as the following methodological questions:

---

multilingual transfer dictionaries.

- *Sufficiency*: "whether a dictionary is a strong enough knowledge base for English"

- *Extricability*: "whether it is possible to specify a set of computational procedures that operate on an MRD and extract, through their operation alone and without any human intervention, general and reliable semantic information on a large scale and in a general format suitable for, though independent of, a range of subsequent NLP tasks"

- *Bootstrapping*: whether it is possible to create the initial information on which the MRD-to-MTD procedures rely from the dictionary itself.

Wilks et al. answer all these questions in the affirmative. But as briefly noted earlier, a single human-oriented dictionary can hardly be considered sufficient for supporting a realistic application. Even if we were to agree that the *Longman Dictionary of Contemporary English* (LDOCE; Procter et al. 1978) can be used for extracting a general ontology, it is not a useful source of specialized domain information, abbreviations or proper names. Moreover, one can find better sources for synonymy and hyperonymy information, collocations, idioms and so on. In addition to LDOCE, Longman has published, for example, a thesaurus-like *Lexicon of Contemporary English* (McArthur 1981) as well as a *Dictionary of Phrasal Verbs* (Courtney 1983) and a *Dictionary of English Idioms* (Long et al. 1979). A comparison between an output of Slator's Lexicon Producer program and the contents of a lexicon entry in a system such as KBMT-89 shows that the latter contains a significantly larger amount of knowledge. One can also argue for using machine-readable *encyclopedias* alongside MRDs (cf. Amsler, forthcoming; Walker 1987). An existing, handcrafted domain model (such as, for instance, a rule base for an expert system or a handcrafted computer-oriented encyclopedia, as in the CYC project (Lenat and Guha 1988) or a set of *core theories* of the world, as advocated by the TACITUS project (e.g., Hobbs et al. 1987)) can serve as the basis for at least some computational-lexicographic work. Finally, to serve a realistic-sized domain, lexical knowledge acquisition systems will routinely have to make use of *text corpora* from this domain as training texts on which to test and improve an emerging dictionary.

The extricability assumption has been partially shown correct by the fact that the programs by Plate, Guo and Slator (see Wilks et al. 1990)—as well as other programs (such as Chodorow et al. 1985)—already produce useful and largely reliable information. Thus, in the New Mexico environment the output of the MRD-to-MTD program by Slator produces dictionary entries used in at least two consumer programs—meta5 (Fass 1988) and PREMO (Slator 1988). However, the amount of knowledge provided for MTDs by Slator's LDOCE parser is somewhat limited. Many selectional restrictions and preferences are left out of the definitions. In order to be successful, the tree interpreter routine used by Slator for adding such information through analysis of *differentia* in LDOCE has to rely on a very detailed and extensive set of heuristic rules for meaning assignment to nominal, adjectival, prepositional and other modifiers. The acquisition of this set of rules is difficult to automate. At the same time, their availability is a prerequisite for producing comprehensive MTDs. Complete extricability remains, thus, a research objective, not a reality. Even partial extractability, however, can prove valuable for reducing the effort of compiling an MTD.

The further requirement of format generality (and therefore transportability) is more difficult to meet in practice without developing systems for translation among different knowledge representation languages. Even when such systems are developed, the added complexity of software maintenance will be a strong vote against this method of achieving knowledge shareability. A better solution may be to adopt standards for lexical entries and eventually knowledge representation languages.

Finally, internal bootstrapping will only work for closed knowledge repositories, such as LDOCE. Not all lexical units in text corpora used for testing and tuning an application can be expected to appear in an MRD. Whether additional concepts can be described using the primitives derived from an MRD (such as the set of modified controlled vocabulary items in LDOCE, as used by Guo's program (Wilks et al. 1990)), or whether additional primitives will have to be introduced, remains an open question to be treated empirically.

One way to make the MRD-to-MTD research results more usable today is to relax some or all of the above methodological assumptions, especially that of sufficiency. This will, however, make building automatic MRD-to-MTD transformation systems more difficult. A more realistic and practically feasible way of making this research more useful in the immediate future is, at least temporarily, to *forgo the requirement of complete automation.*

The gap between the immediate needs of the application systems and the current capabilities of the MRD-to-MTD systems can be bridged in a mixed-initiative knowledge acquisition system that would allow for human augmentation of results obtained through automatic processing of human-oriented knowledge repositories such as dictionaries of various kinds, encyclopedias and corpora.

Just as in KBMT-89, where the augmentor is used for improving and enhancing the results of automatic text analysis, in a hybrid knowledge acquisition environment a similar module can be used to augment the candidate MTD entries produced by an MRD-to-MTD system. In such an environment, the human knowledge enterer will have interactive access to a variety of machine-readable information resources, including MRDs, encyclopedias and corpora. Current advances in the design of interfaces facilitate the integration of all these diverse resources in a single workstation. By the same token, the human user will have a window into the existing portions of the MTDs. Several components of a mixed-initiative system already exist in the KBMT-89 knowledge-acquisition environment.

4.3 A Multipurpose Processing and Acquisition Environment

Knowledge acquisition applies to each of the static knowledge sources—domain models, lexicons and grammars. Acquisition can be carried out both as an off-line activity and in an incremental fashion, especially during the testing stages of a natural language processing system.

The nature of the dictionaries, ontologies and grammars also depends on the particular application. In fact, depending on a theoretical approach taken to certain parts of the analysis and generation tasks, even the boundaries between the grammars and the dictionaries on the one hand, and the dictionaries and the ontologies on the other, may sometimes be blurred. In some approaches the morphological information about lexical units is stored in the grammars; in others it is stored in the dictionaries. In some approaches most syntactic knowledge is stored in the grammars. In some others (notably, in the unification-oriented approaches), much of the syntactic knowledge is stored in the lexicon. In terms of lexico-semantics, some approaches consider the meanings of natural language units to be instances of concept types stored in ontological models; in other systems the importance of the ontological model is downplayed and the language in which lexical meanings are explained is that of word senses.

Recall figure 1.6 from chapter 1. The single arrows in it represent data flow from static knowledge sources to processing modules, with the exception of the link between the ontology and the lexicons. This connection can have two facets. First, some parts of the knowledge required in dictionary entries can be physically stored in the ontological models, because the meanings of open-class items can be interpreted as instances of particular ontological concepts. Second, all practical natural language processing systems expect their ontologies and lexicons to grow as they are used. Therefore, there is a knowledge acquisition importance to the connection between the ontology and the lexicons. The acquisition operations can be initiated on either side of the arrow. If a new open-class lexical unit is to be introduced into the system, it first is entered into the lexicon; then its meaning is interpreted in terms of either existing ontological concepts or a new set of concepts that must be included in the ontology in order to express this meaning. Conversely, if it becomes clear that the ontology for a particular application needs to be expanded, a set of new concepts has to be added to the ontology. After this is done, it becomes necessary to add to the lexicon entries (or entry parts) that realize the meanings of the new concepts in the natural languages in the system. Moreover, in multilingual systems it is beneficial to store as much semantics as possible in the ontology, referenced through the lexicon, since this knowledge can be represented once and reused for every language, both for analysis and generation.

Acquisition of ontologies and lexicons in most systems is typically manual and is usually performed in an "off-line" mode, with the processing system turned off. This means that natural language processing systems are not usually designed for "on-the-fly" updates of their grammar and lexicon support. In the advanced state-of-the-art natural language processing environments special background acquisition support systems are designed and implemented. Figure 4.1 illustrates the process of grammar, lexicon and ontology acquisition in such systems. Usually, there are two types of interfaces—one for grammar acquisition and another for dictionary acquisition. The latter is sometimes also used for specifying ontologies in those NLP systems that rely on ontology acquisition for their operation. Grammar acquisition interfaces allow for quick browsing through sets of grammar rules and types of structures that these grammars generate. An example of this type of system is the Intercoder interface of the METAL machine translation system (Liro 1989).

Similarly, current ontology and lexicon acquisition systems are typically manual. (There are several experimental systems attempting automatic lexicon acquisition, notably Wilks et al. 1990. However, they are not yet sufficiently general to support a realistic application.) A typical manual interface for lexicon and ontology acquisition includes a graphics interface with browsing capabilities to allow the representation of ontological concepts and lexicon entries as networks of nodes and links, thus facilitating comparison, search, generalization and information retrieval. An advanced acquisition system can also contain other means of access to the knowledge—for instance, a query subsystem that allows information retrieval through a menu-oriented and/or command-language interface. To support modification of the knowledge base, an acquisition system must also support an editor, preferably structured to reflect the basic data organization in the system (for

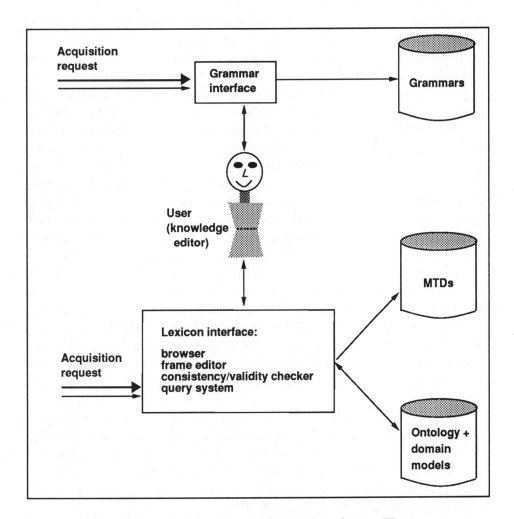

Figure 4.1: **Standalone knowledge acquisition interfaces. The grammar acquisition interface permits rapid browing through rule sets. Lexicon and ontology interfaces can include browsers, editors, consistency/validity checkers and query subsystems.**

example, representation systems can be either frame-based or rule-based). Finally, such a system will benefit from an automatic means of checking the validity of a newly introduced knowledge element as well as its consistency with objects already existing in the knowledge base. The preceding functionalities are all present in the knowledge acquisition system Ontos (e.g., Monarch and Nirenburg 1989) or the BBN knowledge acquisition environment (Abrett 1987; Burstein 1990; Zeitz 1987).

The recent growth of interest in creating on-line lexical resources and their corresponding user interfaces suggests a number of new possibilities for enhancing the productivity of the knowledge acquisition components in natural language processing systems. The main ways in which knowledge acquisition productivity can be enhanced is by allowing the knowledge engineer to consult on-line reference materials. Figure 4.2 illustrates an enhanced knowledge acquisition environment, which includes interfaces to machine-tractable dictionaries and encyclopedias as well as to textual corpora. Ontologies are consulted during the acquisition of MTD entries, but the lexicon acquisition interface is also used for updating the ontology itself. The unshaded barrels in the figure represent static knowledge sources that are used as aids in the acquisition of those static knowledge sources used in actual processing. The use of textual corpora is extremely helpful for determining lexical collocations and selectional restrictions on co-occurrences of various word senses through statistical processing. On-line encyclopedias help shape ontologies and domain models. Machine-readable dictionaries, with appropriate search and retrieval facilities, provide a convenient means of deriving candidates for word-sense delimitation and other relevant information for entries of machine-tractable dictionaries.

At present, there are no knowledge acquisition environments for natural language processing that feature all of the above functionalities. It is, however, completely within the state of the art to put together a system of this sort—for instance, by combining Ontos with an MRD interface such as Wordsmith (Neff and Byrd 1987) and a set of corpus-processing routines such as those used by the IBM speech processing group (P. Brown et al. 1988).

A major problem for current natural language processing systems is their brittleness or inability to deal with unconstrained input. A large part of this problem is due to the incompleteness of grammars and lexicons—indeed it is to be expected that at any given time in a natural language application that covers a broad domain, previously unencountered lexical units and syntactic constructions would appear in input texts. In current systems, when such a situation occurs, there are two typical strategies. First, the processing system can be built in such a way that it

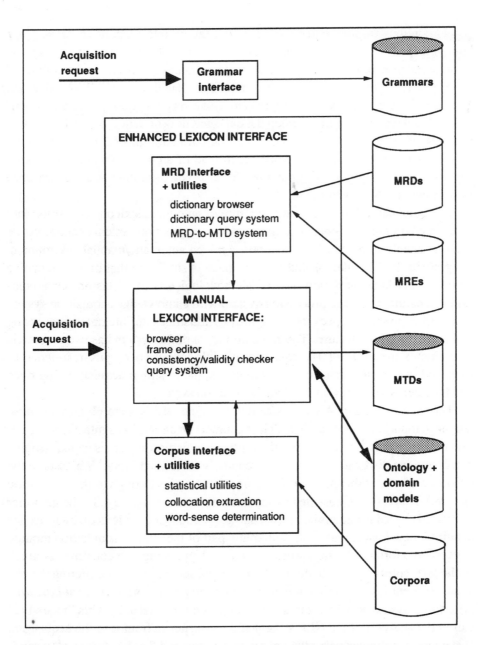

Figure 4.2: **Enhanced standalone knowledge acquisition interfaces. This includes interfaces to machine-tractable dictionaries and encyclopedias and textual corpora. Thick arrows represent control flow and thin arrows data flow. The link between the lexicon acquisition interface and the ontology represents both data and control flow.**

would continue to process the input without taking into account an "offending" component. This approach enhances the robustness of the system at the expense of potential inaccuracies in its processing. The strategy has been successfully used in the EPISTLE, CRITIQUE and PLNLP systems (e.g., Heidorn et al. 1982). Another way of dealing with unexpected input is to evoke specially designed "emergency" fail-soft and recovery routines when the expected flow of data is broken. A simple example of such a routine may be a spelling correction program, which would, for instance, suggest using the word *the* instead of an unknown and unexpected input string 'hte'. See Weischedel 1987 for a survey of problems and approaches to treatment of ill-formed input.

It is quite natural to introduce a measure of automatic lexicon acquisition into such an environment. Since automatic lexicon acquisition systems cannot yet be used separately in practical applications, a mixed automatic/manual environment suggests itself. The idea behind this approach is similar to that of an interactive editor in a machine translation system. Methodologically, this decision means combining a natural language processing system with a knowledge acquisition system and corpus processing packages. Figure 4.3 illustrates an integrated processing and acquisition architecture. The acquisition side of the system has two automatic components, the MRD-to-MTD acquisition module and a set of corpus treatment utilities, and two manual acquisition components, the grammar acquisition interface and the manual ontology and lexicon acquisition system.

The system in figure 4.3 works as follows. The NLP system obtains a natural language input and processes it until it encounters an unfamiliar syntactic construction or lexical unit.[4] At this point, the on-line acquisition system is called. (In this discussion we disregard the cases of genuinely ill-formed input. We assume the existence of a filter that passes only appropriate queries through to the acquisition system.) This call is represented by the thick, solid line in figure 4.3. The grammar interface is called for grammar knowledge acquisition, and the lexicon interface for acquiring new lexical units. The automatic part of the lexicon acquisition module suggests the format of a new word sense and then attempts to construct as much of the MTD entry as possible through parsing and semantically interpreting the relevant MRD entries. This functionality is supported by *the same natural language processing system* to which the acquisition system is attached. This "recursive" call to the analyzer of the NLP system and the response from it to the acquisition system are represented using the dotted lines in figure 4.3. The MRD-to-MTD mod-

---

[4]If no unfamiliar constructions or lexical units are found, the on-line acquisition system is not called, and the processing is the same as in a system with the architecture illustrated in figure 1.6 in chapter 1.

ule of the lexicon interface serves as the reasoning system in this version of the NLP system, while the generator is not required for it since the desired output is, in fact, a symbolic structure and not natural language text. When the automatic MRD-to-MTD interface ends its processing, typically, additional work is needed to produce a complete and correct MRD entry. Therefore, the MRD-to-MTD interface triggers the manual acquisition interface for control and actual incorporation into the lexicon.

During the operation of the reasoning system it can come to pass that a certain decision cannot be made because of insufficient detail in the ontological model. In this case there is an option of calling the acquisition system to augment the ontology.

During the operation of the generator, in cases when it is not possible to eliminate lexical synonymy, a search in a textual corpus can be used to determine the preferential lexical selection in a given context by comparing the frequencies of collocations of each of the elements in the set of lexical realization candidates with the lexical selections for units in the sentential context. Queries of this sort can be formulated automatically, but when their results should be recorded in the MTDs (as fillers of the lexical collocation slots of various word senses), it is necessary, just as in the case of automatic MRD-to-MTD conversion, to include a human quality-control step.

If we look at the automatic MRD-to-MTD systems in greater detail, we notice that they are architecturally identical to those natural language processing systems for which we have been discussing knowledge acquisition support. Indeed, their inputs are texts of entries in human-oriented MRDs, and their outputs are entries in MTDs. The reasoning component connecting the analyzer of MRD entries and the generator of MTD entries is the interactive knowledge acquisition system illustrated in figure 4.2. This observation suggests a novel design for a combination processing/acquisition system in which processing modules originally designed for one of the processing modes are at least partially reusable in the other. Ideally, one and the same system can be used both for processing and for acquisition.

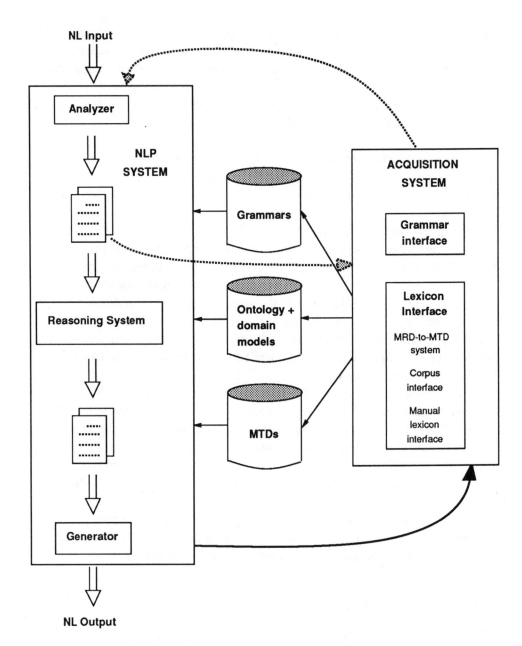

Figure 4.3: **An acquisition system coupled with an NLP system. The system obtains natural language input and processes it until an unfamiliar syntactic construction or lexical unit is encountered. Then, the on-line acquisition system is called (thick, solid line). Calls to and responses from the analyzer are represented by dotted lines. Other connections are marked with thin lines.**

Chapter 5

Source Language Analysis

5.1 The Phases of Natural Language Analysis

Natural language analysis is the process of mapping between a natural language text and a representation of its form and/or content. This representation can be a syntactic structure representation, a representation of the text's propositional meaning, a comprehensive interlingua text (consisting of unambiguous semantic propositions and discourse/pragmatic information) or some specialized representation geared at a particular application. In knowledge-based machine translation, the analysis stage is expected to produce a complete interlingua text. In essence, the quality of the translation depends upon the depth and quality of the analysis. Most transfer-based MT systems stop at a syntactic representation, often augmented with semantic markers (such as case markers for verb arguments), although the trend is toward ever-deeper semantic analysis.

A comprehensive system of natural language analysis, such as an analysis module of a knowledge-based machine translation system, must include the following basic components:

- *Morphological analysis*: the decomposition of words into their uninflected root forms, performed at the word level. There are many morphological phenomena: almost all languages have inflectional morphology; the majority have some form of derivational morphology; and some have special phenomena such as clitic attachment (as in *entregarselo* in Spanish, where *se* and *lo* are clitic pronouns attached to the infinitive *entregar*). A number of general models of morphological processing have been investigated. At the theoretical level, the most popular approach to morphology is the so-called two-level approach (Koskenniemi 1983; Karttunen 1983). In practical systems many other, less general and more language- and task-specific approaches have been used. In KBMT-89, for instance, a compilable Lexical Functional Grammar (CLFG) in character-based mode has been used for morphological analysis of Japanese.

- *Syntactic analysis*: the extraction of all well-formed syntactic structures and dependencies for a source text, performed at the sentence level. In the MT environment, a grammar must be written for each source language, in one of the many current grammar formalisms, such as, for instance, Lexical Functional Grammar (Kaplan and Bresnan 1982), Generalized Phrase Structure Grammar (GPSG; Gazdar et al. 1985), Head-driven Phrase Structure Grammar (HPSG; Pollard and Sag 1987), Definite Clause Grammar (Pereira and Warren 1980), Tree-adjoining Grammar (Joshi et al. 1975; Kroch and Joshi, forthcoming) or Government-and-Binding-related Grammars (Dorr 1988; Fong and Berwick 1991). The use of a "canonical" formalism facilitates the use of a single grammar interpreter applicable to any language whose grammar is defined in the selected formalism.

- *Semantic analysis*: the creation of knowledge structures in a text-meaning representation language (interlingua in MT) that reflect the meanings of lexical units in the source text and semantic dependencies among them, performed at the sentence level but often having to take into account suprasentential contexts. Semantic analysis procedures are typically developed for a particular domain (e.g., medicine, finance, computers), though general, "common sense" semantic knowledge is also used. The existence of canonical formalisms for encoding world knowledge and text meaning enables the use of a single universal semantic *interpreter* with different knowledge sources for each domain.

- *Pragmatic or discourse analysis*: suprasentential analysis leading to the resolution of anaphors, ellided phrases, deixis, as well as the attribution of intent and speech acts. In its full form, discourse analysis leads to the creation of a text-meaning structure in a representation language with the various domain-oriented and rhetorical relations among the elements of a text, including coreference of noun phrases and anaphors, causal and temporal relations, topic/comment structure and so forth. The state of the art in pragmatic and discourse analysis is not as well developed as the other three phases of language analysis.

In many early approaches to knowledge-based machine translation the syntactic stage of natural language analysis was de-emphasized (e.g., Wilks 1973; Carbonell et al. 1981). This led to the widespread, if false, belief in the field that knowledge-based machine translation claimed not to take into account syntactic knowledge about the source language in the process of analysis. In reality, the syntactic information was never neglected. Simply, early knowledge-based machine translation approaches made the architectural decision not to develop an *autonomous* syntactic module and instead performed the necessary syntactic processing and the semantic interpretation tasks in a single analysis module.

As the field of knowledge-based machine translation developed, other architectures gradually evolved. One important influence was the development of lexicon-oriented, often unification-based, syntactic parsing methods (by Kaplan, Shieber, Kay, Karttunen, Tomita, etc.). It became worthwhile to experiment with the elegant and general data structures and algorithms developed in this tradition, to determine whether they can be naturally and usefully extended and modified to encode and manipulate semantic constraints as well as syntactic and morphological knowledge.

The developments in the fields of knowledge representation and acquisition of very large knowledge bases, as well as in computational lexicography, have led knowledge-based machine translation workers toward the idea of developing dedicated and nonimported data structures and algorithms for each of the components of the analysis system. While syntactic processing uses syntactically oriented representations, semantic and pragmatic representations are encoded in independently motivated formats.

One cluster of knowledge-based machine translation projects stemming from the above methodological ideas uses the Tomita parsing method within the universal parser architecture for syntactic analysis (Tomita 1986a; Tomita and Carbonell 1987; Carbonell and Tomita 1987). In all knowledge-based machine translation systems one of the main architectural and control tasks was deriving semantic dependencies among elements of the interlingua texts from syntactic dependencies among elements of syntactic representation. This task is known as *linking* or *syntax-to-semantics mapping* (See chapter 7 of Goodman and Nirenburg 1991; and Mitamura 1989). In the original CMT translation system for the doctor-patient communication domain the linking was performed into a basic case-frame representation (Carbonell and Hayes 1987).

5.2   Analysis Algorithms

A large number of natural language analysis algorithms have been developed. These algorithms are often called "parsing methods" or "parsers." Most of these are purely syntactic in nature. Parsing algorithms include the various versions of context-free grammar interpreters, augmented transition networks, case-frame instantiation systems, definite-clause grammar interpreters and unification grammar interpreters. Many of these methods have been applied to source language analysis in various machine translation systems. However, most practical systems use algorithms based on context-free parsing. Efficient context-free parsing algorithms include the Cocke-Younger-Kasami algorithm (Younger 1967), Earley's algorithm (Earley 1970) and the generalized left-right (GLR) algorithm (Tomita 1986a, 1987b). This section gives a brief description of the generalized LR algorithm—essentially an augmented form of efficient LR parsing—which forms the core of syntactic analysis for the various KBMT systems at Carnegie Mellon University's Center for Machine Translation. For a discussion of many different parsing algorithms the reader is referred to Carbonell and Hayes 1987, Winograd 1983 and Tomita 1991. Here we review one technique, GLR parsing, that is both efficient and proven in an MT setting.

5.2.1   The Generalized LR (Tomita) Algorithm

LR parsing is known as a very efficient parsing algorithm and has been extensively used in programming language compilers. The LR parsing algorithm is a shift-reduce parsing algorithm and its grammar is precompiled into a parsing table. No backtracking or search is involved, and the algorithm is fully deterministic and runs in linear time. The standard LR parsing algorithm, however, can deal with only a small subset of context-free grammars, called *LR grammars*. These are often sufficient for programming languages, but clearly not for natural languages. If, for example, a grammar is ambiguous, then its LR table would have multiple entries; in this case, deterministic parsing would no longer be possible.

Figures 5.1 and 5.2 show an example of a non-LR grammar and its LR table. Grammar symbols starting with '*' represent pre-terminals (i.e., symbols that expand only into terminals). Entries 'sh*n*' in the action table (the left-hand side of the table) indicate that the action is to "shift one word from input buffer onto the stack, and go to state *n*." Entries 're *n*' indicate that the action is to "reduce constituents on the stack using rule *n*." The entry acc stands for the action "accept," and blank spaces represent "error." The goto table (the right-hand side of the table) determines which state the parser should go to after a reduce action.

```
(1)  S  --> NP   VP
(2)  S  --> S    PP
(3)  NP --> *n
(4)  NP --> *det *n
(5)  NP --> NP   VP
(6)  PP --> * prep   NP
(7)  VP --> *v   NP
```

Figure 5.1: **Example of a simple ambiguous grammar.**

The LR parsing algorithm pushes state numbers (as well as constituents) onto the stack; the state number on the top of the stack indicates the current state. The exact definition and operation of the LR parser can be found in Aho and Ullman 1977.

We can see that there are two multiple entries in the action table, at rows for states 11 and 12 for the column labeled *prep. Roughly speaking, this is the situation in which the parser encounters a preposition of a PP right after an NP. If this PP does not modify the NP, then the parser can go ahead to reduce the NP to a higher nonterminal such as PP or VP, using rule 6 or 7, respectively (re6 and re7 in the multiple entries). If, on the other hand, the PP does modify the NP, then the parser must wait (sh6) until the PP is completed so it can build a higher NP using rule 5.

To cope with the nondeterminism, the GLR parsing algorithm uses a *graph-structured stack*. Three key notions subsumed by graph-structured stacks are splitting, combining and local ambiguity packing. When a stack must be reduced (or popped) in more than one way, the top of the stack is *split*.

When an element needs to be shifted (pushed) onto two or more tops of the stack, it is done only once by *combining* the tops of the stack. This corresponds to the end of a local ambiguity. For instance, a PP that can be attached at two places would cause a stack split, both of whose branches would recombine at the end of the PP.

Finally, shared structure across split stacks is combined, though the attachment points remain distinct. This is *local ambiguity packing*.

With this graph-structured stack, the nondeterminism caused by multiple entries in the LR parsing table can be handled efficiently in polynomial time. Further description of the GLR algorithm may be found in Tomita 1986a and 1987b.

State	*det	*n	*v	*prep	$	NP	PP	VP	S
0	sh3	sh4				2			1
1				sh6	acc		5		
2			sh7	sh6			9	8	
3		sh10							
4			re3	re3	re3				
5				re2	re2				
6	sh3	sh4				11			
7	sh3	sh4				12			
8				re1	re1				
9			re5	re5	re5				
10			re4	re4	re4				
11			re6	re6,sh6	re6		9		
12				re7,sh6	re7		9		

| Action table | Goto table |

Figure 5.2: **LR parsing table with multiple entries (derived from the grammar in Figure 5.1.)**

5.3 Augmented Context-Free Grammars

So far, we have described the parsing process as a pure context-free parsing algorithm. In practice, however, each grammar rule needs to be augmented in one way or another to perform extra computation which cannot be otherwise performed within the pure context-free framework. We attach a function to each grammar rule for this augmentation. Whenever the parser reduces constituents into a higher-level nonterminal using a phrase structure rule, the function associated with the rule is evaluated. The functions handle aspects such as construction of a syntax/semantic representation of the input sentence, passing attribute values among constituents at different levels and checking syntactic and semantic constraints, including subject-verb agreement, case-role assignments and semantically permissible PP attachments.

If the function fails, the parser does not do the reduce action with the rule. If the function returns a value, then this value is given to the newly created nonterminal. The value includes attributes of the nonterminal and a partial syntactic/semantic representation constructed thus far. Notice that those functions can be precompiled into machine code by standard compilers.

It is in general very tedious to create, extend and modify augmentations written in LISP or, worse yet, a lower-level programming language. The functions should be generated automatically from more abstract specifications. We have implemented a compiler that compiles augmentations in a higher-level notation into LISP functions for CLFG notation, as discussed below.

5.3.1 Computational LFG for Source Language Analysis

Effective KBMT requires the development of a computationally oriented version of a unification-oriented grammar, the CLFG, which we used with the universal parser architecture in the KBMT-89 project.

CLFG is a modified version of LFG (Kaplan and Bresnan 1982), developed especially for practical natural language analysis. In essence, CLFG optimizes flexibility for the grammar writer and efficient compilability at the expense of some theoretical elegance. CLFG uses pseudo-unification operators in natural language analysis in KBMT in the context of the generalized LR parser and compiler. Pseudo-unification refers to tree-to-tree matching, whereas full unification refers to standard graph matching, including shared substructures. Pseudo equations are constraint relationships checked by the pseudo-unifier. The entire system (compiler and run-time modules) is written in device-independent COMMONLISP, and has been in regular use for several years in multiple projects at several sites.

Consider the following example of grammar rule for parsing a declarative sentence in English:

```
(<DEC> <==> (<NP> <VP>)
     (((x1 case) = nom)
      ((x2 form) =c finite)
      (*OR*
        (((x2 :time) = present)
         ((x1 agr) = (x2 agr)))
        (((x2 :time = past)))
      (x0 = x2)
      ((x0 subj) = x1)
      ((x0 :mood) = dec))))
```

The rule consists of a context-free phrase structure description and a cluster of *pseudo-equations*. This is the case with all CLFG rules.

The nonterminals in the phrase-structure part of the rule are referenced in the equations as $x0 \ldots xn$, where $x0$ is the nonterminal in the left-hand side (here, <DEC>) and xn is the nth nonterminal in the right-hand side (here, $x1$ represents <NP> and $x2$ represents <VP>). The pseudo-equations are used to check certain attribute values, such as verb form and person agreement, and to construct an f-structure. In the example, the first equation states that the case of <NP> must be nominative, and the second equation states that the form of <VP> must be finite.

The third equation (ensemble) states that one of the following two must be true: (i) the time of <VP> is present and agreements of <NP> and <VP> agree, or (ii) the time of the <VP> is past. If all these conditions hold, let the f-structure of <DEC> be that of <VP>, create a slot called `subj` and put the f-structure of <NP> there; and let `:mood` be declarative.

Grammar compilation is the key to parsing CLFG efficiently. External semantic constraints may be converted into constraint equations (for instance, case-role constraints can be represented exactly like syntactic agreement constraints in the example above). The context-free phrase structure rules are compiled into an *augmented LR parsing table*, and the equations are compiled into COMMONLISP functions and further compiled to machine code by the COMMONLISP compiler, as discussed in the following section.

5.3.1.1 Compiling CLFG into Tomita-Style LR Tables

CLFG notation is automatically compiled into a multientry, functionally augmented LR table. The context-free part is compiled in the standard LR/Tomita manner, and the equations are compiled into LISP functions. As an example, consider the CLFG rule in the previous section, and its compilable form, below. We generate only nondestructive functions with no side effects to make sure that a process never alters other processes or the parser's control flow. A generated function takes a list of arguments, each of which is a value associated with each right-hand side symbol, and returns a value to be associated with the left-hand side symbol. Each value is a list of f-structures, in case of disjunction and local ambiguity. A grammar rule in LFG-line notation follows:

```
(<S>  <==>  (<NP> <VP>)
      (((x1 case) = nom)
       ((x2 form) =c finite)
       (*OR*
        (((x2 :time) = present)
         ((x1 agr) = (x2 agr)))
        (((x2 :time) = past)))
       ((x0) = (x2))
       ((x0 :mood) = dec)
       ((x0 subj) = (x1))))
```

The constraint equations in the grammar rule above are automatically compiled into the following LISP code. Fortunately, grammar writers need only work with the LFG-like representation above.

```
(<S> <==> (<NP> <VP>)
(LAMBDA (X1 X2)
 (LET ((X (LIST (LIST (CONS (QUOTE X2) X2) (CONS (QUOTE X1) X1)))))
  (AND
   (SETQ X (UNIFYSETVALUE* (QUOTE (X1 CASE)) (QUOTE (NOM))))
   (SETQ X (C-UNIFYSETVALUE* (QUOTE (X2 FORM)) (QUOTE (FINITE))))
   (SETQ X (APPEND
             (LET ((X X))
              (SETQ X (UNIFYSETVALUE* (QUOTE (X2 :TIME)) (QUOTE (PRESENT))))
              (SETQ X (UNIFYVALUE* (QUOTE (X2 AGR)) (QUOTE (X1 AGR))))
              X)
             (LET ((X X))
              (SETQ X (UNIFYSETVALUE* (QUOTE (X2 :TIME)) (QUOTE (PAST))))
              X)))
   (SETQ X (UNIFYVALUE* (QUOTE (X0)) (QUOTE (X2))))
   (SETQ X (UNIFYSETVALUE* (QUOTE (X0 :MOOD)) (QUOTE (DEC))))
   (SETQ X (UNIFYVALUE* (QUOTE (X0 SUBJ)) (QUOTE (X1))))
   (GETVALUE* X (QUOTE (X0)))))))))
```

5.3.2 Enhancements for KBMT

To use the Tomita parser and compiler for the KBMT universal parser, whose architecture is described later, some enhancements to the basic process were required. First, the constraint equations grew to include semantic and pragmatic constraints used for lexical disambiguation, structural attachment disambiguation and case-role assignment. These constraints can be hand coded into the grammar (usually for small, restricted domains) or automatically extracted from the semantic domain model in the unifying compilation step of the universal parser architecture (see following). Second, the Tomita algorithm operates in character-based mode, which is necessary for morphological analysis. At the syntactic and semantic levels however, it is far more natural and efficient to operate at the word level, and the modified Tomita parser will do both. Finally, tracing, debugging and grammar management tools were added to cope with large-scale, multiperson development efforts.

5.4 Integration of Syntactic and Semantic Analysis

Most parsing methods in natural language processing have been developed without any special concern for MT, although many could be, in principle, applied to this task. In contrast, the *universal parser architecture* discussed below has been developed with knowledge-based machine translation in mind. Its design has been influenced by the following methodological considerations.

Syntactic and semantic analysis may be conceptually independent processes, but efficiency considerations in building comprehensive analyzers require their co-operation: formation of semantic structures usually depends on results of syntactic processing, while resolution of certain syntactic ambiguities is impossible without semantic knowledge.

The number of syntactic ambiguities derived while parsing a typical sentence using a realistic-size grammar can be quite large. Additionally, when lexical ambiguity is taken into account, the number of possible readings grows as a product of the number of senses listed in the lexicon for each of its words. Syntactic analysis alone can produce hundreds or even thousands of readings. Hence, it is essential to reduce the number of candidates as early as possible in the analysis process. One approach to this task is to integrate, at processing time, the syntactic and semantic analysis, using the latter to constrain the former.

There are at least two ways of attaining this goal. First, one can write a combined syntactico-semantic grammar. Some early approaches to natural language analysis took this road, including the word-expert parsing paradigm (Small and Rieger 1982), conceptual analysis (Riesbeck 1975) and case-frame instantiation (Hayes and Carbonell 1983). In practice, writing a combined grammar of this sort is conceptually tedious. Moreover, if n languages and m domains are to be covered, then nm such grammars will be required. Second, it would be much better to define independently a syntactic grammar for each language and a semantic model for each domain. The central question is how to accomplish full independence of syntactic and semantic information at definition time, and yet allow their integrated application at run time, providing both run-time efficiency and reusability of knowledge (permitting a syntactic grammar to be used for all domains and a domain model to be used for all languages).

There are in turn at least two ways of attaining these goals. One of them is the use of a blackboard architecture with syntax and semantics embodied in different knowledge source classes and producing units on different, though publicly accessible, blackboards. This architecture is discussed in chapter 6. The universal parser architecture offers the other solution.

5.4.1   The Universal Parser Architecture

Certain formalisms facilitate the integration of syntactic and semantic knowledge, most notably the unification grammar approaches such as Functional Unification Grammar (FUG; Kay 1985), HPSG, LFG and CLFG. Earlier case-frame parsing methods (Simmons 1973; Carbonell et al. 1985; Hayes et al. 1987) also enabled unified processing of syntactic and semantic information, but did not provide for an explicit syntactic grammar separate from and independent of the domain semantics.

As depicted in Figure 5.3, the universal parser can be seen as a data-driven *parser factory*. Its "assembly line" produces run-time parsing systems from prefabricated components—syntactic grammars written in the CLFG format and domain specifications written in FRAMEKIT (Nyberg 1988) via the ontology representation interface Ontos (Monarch and Nirenburg 1988). Every domain specification is supplemented with a lexicon that facilitates the analysis and realization of the domain model entities in each language, and with a set of linking rules for each language.

The assembly process is as follows. First, a language and a domain are selected. Second, the grammar for the selected language and the domain specification, together with the corresponding lexicon, are loaded into a unifying compiler, along with an additional, general-purpose knowledge base, the ontology. The ontology covers the most general conceptual entities, namely those that transcend the particular domains—for instance, such concepts as *move* or *artifact*. Third, the compilation proceeds in various phases, producing a functionally augmented context-free grammar, and subsequently a multientry, functionally augmented LR table. The CLFG equation unifications are compiled to LR-table-driven executable code. This process results in a very large, precompiled morphological-syntactic-semantic grammar in the format of an LR table with associated functional constraints, enabling efficient run-time parsing that is fully equivalent to the much less efficient direct interpretation of the grammatical and semantic knowledge sources.

Finally, the Tomita algorithm is used as the run-time parser on the compiled CLFG to process source texts into their corresponding semantic representation using the compiled LR table, with functional augmentations.

The universal parser architecture is designed to cover the processes of syntactic parsing and linking. Meanings of heads of grammatical phrases and many of their modifiers can be obtained by generating instances of corresponding ontological and domain-model concepts, through the mediation of the lexicon and the grammar. Of course, in the cases of syntactic ambiguity, additional knowledge (such as semantic constraint checking) is brought to bear. (For discussion of the implementation of the universal parser architecture in KBMT-89, see chapter 7 of Goodman and Nirenburg 1991.)

After the parser completes its work, additional processes are called up to finish the semantic processing. These eliminate any residual lexical ambiguities that require extrasentential context, and process such semantic phenomena as modality, aspect, time and reference. Pragmatic phenomena, including speech acts, speaker

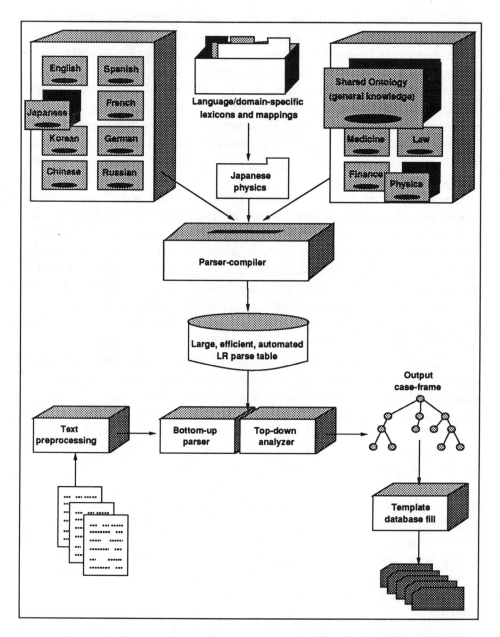

Figure 5.3: **Universal parser architecture for analysis. A selected grammar and domain model are compiled into a large but efficient run-time syntactic-semantic tabular generalized LR grammar.**

attitudes and discourse relations are also treated at this post-analysis phase, as is the reformatting of parser output into a specially designed interlingua language. KBMT-89 is a system organized around these principles—processing in a universal parser environment followed by a set of additional, specialized modules. Since achieving throughput in a realistic domain was the major goal of the KBMT-89 project, it became necessary to add human intervention to the post-analysis process—within the present state of the art not all of the interlingua components can be derived automatically. (For details about the interactive *augmentor* as a component of a practical KBMT system, see chapter 8 in Goodman and Nirenburg 1991.) The KBMT-89 architecture, including the universal parser, is represented in figure 5.4.

5.5 Beyond the Universal Parser Architecture

Some more recent experiments in knowledge-based machine translation, such as the DIONYSUS system at Carnegie Mellon University, venture beyond sentence boundaries at the analysis phase to detect and represent a wide variety of text-level pragmatic, rhetorical and stylistic features, as well as local intersentential discourse links. To support this type of processing, further enhancements were added to the format and content of the interlingua text. The features of the enhanced interlingua text language, TAMERLAN, used in DIONYSUS were described in chapter 3. Some elements of pragmatic and discourse knowledge are not properly a part of ontology, and therefore, the lexicon has grown richer (see chapter 4 for discussion).

Many components of a comprehensive representation of meaning in natural language do not directly correspond to ontological reality and are not obtained through the general process of instantiating ontological and domain-model concepts corresponding to meanings of individual lexical units in the input. In chapter 4, the reader saw examples of lexicon entries that contained (sometimes exclusively so) mappings of lexical unit meanings not into instances of ontological concepts but rather into particular values of speaker attitudes or rhetorical relations; mappings into pragmatic factors, including stylistic information, or speech acts; and mappings into speaker intention-parameters of the discourse situation.

In order to support a deep-understanding module whose results are complex structures that account for a wide variety of natural language meaning, a large number of language phenomena should be formally described. As we have already mentioned, significant progress has been made recently in the field of computational linguistics with respect to the theories of syntax. Semantic and pragmatic phenomena have traditionally been less amenable to comprehensive computational analysis. It does not seem plausible that an integrated semantic theory that covers

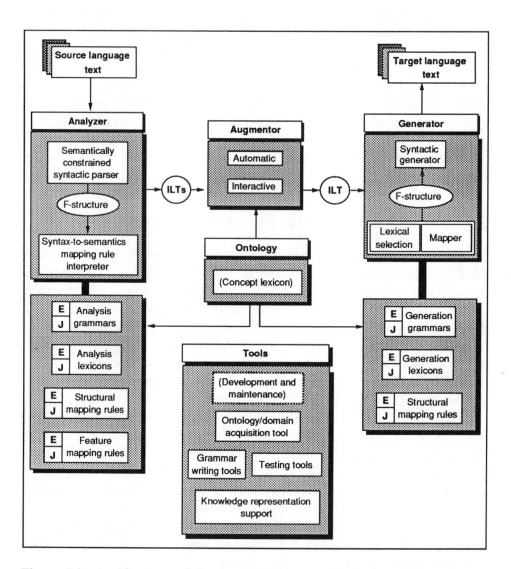

Figure 5.4: **Architecture of the** KBMT-89 **system. First, knowledge sources (grammars, lexicons, mapping rules, ontologies) are created with specialized tools such as Ontos. Second, knowledge sources are compiled where possible for run-time efficiency. Third, work flows from source text to run-time analyzer, to interactive augmentor, to run-time generator, and finally to finished target text (without need for usual MT postediting).**

all of lexical and compositional phenomena, as well as various pragmatic considerations, will be formulated in the near future. This assessment becomes even more
evident if one recognizes the need for any theory to provide methods of automatic
disambiguation of the multiple meaning facets of natural language texts. At the
same time, linguistics has accumulated a significant body of knowledge about the
various semantically laden phenomena in the natural languages (see Raskin 1987
for a discussion of how this body of knowledge can be applied to computational
analysis).

The foregoing suggests that a more feasible method for building comprehensive
computational systems for language understanding and generation will not attempt
a single unifying theory but rather will, first, develop a large number of specialist *microtheories* that address a particular linguistic phenomenon in a particular
language or group of languages and, second, provide a computational architecture that allows the integration of the operation of all the modules based on these
microtheories. (Microtheories are discussed briefly in chapter 2 of Goodman and
Nirenburg 1991; see also Nirenburg et al. 1987.) Thus, one can envisage a microtheory of time, another of modality, a third of speech acts, a fourth of causality,
a fifth of speaker attitudes and so forth.

A good method of integrating microtheories is to use the blackboard computational architecture, in which a number of processing modules co-exist and,
using a variety of background-knowledge modules, collectively produce the desired output.[1] Constraints from different modules may coexist in the working space
on various public data structures, the blackboards. Formulating process control
methods becomes a central task in this environment (cf. Emele and Zajac 1990
for an approach to tracking dependencies among partial descriptions belonging to
different levels of representation). Moreover, since access to all types of data is
facilitated through the blackboards, new possibilities appear for the formulation of
constraints and preference rules for choosing among several candidate solutions at
any stage of the processing.

The preceding should be seen to point toward the desirability of dynamic
control, that is, changing control strategies depending on the actual data. One
good candidate architecture is agenda-style control. For use in DIONYSUS, a special blackboard control system, DIBBS (Leavitt 1990; Leavitt and Nyberg 1990)
was developed to facilitate access to all extant candidate partial analyses and

---

[1]There is hope for the grand unification of microtheories in coming decades, a hope analogous
to that of physicists for a unifying field theory. But physics has seen much progress without
having arrived at a complete unification of forces. We hope that comparable progress will occur in
computational linguistics—a much younger science.

thus makes the formulation of complex heuristics easier. The architecture of a blackboard-oriented natural language analysis system with agenda-style control (such as DIONYSUS) is illustrated in figure 5.5. In this figure, the processes are computational realizations of the various microtheories derived for the corresponding linguistic phenomena. These processes operate using data from the background knowledge repositories, such as grammars and dictionaries, as well as the intermediate results stored on the universally accessible set of blackboards. In designing and implementing blackboard-oriented systems it is important to use the same knowledge representation language to store the knowledge used by the discovery procedures associated with the various microtheories and to record their outputs (which could and would be used as inputs by other heuristics) on the blackboards. In fact, making sure that the microtheories can "talk to each other" may the most important task for developers of blackboard-oriented natural language processing systems.

As the field of knowledge-based machine translation develops, new and more sophisticated methods will be introduced and, possibly, broader and better-organized static knowledge sources will emerge. It is important, early in the system-building process, to design and implement a flexible architecture capable of accommodating experimentation with alternative microtheories and of evolution following the advances in the state of the art. DIONYSUS blackboard/agenda control provides one example of such a flexible architecture.

5.6 Concluding Remarks

The past 20 years or so have seen a number of changes in our approach to analysis in knowledge-based machine translation. We have given a very brief survey of trends in this area of machine translation research. We observed that analysis modules of knowledge-based machine translation systems have become progressively more sophisticated in their computational architectures and representation substrates; the sizes of the various knowledge bases (world models, lexicons, grammars, etc.) have grown significantly, and the coverage of language phenomena has become significantly broader.

The main points discussed in this chapter can be summarized as follows:

- Multiple knowledge sources (morphological, syntactic, semantic, pragmatic) must be brought to bear in a coordinated fashion for successful source language analysis into unambiguous interlingua representations.

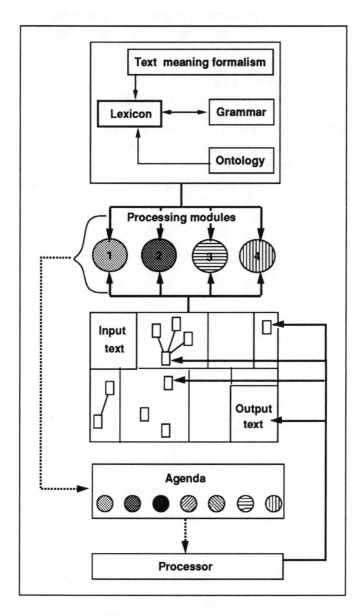

Figure 5.5: **Architecture of a blackboard-oriented natural language analysis system with agenda-style control. Using data from background knowledge sources (lexicons, grammars, etc.) and blackboards, the system automatically realizes microtheories for various linguistic phenomena.**

- One approach, the universal parser architecture, permits segregated knowledge-source development but integrated run-time application via the unifying precompiler.

- Another approach, used in DIONYSUS, utilizes a blackboard architecture for dynamic control and integration of knowledge sources at run time.

- Treatment of many linguistic phenomena can take the form of self-contained microtheories whose computational implementations are integrated into a comprehensive analysis system by making them separate knowledge sources that use a common set of blackboards for obtaining background knowledge and posting results.

Chapter 6

Target Language Generation

The process of natural language generation, in its unconstrained form, starts with the specification of the "need to communicate," the propositional goals for a target language text, and a pragmatic profile of the speech situation—knowledge about the speaker/author (or, more generally, text *producer*), the hearer/reader (text *consumer*), the style of communication and so on (cf. DiMarco and Hirst 1988; Hovy 1987, 1988b; McDonald 1986). A generator then must perform the following tasks:

1. *Content delimitation:* The system must select which of the active propositional and rhetorical goals should be overtly realized in text and which should be left for the human consumer to infer (e.g., McKeown 1985).

2. *Text structuring:* The system must determine the order of propositions and the boundaries of sentences in the target language text (cf. Hovy 1988a).

3. *Lexical selection:* The system must select open-class lexical units to be used in the target language text (e.g., Goldman 1975; Granville 1983; Jacobs 1985 ; Kittredge et al. 1988; Nirenburg 1987c; Ward 1988).

4. *Syntactic selection:* The system must select syntactic structures for the target language clauses (e.g., Mann 1983; McDonald 1983; Meteer et al. 1987) and perform closed-class lexical selection according to syntactic structure decisions (e.g., Pustejovsky and Nirenburg 1987).

135

5. *Coreference treatment:* The system must introduce anaphora, deixis and ellipsis phenomena when appropriate (e.g., Derr and McKeown 1984; Sondheimer et al. 1990; Werner and Nirenburg 1988).

6. *Constituent ordering:* The system must establish the order of syntactic constituents in a sentence (e.g., Hovy 1988a; Kenschaft 1988).

7. *Realization:* The system must map from syntactic representations with lexical insertions into surface strings (e.g., Tomita and Nyberg 1988).

It has been observed that all the above processes, with the exception of realization, are best interpreted as *planning* tasks. Thus, a relatively early system developed by Appelt (1985), was built essentially as an application of NOAH-style planning (Sacerdoti 1977). Much of the subsequent work on planning in natural language generation (e.g., McKeown 1985; Paris 1988; Moore and Paris 1989), however, concentrated predominantly on content and rhetorical planning. The distinction between the two was underscored by Hovy (1988b), who argued that while is best performed with the help of an hierarchical planner, a different, data-driven "restrictive" planner is best suited for the rest of the planning tasks. The reason for this is that tasks 2 through 6 perform selection out of a set of alternative expressive means, based on dynamically determined heuristics that depend on the state of a number of different planning processes. If we accept this taxonomy,[1] then the three top-level stages in the generation process can be identified as:

- Content delimitation (task 1)

- Text planning (tasks 2 through 6)

- Realization (task 7)

Many "traditional" natural language generators concentrate primarily on the problem of realization. Inputs to a realization component are typically syntactic dependency structures with lexical items inserted. A realization module usually uses a grammar of the target language to produce the output string from this input. Inputs to the realization module are produced by text planners. Major tasks in building realization modules include the choice of the most appropriate grammar formalism and control structure. The grammar formalism must have expressive

---

[1]This definition follows the insight that the best way to specify stages in generation is in terms of types of processing each stage performs (David McDonald, personal communication; cf. also Meteer 1989).

power sufficient for deriving fluent output. The control structure must be flexible enough to facilitate search, but at the same time it must be sufficiently constraining if efficiency is a central concern. (These issues have been discussed in detail in McDonald 1983, 1986, among others.)

Together with the predominantly syntactic concerns of realization, the text planner forms the central part of a natural language generator. It is the task of the planner to determine all the content-related and rhetorical means of realizing text. Hovy (1987) has introduced the concept of rhetorical goals in text generation, which was in part motivated by his interest in style and especially *slant* of the generated text. These phenomena are probably best dealt with by setting static parameters for an instance of text generation (though some researchers chose a more dynamic approach to style, e.g., McDonald and Pustejovsky (1985); and some others committed themselves to a stylistic grammar, e.g., DiMarco and Hirst (1990)). These parameters refer exclusively to the producer, the consumer or the dialogue situation itself. It is from this perspective that Hovy's insights about rhetorical goals were used in the DIOGENES research project at Carnegie Mellon University. The pragmatic factors component of the text-meaning representation language TAMERLAN is, in fact, a modified version of these rhetorical goals.

Moore and Paris (1989) argue that planners have to take into account not only rhetorical and attentional information (current dialogue context), but also *intentional* information about the producer's goals and plans that are to be realized through text or dialogue. In their work they draw on a number of studies from the field of natural language *understanding*. Researchers in natural language understanding have investigated the use of full-fledged planning architectures to analyze the producer's domain plans (planning physical and mental actions in an application environment) and discourse plans.

It is clear that if rhetorical plans are treated by the same mechanism as domain plans, dynamic planning (not only parameter-driven constraint satisfaction, as described in Hovy 1988b) should be used for the above tasks 2 through 6 as well. In order to build a natural language generation system using such a planning paradigm, it is necessary first to develop a conceptual model of processing that ties together all of the background knowledge elements and processing modules. The environment required for knowledge-based machine translation already contains a set of knowledge prerequisites for most of the needs of natural language generation.

Generation in machine translation does not require a delimitation stage. Indeed, the input to the generation stage is, in knowledge-based MT, a text in a formal text-meaning representation language, or interlingua. The analysis stage of a machine translation system thus serves as the content delimiter for its generation side. As a result, the machine translation generator can concentrate on text planning and realization. In what follows we describe text planning and realization in machine translation generation using as the example the approach of the DIOGENES project (Leavitt et al. 1991).

6.1   Text Planning

Depending on the presence of various rhetorical and domain relations in the input interlingua text, the propositional content of the text can be rendered in different ways. Propositions can be grouped variously among target language sentences, with a variety of conjunctions generated to flag the cohesion among the realizations of the propositions. The number of possible paraphrases of a single set of propositional meanings differing only in text structure, with no variability of lexical material, can be quite large:[2]

(6.1)   a. A boy threw a ball. The ball hit a car. The fender got dented.

b. A boy threw a ball. The ball hit a car <u>and</u> the fender got dented.

c. A boy threw a ball. The ball hit a car, <u>denting</u> the fender.

d. A boy threw a ball <u>which</u> hit a car <u>and dented</u> its fender.

e. A boy threw a ball. It hit a car <u>whose</u> fender got dented.

f. A boy's throwing of a ball caused the latter to hit a car and dent the latter's fender.

g. A ball thrown by a boy hit a car and dented its fender.

h. The car whose fender got dented was hit by a ball thrown by a boy.

i. A boy dented a car's fender by throwing a ball at it.

j. A car's fender was hit and dented by a ball thrown by a boy.

k. A car was hit by a ball thrown by a boy, as a result of which its fender got dented.

---

[2]Note that the combinations of all possible variants would yield thousands of sentences, not just the 11 sampled here.

MEANING	REALIZATION
Propositional meaning:	
- domain objects, events, and their properties	open-class lexical units
- aspect	open- and closed-class units
- time	closed-class units; tense markers
	and sentence and clause order
- causality	closed-class units; sentence, clause order
Pragmatic meaning:	
- speech acts	open- and closed-class lexical units
- focus	lexical units; sentence, clause, word order
- modality	closed-class lexical units
- discourse cohesion	closed-class units; sentence, clause order
Coreferentiality:	use of definite descriptions, anaphora, deixis
	and ellipsis

Table 6.1: **Meanings and their realizations in English. The connection between types of meanings to be realized and expressive means of a language is a many-to-many relationship.**

Interlingua texts contain a wide variety of meanings, each of which has a set of associated expressive means in every target language. The types of input meaning and their typical means of target language realization are illustrated in table 6.1.

The task of a text planner is, thus, to decide on the type of realization for every input unit and to then to plan out the text structure (which involves lexical realization of such closed-class lexical items as conjunctions) and the lexical realization of open-class target language lexical items.

Figure 6.1 shows the structure of the text planning component of a knowledge-based machine translation system. The initial text plan is produced through the operation of the text structure module and the lexical selector on an interlingua input. The former component relies on a set of text structure rules and the latter on a lexicon and an ontology. After the initial text plan is produced it becomes possible to decide on appropriate ways of treating coreference. If the input contains, say, four references to a particular object within one text, then the text planner will decide which of those instances to realize directly, which to pronominalize (if it is a noun), which to elide and which to render through a definite description. Such a decision can be made only when the linguistic context is already (at least partially) determined. Prior decisions about sentence boundaries and sentence composition, the presence or absence of additional coreference sets and other contextual features will influence reference realization decisions.

A complete text plan is next given as input to the module that selects and

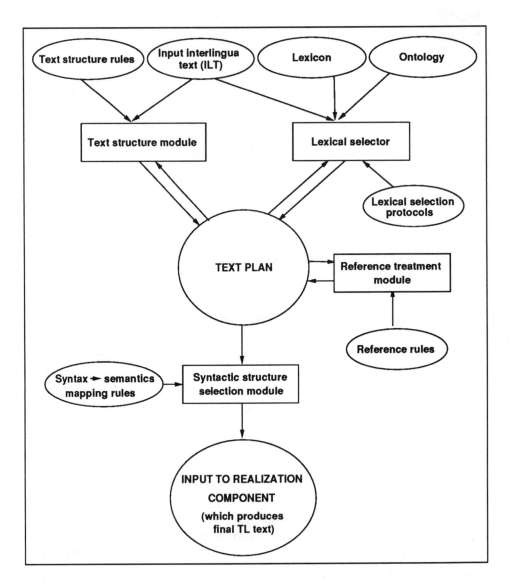

Figure 6.1: **A schematic view of text planning. The text structure module and lexical selector operate on an ILT to produce an initial text plan. This plan is used for treatment of coreference. A complete text plan is conditioned by semantics-to-syntax mapping rules operating on the syntactic structure selection module. The output of this process constitutes input to the system's realization component, which, in turn, produces target language text.**

actually builds the representation of the syntactic structures of the output text. A set of semantics-to-syntax mapping rules is used for this purpose, many of which are inverses of similar linking rules used in analysis. Some types of syntactic structures can incorporate information about constituent ordering (the order of adjectives inside a noun phrase or of prepositional phrases in a sentence). In some other approaches (notably, standard Lexical-Functional Grammar) the order is not constrained and corresponding decisions are left to the realization component. Information about ordering must already be available at the time of reference resolution. Therefore, ordering decisions are not concentrated in a single processing module, but rather are distributed among the rest of the modules.

6.2 Text Plan Formalism

The text planning process in knowledge-based machine translation accounts for the differences among realization strategies for the various ILT input meanings. The results of this process can be incorporated in a more general realization process. Alternatively, the results of text planning can be encoded in a text plan, an expression in a specially developed text plan language.

In what follows we describe TPL, one possible format for a text plan language, as used in the DIONYSUS project (Nirenburg and Defrise, forthcoming, a). A different, less expressive and more economical language is used, for instance, in SPOKESMAN (Meteer 1989). The major structures defined for the text plan language are the text structure frame (TSF), the plan-sentence, the plan-clause, the plan-role and the plan-modifier.

```
(TSF
   (has-as-part <S_#>+))
```

The text structure frame lists the plan-sentences. The order in which the sentences appear in this frame is the order in which the corresponding target language sentences will appear in the target text. This ordering gets established based on partial orderings posited at the sentence level.

```
(S_#
   (clauses (C_# [(conj_# C_##)+]))
   (textual-before (S_# S_##)+)
```

The plan-sentence consists of a number of clauses. If it is compound or complex, or if it contains a parenthetical, it is necessary to specify the way in which its clauses are actually connected. It is here that the results of the lexical selection of conjunctions (which include the comma, the dash, parentheses and the semicolon) is recorded. The *textual-before* property of the plan-sentence reflects the relative position of the corresponding target language sentence in the target text. This property has not previously been used in a machine translation system. This is because it was universally assumed that the order of sentences in the target text should follow that in the source text. Such a heuristic is quite acceptable in the absence of text planning (that is, typically in systems where processing never transcends sentence boundaries). Nevertheless, it is generally desirable to be able to manipulate sentence order (as well as internal configuration of sentences—the way they combine clauses) to enhance quality of translation output. As any human translator knows, quite often the most appropriate translation involves a partial restructuring of the source text at the level of sentences and clauses.

```
(C_#
  (head <word-sense>)
  (realization {elliptical | deictic |
               lexical-direct | lexical-descriptive})
  (features <feature-value>* )
  (roles (<role-name> [<R_#> | <C_#>])*)
  (modifiers <MOD_#>* <R_#>* <C_#>*)
  (textual-before C_# <C_##>+))
```

The value of the `head` property of the plan-clause is a word sense in the target language. Lexical realization of this word sense can be either direct lexical (from the lexicon), descriptive lexical, deictic (e.g., pronominal) or elliptical (i.e., not realized). The actual value of this property is determined by the reference treatment module. The `features` property of the plan-clause contains a list of syntactic features that are determined as a side effect of the operation of text planning rules. A plan-clause typically contains a number of plan-roles and modifiers, listed in the plan-clause frame. Clause modifiers can be plan-modifiers or they can be plan-roles or even plan-clauses.

```
(R_#
  (head <word-sense>)
  (realization {elliptical | deictic |
  lexical-direct | lexical-descriptive})
  (features <feature-value>* )
  (roles (<role-name> <R_#>)*)
  (modifiers <MOD_#>* <C_#>* <R_#>*)
  (textual-before MOD_# | C_# | R_# (MOD_# | C_# | R_#)+))
```

```
(R_#
  (head $SET$)
  (elements <R_##>+)
  (type {and | or})
  (realization {elliptical | deictic |
                 lexical-direct | lexical-descriptive})
  (features <feature-value>* )
  (textual-before R_# <R_##>+))
```

Plan-roles come in two types—those headed by individual word senses and those headed by a set of word senses. In the latter case, the partial ordering in the set plan-role is done in terms of the order of the component plan-roles, whereas in single word-sense plan-roles the relative ordering is specified in terms of other sentence modifiers. The types of lexical realization remain the same for both types of plan-roles, since there are direct lexical means of realizing the concept of a set, depending on the nature of set elements and the style of the text. In addition to "simple" individual modifiers (e.g., adjectives, prenominal nouns), role modifiers can be realized as other roles (realized through prepositional phrases) or as clauses (typically, relative clauses).

```
(MOD_#
  (head <word-sense>)
  (realization {elliptical | deictic |
                 lexical-direct | lexical-descriptive})
  (features <feature-value>* )
  (modifiers <MOD_#>* <R_#>*)
  (textual-before MOD_# <MOD_##>+))
```

Modifiers can have their own modifiers (e.g., adjectives can be modified by adverbs or by prepositional phrases).

To illustrate the use of the text plan language, we include the following text plan for the sample text first presented in chapter 3.

```
(TSF
   (has-as-part S_1 S_2))
(S_1
   (clauses C_1 and C_2)
   (textual-before C_1 C_2))
```

The clauses slot of the sentence frame already contains the lexical realization of the conjunction.

```
(C_1
   (head +drop-v1)
   (features
      (voice active)
      (mood imperative))
   (realization  lexical)
   (roles (agent r_0)
          (theme r_1)))
```

Here, +drop-v1 means "the first verbal sense of *drop*."

```
(r_0
   (head +consumer-n1)
   (realization pro))
```

Here, consumer-n1 is a special word sense used to refer to any reader of the text.

```
(r_1
   (head +shop-n1)
   (realization lexical)
   (features
      (ref def)
      (number sg))
   (modifiers r_2 mod_2))
(r_2
   (head +dunkin_donuts-n1))
(mod_2
   (head +favorite-adj1)
   (realization lexical)
   (modifiers r_3))
(r_3
   (head +consumer-n1)
   (realization pro)
   (features
      (person 2)
      (number sg)))
```

The preceding will be generated as *your favorite Dunkin' Donuts shop.*

```
(C_2
  (head +find-v1)
  (realization lexical)
```

```
(features
   (voice active)
   (tense future)
   (mood declarative))
(roles
   (experiencer r_3)
   (theme r_4))
(modifiers mod_3))
(r_4
   (head $set$)
   (type *plan-role)
   (subtype and)
   (elements r_4 r_5 r_6 r_7)
   (textual-before r_4 r_5 r_6 r_7))
(mod_3
   (head +only-adv1)
   (modifiers mod_4)
   (realization lexical))
(mod_4
   (head +not-neg1)
   (realization lexical))
(r_4
   (head +donut-n1)
   (realization lexical)
   (features
      (number pl)
      (ref indef))
      (modifiers mod_5  C_3) )
(mod_5
   (head +fresh-adj1)
   (realization lexical))
(C_3
   (head +make-v1)
   (realization lexical)
   (features
      (voice passive)
      (mood declarative))
   (theme r_8)
   (modifiers r_9))
(r_8
   (head +donut-n1)
   (realization ellipsis))
```

If realization in the role r_8 is posited as pro, it will be realized through the relative pronoun *which* because C_3 is a relative clause—it is among the modifiers of the role r_4.

```
(r_9
    (head +hand-n1)
    (features
        (number sg)
        (prep (root by)))
    (realization lexical))
```

Note that the feature `ref` is not specified in the role r_9. This means that *hand* will be generated instead of *the hand* or *a hand*.

```
(r_5
    (head +Munchkin-n1)
    (realization lexical)
    (features
        (number pl)
        (ref indef))
    (modifiers mod_6) )
(mod_6
        (head +fresh-adj1)
        (realization lexical))
(r_6
    (head +smell-n3)
    (realization lexical)
    (features
        (number sg)
        (ref def))
    (modifiers  mod_7)
    (domain r_10))
(mod_7
    (head +delicious-adj1)
    (realization lexical))
(r_10
    (head +coffee-n2)
    (realization lexical)
    (features
        (ref indef)
        (number sg))
    (modifiers mod_9))
(mod_9
    (head +fresh-brewed-adj1)
    (realization lexical))
(r_7
    (head +thing-n1)
    (realization ellipsis)
    (features
        (number pl)
```

```
       (ref indef))
    (modifiers mod_10))
```

The role `r_7` renders *more things*, with *things* ellided.

```
(mod_10
   (head +more-det1)
   (realization lexical))
(S_2
   (clauses C_4))
(C_4
   (head +find-v1)
   (realization lexical)
   (features
       (mood declarative)
       (tense future)
       (voice active))
   (experiencer r_11)
   (theme r_12)
   (modifiers mod_11))

(r_11
   (head +consumer-n1)
   (realization pro)
   (features
       (number sg)
     (person 2)))
(mod_11
   (head +also-adv1)
   (realization lexical))
(r_12
   (head +shop-n1)
   (realization lexical)
   (features
       (number sg)
       (ref indef))
   (modifiers  mod_12 mod_13 r_13)
   (textual-before mod_12 mod_13 r_13))
```

The role `r_12` renders *a fresh new Dunkin' Donuts shop*. It is interesting to note that the article is indefinite (`ref indef`) which supports the knowledge representation decision (see chapter 3) to represent objects with time stamps. The shop has been mentioned before in the paragraph (*Drop by your favorite Dunkin' Donuts shop*), but now the reference is to the remodeled shop, hence the indefinite article.

```
(mod_12
 (head +fresh-adj1)
 (realization lexical))
(mod_13
 (head +new-adj1)
 (realization lexical))
(r_13
 (head +dunkin_donuts-n1)
 (realization lexical))
```

6.3   Decision Knowledge in Text Planning

Text planning in DIONYSUS is rule-based. Text structure rules create elements of a text plan based on the input interlingua text and those parts of a text plan that have already been determined. Another task performed by text structure rules is to make sure that every component of the input has been used in at least one rule application. In other words, every input component must be taken into account in generating a target text. As a result, some text structure rules not only determine the target language lexical dependency structure, but also serve as triggers of lexical selection protocols on components of input, such as relations or attitudes.

As an example, consider a text structure rule that creates a simple conditional sentence using the English lexemes *if* and *then*. This rule is used when there is a condition relation in the input, when the output text need not be overly colloquial or colorful and when the condition is still valid, in the opinion of the speaker.

Text Planning Rule 1: Simple-conditional
   If

      (a)   There is a `condition` relation between two input clauses (or two sets of clauses), C_j and C_k;

      (b)   The `formality` pragmatic factor is greater than or equal to 0.5 and the `color` pragmatic factor is less or equal to 0.5; and

      (c)   The epistemic attitude to C_j is unity (the maximum value), that is, the condition stands at the time of speech (not as in "had you gone to ... you would have ...") —

then:

      (d)   Create the frame:

```
(S_i
   (clauses C_j C_k))
```

(e) Whenever C_j and C_k are instantiated, add filler mod_l toC_j:

```
(mod_l
   (head +if-conj1)
   (realization lexical))
```

and filler mod_m to C_k:

```
(mod_m
   (head +then-conj1)
   (realization lexical))
```

(f) Add textual relation (textual-before C_j C_k)

The triggering conditions for the second example rule are similar to those of the first one. The only difference is the presence in the input of a producer-intention value that characterizes the input as the instance of a speech act of the threat, assurance or promise type. In this case we opt to produce not an *if ... then* sentence but rather a sentence of the *imperative-future* type, for example, *Open this book, and you will not be able to put it down till you finish it.*

Text Planning Rule 2: Imperative-future

If

(a) There is a condition relation between C_j and C_k (or between two sets of clauses);

(b) formality is less than or equal to 0.5 and color is greater or equal to 0.5;

(c) The epistemic attitude to C_j is default (that is, (a));

(d) The producer-intention in the input is (is-a *comissive-act) (e.g., a promise or a threat) —

then:

(e) Create the frame:

```
(S_i
   (clauses C_j C_k))
```

(f) Add feature (mood imperative) to C_j
   and features (mood declarative) (tense future) to C_k;

(g) Add textual relation (`textual-before C_j C_k`).

The following sample planning rule deals with a class of relative clauses. This rule is for transformation, not instantiation.

Text Planning Rule 3: Passive-relative

If

    (a) The value of the theme role in `C_i` is coreferential with the value of the theme role in `C_j`; and

    (b) There is no agent role in `C_j`—

then:

    (c) in the plan-role frame for the theme of `C_i` add the filler `C_j` to the `modifiers` slot

    (d) In `C_j` add features (`voice passive`) (`mood declarative`) and change the value of realization to `lexical`; and

    (e) In `C_j.theme` change the realization to `elided`.

Finally, the following rule produces a lexical realization of an attitude (if the value of `force` is less than or equal to 0.5, the median point on the scale, then the attitude is not lexically realized and is expected to be inferred by the reader/hearer).

Text Planning Rule 4: Lexically realized attitude

If

    (a) Input contains an attitude of type evaluative whose value is 1 (highest) and whose scope is a plan-role; and

    (b) The pragmatic factor `force` is greater than 0.5 —

then:

    (c) Create the frame

```
(mod_a
  (head <lexical-unit>)
  (realization lexical))
```

    (d) Lexically select for evaluative attitude and record the result in the head slot of `mod_a`

As the number of text structure rules increases, so does the expressive power of a generator. Text plans, unlike interlingua texts that serve as inputs to generation in machine translation, are language-dependent because the differences with respect to meaning realization in various languages transcend those in lexical selection. However, inasmuch as the various languages have similarities in basic sentence types, text structure rules developed for one language can be modified and reused in generating another. In general, a set of text structure rules for one language can be used as a template for creating a set of similar rules in a second, related language. As a result of using the "copy and edit" method instead of creating a set of rules from scratch, the efficiency of knowledge acquisition can be improved significantly.

6.4 Lexical Selection

Natural language generation systems typically operate with relatively simple lexicons. It is difficult to judge *a priori* what level of lexicon detail is appropriate for a particular application, especially if the texts to be generated are open ended. The morphological and syntactic adequacy of output have until recently been the focus of attention in natural language generation. After all, syntactic and morphological errors cannot be tolerated in the generated text, while the tolerance for a less-than-perfect word choice seems to be much higher. This is why, in many cases, advanced experimental generation systems (e.g., Mumble (Meteer et al. 1987); TEXT (McKeown 1985); Nigel (Mann 1983); and others) treat lexical selection more like lexical mapping, where a unit of conceptual input is mapped, one to one, into a word or a phrase. There are, of course, exceptions; for instance, in the treatment of conversives, such as *buy* and *sell*, in systems like KING (Jacobs 1985), and even dating back to the conceptual dependency discrimination nets for verb selection in BABEL (Goldman 1975).

Since some syntactic relations are expressed in natural language through the use of grammatical morphemes, which can be separate words or phrases, this part of the lexicon has been addressed in somewhat more detail than the treatment of open-class lexical items such as nouns, verbs, adjectives or adverbs (see Cumming and Albano 1986; Pustejovsky and Nirenburg 1987; and see the chapters on analysis and generation lexicons in Goodman and Nirenburg 1991 for a discussion of the treatment of closed-class lexical items).

As the generation task shifts from well-defined sublanguages to more general, larger and less structured texts, greater importance is placed on the task of selecting open-class lexical items. Lexicons become larger and more detailed, and as a result the conceptual structures serving as input to the text planning module are potentially realizable by different candidate words or phrases. Resolution of synonymy or near-synonymy thus becomes a central problem in lexical selection.

The four basic types of lexical realizations for open-class lexical items are direct lexical, descriptive lexical, deictic and elliptical. Dealing with lexical realization involves two types of decision—the decision about which of the four realization types to choose in each instance, and the actual mechanics of selecting the lexical unit(s). The latter type of decision for deictic and elliptical realization is relatively straightforward (see Werner and Nirenburg 1988 for a proposal about anaphoric realization of nominals), whereas with the direct and descriptive forms of lexical realization the decisions are complex and involve a number of different types of knowledge. In what follows we describe some problems and methods for direct lexical realization.

Suppose the generator has to express in English an interlingua text whose meaning is glossed in example (6.2).

(6.2)   a person whose sex is male and whose age is between 13 and 15 years

Suppose also that the domain model has *person* as a terminal node, as a result of which the English generation lexicon entries for the lexical units in (6.3) will have to form a synonymy equivalence class.

(6.3)   *boy, kid, teenager, youth, child, young man, adolescent, man, human*

The primary criterion for the resolution of relative synonymy under these circumstances is the proximity between the meaning of the input and the meanings (as described in the generation lexicon) of the elements of the list (6.3). In order to be capable of making choices like this, a generator must possess a "distance"-assigning capability that can be applied to these two meanings.

Inputs to the process of lexical selection of open-class items are values of the head slots in the clauses and roles of the interlingua text. A typical role in the input is the one paraphrased above, which is more precisely written as as follows:

```
(make-frame person_5
  (is-token-of (value *person))
  (sex (value male))
  (age (value (<> 13 15)))))
```

To be able to match the input with the entries in the lexicon, we need to represent them in a compatible formalism, with corresponding slots and value sets. The following frames are versions of the semantic (or meaning pattern) zones of lexicon entries for some members of the set (6.3).

```
(make-frame boy
  (is-token-of (value *person))
  (sex (value male)
       (importance 10))
  (age (value (<> 2 15))
       (importance 4)))
(make-frame kid
  (is-token-of (value *person))
  (sex (value male)
       (importance 2))
  (age (value (<> 5 15))
       (importance 6)))
(make-frame girl
  (is-token-of (value *person))
  (sex (value female)
       (importance 10))
  (age (value (2 15))
       (importance 4)))
(make-frame man
  (is-token-of (value *person))
  (sex (value male)
       (importance 10))
  (age (value (<> 17 120))
       (importance 3)))
(make-frame woman
  (is-token-of (value *person))
  (sex (value female)
       (importance 10))
  (age (value (<> 17 120))
       (importance 3)))
(make-frame human
  (is-token-of (value *person)))
(make-frame adult
  (is-token-of (value *person))
  (age (value (<> 18 120)))
       (importance 9))
```

Note the presence of importance values in many of the lexicon frame slots. This additional parameter ranks the slots in a lexicon frame with respect to the relevance of their values for the identity of a reference. For example, the importance values shown above indicate that the penalty for using the word *boy* to realize an input frame whose *age* slot has a value out of the range (2 to 15) is less severe than the penalty for doing so if the value of the sex slot is out of the allowed range.[3]

---

[3]We take a more relativistic stance than Creary and Pollard (1985), who divide all ontological

One way to evaluate the proximity of the meaning of a lexical unit to that of an element of an ILT is to design a special meaning distance metric. Such a metric was built for KBMT-89, which has a partial instantiation of the general class of lexical meaning metrics outlined here. To construct a meaning-match metric, one should take into account differences in types of properties and property values characterizing a concept. The slots of both the input and the meaning pattern of the lexicon frames correspond to predefined ontological properties (relations and attributes), each of which has a well-defined domain of applicability and a range of values (slot fillers). Syntactically, the slot fillers can be symbols or numbers. The value sets from which slot filler values are taken can be unordered, ordered-discrete or ordered-continuous. The cardinality of slot fillers in meaning frames can be single, for instance, (`male`); enumerated, for example, (`geography history biology`); or a range of values, say, (`<> 0 100`), meaning "between 0 and 100."

We summarize the principles on which such a metric should be built:

- The quality of the match is proportional to the size of the intersection of the fillers for the slots of the same name in input and lexicon frames, normalized by the number of slots present.

- Slots in the meaning pattern of a lexicon entry are rated with respect to their importance for the meaning expressed by the frame; a mismatch on a less important slot has a smaller influence on the overall score of the match.

- A maximum penalty is assigned for a slot that appears in the meaning pattern of a lexicon entry and does not appear in the ILT (such a mismatch reflects meaning incompatibility in which a component of the lexical unit meaning is incompatible with the meaning of input). The penalty is used to favor those realizations that do not add extraneous shades of meaning to the ILT.

- A fraction of the maximum penalty (estimated at 20% of the maximum penalty in the current implementation) is assigned for a slot that appears in the ILT and not in the meaning pattern (such a mismatch reflects meaning incompleteness, that is, a situation in which the meaning of the lexical unit is a (compatible) subset of the meaning of input.[4] The penalty is used to favor those realizations that cover most of the meaning of the ILT frame.

---

properties into either defining or accidental properties.

[4]This heuristic is similar to those employed by other generators, e.g., KING (Jacobs 1985) or PAULINE (Hovy 1988d).

- The quality of a match between two frames is a sum of the quality of the matches of the frame slots, weighted by their corresponding importance values.

One important property of the type of inexact matching that we employ is its relative simplicity. We believe that the nature of the domain (word senses and lexical units) warrants the relatively coarse grain size of the metric and the simple method of combining evidence that we employ. A typical proposition or role frame is realized not by a single lexical unit but rather by a phrase (for example, a full noun phrase, complete with various modifiers). Lexical selection, thus, proceeds in two steps: first, the heads of the phrases (typically nouns and verbs) are selected; selection of modifiers (typically adjectives and adverbs) follows. The above means that our metric favors the best, most complete match of phrase heads so that the need for the selection of modifiers is diminished. If the modifiers contain complete clauses or phrases, their heads are first rendered lexically, and then in standard reverse-descent order.

6.4.1   Collocation and Synonymy

Sentential context influences lexical choice. Contextual relations among lexical units can be expressed as co-occurrence constraints, known as *selectional restrictions*, on the meaning representations of the word senses in question (e.g., whatever fills the subject slot in a clause with *admire* as the main verb should have the semantic property of "human").

Some co-occurrence constraints are not explainable in terms of meaning-related properties. Consider the conceptual operator of *a large quantity of*, a (relative) value for measuring quantities of materials, forces, qualities, properties and so on. It is realized in English in accordance with collocational properties of the lexical units that are used as its operands. Not every quantity can co-occur with every realization of the above operator. Consider the following:

(6.4)   a. *high, wide, large, big, broad, great, enormous, strong*

   b. *amount, difficulty, expanse, selection, voltage*

Now note that we say *high voltage* but *a large amount*. It would be inappropriate for a generation system to produce something like *high selection* or *wide difficulty*.[5]

---

[5]Note that in *analysis* the problem of assigning a similar semantic marker to all the various expressions from the example can, in principle, be tackled through a mechanism of metaphor processing,

The following example illustrates the collocational phenomena from the perspective of a machine translation application. The causative construction with the English noun *influence* requires the verb *exert*; its Russian equivalent *vlijanie* requires *okazyvat'*, and the latter is not a Russian correlate of *exert* other than in the above constructions. The Russian verb is also used with *doverije* ("trust"), *predpochtenije* ("preference") and in some other combinations. The relationship between *influence* and *exert* is collocational.

In some cases the co-occurrence is so difficult to explain that it is declared nonexistent and a multiword lexical unit, an idiom, is installed instead. This happens when the meaning of a phrase is qualitatively different from the meanings of its components, as in the French *chemin de fer—road + iron = railroad*.

The decision whether to consider a certain phrase within the realm of selectional restrictions, collocations or idioms depends on the quality and breadth of the underlying semantic representation, the structure of the dictionary and the processing algorithms. Thus, in one application a collocational constraint may exist stating that while the English *large* collocates with *drink* and *fries*, *big* doesn't. In a system with a finer grain of semantic analysis, *large* will be defined, among other things, as a typical value of the size of food amounts that could be purchased.

Since a complete natural language processing system must treat all contextual relations in its sublanguage, it becomes necessary to provide techniques for handling all types of co-occurrence constraints.[6]

In generation, the role of selectional restrictions becomes less central than in analysis, since the main lexical task is not selecting the appropriate sense for a given word but rather selecting the most appropriate lexical unit from a set of

---

whereby a general heuristic rule is developed for processing metaphorical input belonging a single class, such as, for instance, *a large quantity of* . . . —see Lakoff and Johnson 1980 and Carbonell 1982 for an extensive listing of potential metaphor classes. In generation, however, the task is the opposite, namely to *produce* fluent metaphorical language. Since such production depends not on regularities of meaning, but rather on the idiosyncrasies of meaning realization in the various natural languages, the general rules will be more difficult to come by and formulate.

[6]The role of contextual (syntagmatic) information in natural language processing has been widely recognized. A number of semantic theories have used the idea of selectional restrictions. These include, for instance, those of Katz, Fodor and Postal (Katz and Fodor 1963; Katz and Postal 1964). Note also the work on semantic descriptions (including *Roget's Thesaurus*) and computer programs, both theory oriented (Wilks 1973) and devoted to particular applications (e.g., the many machine translation programs that support a measure of meaning analysis). In computational linguistics this type of knowledge is routinely used to support the task of analysis, not generation. The study of collocations is found in Firth 1957; it is a central part of the meaning-text school of linguistics; cf. Mel'čuk 1974, 1981.

synonyms and near synonyms. Indeed, input semantic representations in natural language generation are are unambiguous, so that a match on selectional restrictions is already assured. Since analysis and generation are typically decoupled in knowledge-based natural language processing systems, there is no trace of which source language lexical unit caused the creation of which ILT element passed to the generation module. Thus, the meaning representation of *colorful* will, at a very plausible level of semantic description granularity, be identical to that of the corresponding senses of *multicolored* or perhaps even *gaudy*.[7] And for all of the above English lexical units, the selectional restrictions will be identical, provided that all of them were formulated at the same level of semantic granularity. If finer-grained distinctions are required for fluent generation, the analysis process and the knowledge representation must be elaborated to capture these distinctions.

Another way of treating synonymy prior to runtime is controlling the vocabulary used by the system. The two types of filtering that can be applied to the vocabulary are the sublanguage approach and stylistic filtering. The former has to do with terminology (thus, *CPU* is an acceptable synonym for *central processing unit* in the sublanguage of computer science, but may not be acceptable—at least, without a special explanation or a definition—in general texts); the latter rules out stylistically inappropriate choices (e.g., the English *swell* will not be an option for realizing the meaning of *very good* in standard journalistic prose, but in the scientific style even *great* is not acceptable, as in *The results of the experiments were great.*

The resolution of synonymy at runtime can occur only if there is a source of knowledge about co-occurrence properties of lexical units that is different from and not covered by the selectional restrictions. If for a particular set of synonyms such knowledge is not available, the system will have to make a random choice. The collocational relationships mentioned earlier are defined not on word senses but rather on actual lexical units in the target language .

6.4.2 The Clause Level

The task of the generator at the clausal level is to use knowledge about collocation relationships of a lexical unit to filter further the set of candidate lexical realizations of an input unit. To support this functionality, the generation lexicon should include

---

[7]The well-known principle of near nonexistence of complete synonymy may be shown to hold only when the granularity of semantic description is not established prior to an act of meaning analysis, so that for any proposed synonymy, arbitrarily subtle distinctions are made to illustrate its imperfections. This condition cannot, however, be met in any computational application, and it is therefore a nonissue for NL generation and KBMT in general.

a set of fields to store the collocations of a lexical item.[8] An example of the lexicon entry with collocation specification follows.

```
(make-frame boy
  (is-token-of (value *person))
  (sex (value male)
       (importance 10))
  (age (value (2 15))
       (importance 4))
  (lexeme (value boy))
  (syntactic-info (lexical-class noun)
                  (noun-type class))
  (morphological-info (plural regular))
  (para-collocation (synonym lad kid child)
                    (antonym girl adult)
                    (hyperonym person))
  (syn-collocation
          (agent-of (value play throw run jump)
                    (strength 0.5))
          (place    (value school playground)
                    (strength 0.5))))
```

6.4.3　Reference Treatment

A central problem in generation is deciding on the type of realization among the abovementioned four possibilities—lexical-direct, lexical-descriptive, elliptical and deictic. The following paraphrase of an interlingua text can serve as an illustration of such a choice.

Clause$_1$: Buy(agent: John$_3$ theme: novel$_7$), time$_1$, focus: novel$_7$ novel$_7$(age: old)

Clause$_2$: Bring(John$_3$ novel$_7$ office$_1$), belong-to(office$_1$ John$_3$), time$_2$: time$_2$ > time$_1$, focus: office$_1$

Clause$_3$: Read(John$_3$ novel$_7$), aspect: inchoative, time: after(time$_2$)

An adequate way of realizing the ILT is given in (6.5).

---

[8]While the ontological domain model underlying the lexicon facilitates the concise specification of selectional restrictions through its inheritance mechanism, the specification of collocations remains less structured. It is a challenge to come up with a notational system for these collocations that would be both concise and not prone to duplicating the information already available through selectional restrictions.

(6.5)   John bought a new novel. He brought the book to his office and started to read it.

There are eight instances of the three object-type concepts (John, book, office) in the case-role slots of the input propositions above. Only one concept (novel) is realized lexically more than once (as *novel* and *book*). In three cases the second instance of the same concept was realized through pronominalization (*he, his, it*) and in one, through an elliptical construction (*<John> started to read it*). This example shows that nonlexical or descriptive lexical realization of propositional content is an integral part of the process of lexical selection in generation.[9]

Decisions on the realization of coreference sets occur in the entire context of the text plan. Thus, in the above example, the fact that the last reference to *novel* was realized through pronominalization was possible because in the final text the word *office* cannot be mistaken for an antecedent of *it*. Had the verb in this sentence been, say, *open* and not *read* (that is, had its selectional restrictions included both *office* and *book*) then the only clue to the reader with respect to the antecedent of would have been thematic (*book* is in focus). In this case the possibility of the mistake on the part of the reader is somewhat higher than in the actual example. But, most importantly, the processing load will increase because the reader will have to spend resources on understanding what the actual antecedent is. Processing load is one measure of text quality—good texts require low processing load.

The realization of the three-element coreference set *novel* in the above example is a typical solution for English—the first instance of the concept is realized through direct lexical means, the second as a definite description and the last is pronominalized. The order in which the clauses are positioned in the output need not necessarily be chronological, as in the following:

(6.6)   John bought a new novel. The book was recommended to him by Bill. He brought it to his office and started to read [it].

6.5 Generator Architecture

Existing generators employ a number of different architectures—integrated or sequential, based on the application of grammar or of general production rules and

---

[9]This fact has been widely recognized in the generation community: to give but one example, Derr and McKeown (1984) address this problem (especially in elliptic realization, but in pronominalization as well) when deciding whether to use a single complex sentence or a set of simple sentences to realize a composite meaning.

so on. In the DIOGENES project we have experimented with blackboard-style control in a cascaded system. Our reasoning in making this choice was as follows. Since generation processes can be in large part decoupled (each input component can be processed, at least partially, in an independent fashion), a generator can benefit from a flexible, opportunistic control structure. One such structure involves the blackboard mode of control, in which a number of processes (known as dynamic knowledge sources) post their findings and obtain their decision knowledge from a set of public data structures called blackboards or blackboard spaces. Control is carried out with the help of an agenda of active knowledge source instances, which are scheduled for application with the help of the special set of control heuristics run by the special (meta)knowledge source called the *scheduler*.

6.5.1 Knowledge Sources

DIOGENES planning tasks are performed by its knowledge sources (KSs), which contain both declarative knowledge (such as lexical selection rules) and the means to apply the knowledge. In this section we describe a sample inventory of KSs and illustrate the process flow in the DIOGENES text planner. In the following description, the KSs are grouped according to the type of processing they perform. The KSs inside a group tend to be more tightly coupled by the control strategy than those belonging to different groups. However, results posted by KS *instances* (KSIs) from other groups can also influence the decisions made by a KS.

Table 6.2 illustrates the nature of the DIOGENES knowledge sources. Each KS is shown along with its group, the blackboard events that trigger its instantiation, its inputs and outputs and the knowledge it uses. This includes static knowledge, such as the lexicons and grammars, and dynamic knowledge, such as the results posted by other KSs on the blackboard.

The task of managing multiple knowledge sources has several characteristics with serious implications for control:

- The knowledge-source instances (KSIs) whose results will become a part of the output can be only partially determined *a priori* based on general expectations.

- Although a large number of KSIs can accumulate on the agenda during the planning process, only a small number will actually have to execute in order for an output to be produced.

- Since the set of KSIs on the agenda is expected to be large, the search space must be limited and extra control knowledge introduced to speed up search.

KS (GROUP)	TRIGGERED BY	INPUT ILT	KNOWLEDGE USED	OUTPUT
GL-Search (LS)	input, definite-description-KS results	input ILT clauses and roles	GL, CL; results of sentence-structure build-NP and select-best	CS
Collocationally constrain (LS)	GL-Search results	CS	GL, select-best results	FCS
Select-best (LS)	collocationally-constrain results	FCS	meaning matching metric	a target language lexical unit
Anaphora-KS (C)	a coreference link in input	input role, select-best results	coreference heuristics	a target language pronoun
Definite-description-KS (C)	a coreference link in input	input role, select-best results	coreference heuristics	a set of constraints for GL-search
Text-structure (TS)	input	input clause, temporal and discourse links	stylistic rules grammar rules	skeleton planner output structure
Build-Clause (SS)	input	input clause	text-structure KS results, grammar rules	clause-level output components
Build-NP (SS)	input	input role; results of open- and closed-class LS and O KSs	results of C KSs, grammar rules	NP-level components of output
Closed-class LS (SS)	input, a new syntactic structure component (result of a SS KS)	results of LS, SS and TS KSs	closed-class lexicon entries	closed-class lexical units
Feature (SS)	as above	input, SS KS results	feature mapping rules	syntactic features in the output
Ordering (O)	as above	unordered set of constituents	constituent ordering heuristics	ordered set of constituents

Table 6.2: **DIOGENES Knowledge Sources. Here, C stands for coreference, CL for concept lexicon, CO for constituent ordering, CS for candidate set, FCS for filtered candidate set, LS for lexical selection, O for ordering, SS for syntactic selection, and TS for text structure.**

To enhance cooperation among the KSIs and address these characteristics of the planning process, we introduce two control strategies: *obviation* and *partial ordering on KSI execution.*

Since many more KSs may be instantiated than are actually required to produce a solution, a control strategy that involves *obviation* becomes a natural choice. Whenever a particular KSI becomes superfluous because of a particular control decision, that KSI may be deactivated on the agenda, so that unnecessary processing may be avoided. Since the obviated KSI is merely deactivated and not removed from the agenda, it need not be reinstantiated if the obviating control decision is retracted later; the obviated KSI can be reactivated simply by reflagging its status as active. Since obviation is triggered by a contextual situation, its treatment is necessarily opportunistic.

In the second control strategy, text-structure KSIs receive first priority, followed

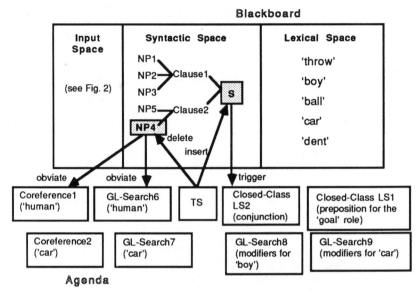

Figure 6.2: **A snapshot of the DIOGENES planner in action. The ordering KSIs are not shown. The sentence that will be produced is "A young boy threw a ball at a big car and dented it." At the present state, several lexical selections have been completed.**

by coreference KSIs with priority 2. The lexical selection KSIs for proposition and role heads have priority 3, as well as the syntactic KSIs (build-clause and build-NP). The lexical selection KSIs for modifiers and the feature KSIs from the syntactic group are assigned priority 4. Finally, textual ordering KSIs receive the lowest priority (5).

Figure 6.2 shows an intermediate state of the system during processing. At the moment just before the one depicted, the processor completed lexical selection of both the proposition heads and the first four role heads. The results were posted on the Lexical Space and the corresponding KSIs were deactivated in the agenda (obviated). These events triggered the instantiation of a number of GL-Search KSs for lexical selection of modifiers in the above input components.[10] The system has also built clause and NP structures using two instances of Build-Clause and five instances of Build-NP. The results were posted on the Syntactic Space and

---

[10]Note that no GL-Search KSI is present for finding the modifiers of *throw*, *ball* and *dent*. This is because the lexical units that were selected completely cover the meanings of the corresponding input units.

the corresponding KSIs were removed. Seven instances of the ordering KS were created (not shown in the figure). An instance of a closed-class lexical selection KS was triggered to select the preposition associated with the realization of the "goal" case role.

Figure 6.2 also shows the results of a Text-Structure KSI—the two clauses will be combined into a single compound target language sentence. The coordination of clauses will be realized lexically, hence *Closed-Class-LS$_2$* is triggered to select the appropriate conjunction. The agent role of the second clause will be realized through ellipsis; as a result, *NP$_4$* is deleted from the Syntactic Space, and the KSIs *GL-Search$_6$* and *Coreference$_1$* are obviated—they are no longer needed.

6.6 Syntactic Selection and Realization

The role of syntactic choice in DIOGENES is to link a completed text plan with a syntactic structure appropriate for that text plan. While the role of text planning is to organize the TAMERLAN text into a set of appropriate clause and role units for realization in the target language, the role of the syntactic choice module is to map completed text plans onto a grammatical functional structure (f-structure) that can then be realized as a surface string in the target language. Syntactic choice is performed after lexical selection (which is, in DIOGENES, part of text planning), and is therefore influenced by decisions already made during lexical selection (e.g., selection of syntactic category for a semantic head, verb argument subcategorization, etc.). The syntactic choice module must satisfy any constraints on syntactic structure that arise due to the nature of the lexical and grammatical knowledge available for the chosen lexemes to be realized.

The relative importance of this step is smaller than in other generation systems since the text planning component performs many of the tasks (such as lexical selection) that are traditionally performed within the syntactic realizer component of a generator. The output of the syntactic choice module is a fully specified f-structure for the target language utterance.

The realization module in DIOGENES applies grammatical knowledge of the target language to an f-structure produced by the mapper module, and generates a surface string in the target language. The output of the realization module is a string of properly ordered, morphologically inflected words that obeys the appropriate rules of punctuation, capitalization and other orthographic conventions.

In an f-structure, constituents are implicitly unordered, and contain explicit syntactic dependency information (agreement features, etc.) that must be present to properly inflect and realize them. The realizer, thus, must take care of word order and morphology. The separation between mapping and realization is essentially a tactical one. The use of a separate level of structure between the mapper and the realizer (the f-structure) allows these two types of tasks to be modularized and developed separately, which promotes conceptual tidiness and orderly knowledge acquisition. Separating the grammar from the mapping rules has the further advantage of enhancing portability—the same syntactic grammar can be used with different sets of mapping rules in different applications of the generator. In DIO-GENES, the realization component is embodied in the GENKIT program (Tomita and Nyberg 1988).

Chapter 7

Speech-to-Speech Translation

The ultimate dream of MT researchers is to build portable multilingual devices that translate accurately between any two spoken languages in real time. Imagine the practical utility—for traveling in foreign countries, attending conferences abroad, making international telephone calls, simultaneously translating movies or broadcasts and so forth. The first step on the arduous road toward automated translation of spoken language is the integration of speech recognition technology into knowledge-based machine translation. The primary reason for requiring KBMT as opposed to other MT methods is that the very idea of postediting a spoken simultaneous translation is absurd. Spoken translation must be as accurate as possible the first time around; since most spoken dialogues are fleeting entities that convey immediate meaning, there is no opportunity for leisurely correction by trained human posteditors.

In this chapter we first review speech recognition in terms of its historical background and current technology. Centrally, we address the issue of integrating speech and natural language analysis in general and in concrete systems. Unfortunately, the integration of speech recognition and language analysis is far from simple—direct end-to-end connection yields poor performance. Instead, both processes must be more tightly coupled with appropriate mutual feedback.

We then present three speech translation systems. Although all three are research projects at Carnegie Mellon University (CMU), they are representative of general approaches to the machine translation of speech. The systems are as follows:

- *SpeechTrans*, with noise-tolerant, generalized left-right (GLR) parsing;

- *Sphinx-LR*, with Hidden Markov Models-LR (HMM-LR); and

- *Neural Network Machine Translation*, with linked predictive neural networks (LPNN).

The systems are described in sections 7.3, 7.4 and 7.5.1, respectively.

7.1   Speech Recognition

Speech recognition is the process of mapping acoustic wave forms corresponding to spoken language into unique sequences of symbols, ideally strings of words. *Speech understanding* is sometimes used to mean only recognition and sometimes to encompass full language analysis.

Speech recognition is a very complex process that requires the discrimination of signals that vary in frequency, amplitude, onset time (phase) and temporal elasticity (speed of utterance) in different ways, by different speakers at different times. There have been many approaches to this task, but there seems to be no simple "magic bullet." Since progress is slow but steady and cumulative, different ways of characterizing system performance have evolved and gained widespread acceptance among researchers.

7.1.1   A Historical Perspective

Speech recognition has been studied fairly extensively for many years. Prototypes of the earliest successful large-scale systems reaching a 1,000-word vocabulary appeared about 1975, at the end of a five-year research plan by the U.S. government's Defense Advanced Research Projects Agency (DARPA). Two well-known examples are HEARSAY-II, which incorporated constraints, mostly syntactic, from language to facilitate recognition (Lesser et al. 1975; Lea, 1980) and HWIM (Woods et al., 1976; Wolf and Woods 1980). The HARPY system was of particular note, as it championed a different approach: It compiled rather than interpreted higher-level knowledge and used the beam-search technique to yield the best performance of the 1975 systems (Lowerre 1976; Lowerre and Reddy 1980). Also in that year, Itakura (1975) of Nippon Telephone and Telegraph introduced the dynamic time warp (DTW) for nonlinear alignment of speech.

In 1982, Wilpon et al. at Bell Labs used clustering techniques to attempt speaker-independent isolated-word recognition. A recognition accuracy of 91%

on a 129-word task was reported. The FEATURE system at CMU (Cole et al. 1983) achieved an accuracy of greater than 90% in English letter recognition without grammar, using a feature-based approach.

In 1985, the IBM Speech Recognition Group addressed a natural very-large-vocabulary task and achieved impressive results. The Tangora system obtained a 97% recognition rate for speaker-dependent recognition of sentences with clear pauses between words, using a 5,000-word vocabulary and a natural-language-like grammar with a perplexity of 160.

Bolt, Beranek and Newman's (BBN) BYBLOS system in 1987 used context-dependent modeling of phonemes and obtained a 93% accuracy on a 997-word continuous task (Chow et al. 1987; Kubala et al. 1988). Using continuous HMM, a sentence recognition rate of 97.1% was achieved without the use of a grammar by Bell Labs on speaker-independent connected digit recognition (Rabiner *et al.* 1988). The Sphinx system at CMU, which uses Hidden Markov Modeling of speech, achieved speaker-independent word accuracies of 71%, 94% and 96% on the 997-word DARPA resource management task, with grammars of perplexity 997, 60, and 20, respectively, in 1988 (Lee 1988).

There are several speech-to-speech MT projects under way throughout the world, primarily in Japan, Europe and the United States. For instance, in Japan, the ATR Interpreting Telephony Research Laboratories were established in 1986 to investigate automatic speech translation aids for overseas communications. Their research program, labeled "interpreting telephony," has the ambitious goal of enabling, in constrained domains, a person speaking one language to communicate readily by telephone with someone speaking another language. The integration of technologies in speech recognition, machine translation and speech synthesis is the focus of their investigations (ATR 1989). Another example is research at British Telecom Research Laboratories, which has been successful in overcoming some practical problems in the recognition, synthesis and translation of speech; their approach employs the use of carefully selected keywords (Stentiford and Steer 1988). The Center for Machine Translation at CMU is also deeply involved in speech-to-speech translation, and has produced several successful, prototype systems; some of these are described in the following sections.

7.1.2 Evaluation Metrics

A speech recognition system is typically evaluated on several dimensions:

- *Vocabulary size*: the number of words in its recognition vocabulary, including all inflected forms, function words and proper names.

- *Word-recognition accuracy*: the percentage of vocabulary items that are recognized correctly.

- *Sentence recognition accuracy*: the percentage of sentences that have all their words correctly recognized. Typically, sentence accuracy is much lower than word accuracy. For instance, if the average number of words in a sentence is 10, and the average recognition accuracy of each word is 90%, then the sentence recognition accuracy is $.9^{10} \times 100\%$, or approximately 35%. However, having a complete sentence enables the use of syntactic and semantic constraints that are not available in isolated word recognition. These constraints improve recognition accuracy by discarding spurious word hypotheses. Occasionally, sentence accuracy is measured in terms of "semantic" accuracy. That is, even if a function word is misrecognized, or if the wrong inflection of a content word is hypothesized, the sentence is still considered to be correctly recognized as long as the underlying message is conveyed accurately.

- *Degree of speaker independence*: whether a potential user needs to train or tune the system with examples of his or her voice. The first speech recognition systems functioned only for a particular speaker. Speaker-trainable systems were then developed. Such systems are exposed to a substantial amount of speech from a given speaker in a training phase and are tuned to recognize speech from that particular speaker. Speaker-independent systems, which are clearly more challenging to develop, represent a very active line of research.

- *Performance*: how fast speech is recognized by the system (real time being the objective), and how fast can it be trained to handle new vocabulary or new speakers.

The HARPY system, for instance, was speaker dependent but trainable, had a vocabulary of 997 words, a word-recognition accuracy of 90%, and performance 20-fold slower than real time. Modern speech recognition systems seek to improve their performance in all of these dimensions, although there are clear tradeoffs, as for instance between vocabulary size and word-recognition accuracy. Therefore, different projects rank the importance of each dimension differently, and so each explores a somewhat different part of the logical space of speech recognition technologies.

Many different technologies have been evaluated for the low-level speech recognition task of mapping digitized acoustic wave forms, first into phonetic labels and

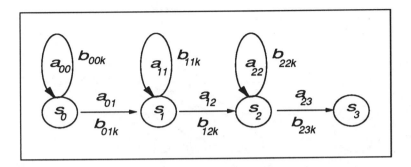

Figure 7.1: **Example of a Hidden Markov Model.**

then into words from a pre-established vocabulary. These methods range from template matching using dynamic time warping (DTW) (Itakura 1975), Hidden Markov Models (Levinson et al. 1983; Poritz 1988; Rabiner et al. 1988) and connectionist networks (Lippmann 1989; Lippmann and Gold 1987; Waibel et al. 1988 a and b, 1989 a and b; Leung and Zue 1988; Bourlard and Wellekens 1989; Franzini et al. 1989, 1990; Jain and Waibel 1990). Here we review the latter two, as they have proven to be the most promising approaches. The reader is referred to the respective references for more comprehensive and detailed assessments.

7.1.3 Hidden Markov Models

An example of a Hidden Markov Model is shown in figure 7.1. A model has a collection of *states* connected by *transitions*. In speech recognition, a state typically represents recognition of a given phoneme (a word fragment), and a sequence of states traversed via legal transitions can represent a word recognized by the system. Two sets of probabilities are attached to each transition. One is a *transition probability* a_{ij}, which denotes the probability of taking a transition from state i to state j. The other is an *output probability* $b_{ij}(k)$, which denotes the probability of emitting symbol k when taking a transition from state i to state j.

Formally, a Hidden Markov Model M is defined by a 4-tuple $M = (S, Y, A, B)$ where

- S is a set of states $\{s_i\}$ including an initial state S_I and a final state S_F.

- Y is a set of output symbols.

- A is a set of transitions $\{a_{ij}\}$ where a_{ij} is the probability of taking a transition from state i to state j, and $\sum_j a_{ij} = 1$.

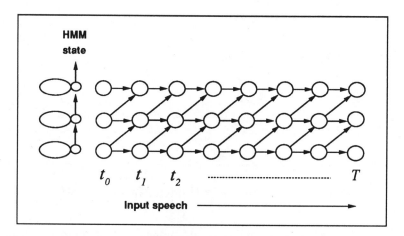

Figure 7.2: **A trellis diagram encodes all possible state transitions used in training the transition probabilities in a Hidden Markov Model.**

- B is the output probability distribution $\{b_{ij}(k)\}$ where $b_{ij}(k)$ is the probability of emitting symbol k when taking a transition from state i to state j, and $\sum_k b_{ij}(k) = 1$.

Typically, *vector quantization* (VQ) (Linde et al. 1980) is used as the acoustic front end for HMMs. Vector quantization is a discrete representation of spectral space. A set of fixed prototype vectors is called a *codebook*, and an output symbol of a model comes from these prototype vectors.

The trellis diagram in figure 7.2 shows all possible state sequences. Each circle includes the cumulative probability at a particular state and time, and the task of tuning an HMM is to find the maximal probability model given sample speech input. Then, the job of recognizing speech is one of finding the maximal probability path through the states and transitions given a new input stream. One method of computing this path is the Viterbi algorithm (cf., e.g., Forney 1973).

HMMs can of course be constrained by other knowledge sources (phonemic, lexical, grammatical, etc.) that can, before training, rule out many of the possible transitions; this increases the precision and efficiency of the resultant HMM.

7.1.4   Neural Networks

The neural network (NN) approach to speech processing seems promising because it forms a computational model that is arguably close to the human cognitive mechanism which performs the recognition task with apparent ease. A neural network is a collection of interconnected, simple processing elements that integrate their inputs and broadcast the results to the units to which they are connected. The aggregate response of these elementary units forms the response of the entire network.

Recently, an increasing number of researchers have begun to suggest that neural networks, with their learning abilities, noise-tolerant behavior and graceful degradation, may just have the ability to overcome some of the limitations of conventional speech processing techniques. A significant amount of effort has been put into the development of speech recognition systems using promising connectionist models (e.g., Lippmann 1989; Lippmann and Gold 1987; Waibel et al. 1988 a and b, 1989 a and b; Leung and Zue, 1988; Bourlard and Wellekens 1989; Franzini et al. 1989, 1990; Jain and Waibel 1990). Most of the current applications of NN to speech processing are still in low-level phoneme recognition.

One speech recognition problem that a network must address is that of time variation. In other words, how should time-variant features of speech be managed in the NN architecture, and how should time-warped speech signals be responded to correctly? The network must provide a good representation of the temporal relationships between acoustic events and provide for invariance under translation in time (i.e. detect acoustic events independent of their precise location in time).

A *time delay neural network* (TDNN) structure has been designed to cope with these problems (Waibel et al. 1988 a and b; Lang 1989). The basic unit used in many neural networks computes the weighted sum of its inputs and then passes this sum through a nonlinear function. In TDNN units, the history of current input features is considered in addition to the weighted sum of these features. This is done by introducing varying delays on each of the inputs and "weighting" the versions with a separate weight. For instance, in figure 7.3, the delays are introduced at $D_1, \ldots, D_N$, as shown. The J inputs are multiplied by several weights: one for each delay and one for the undelayed input. That is, a total of $(N+1) \times J$ weights will be needed to compute the weighted sum of the J inputs, with each input measured at $N+1$ different points in time. In this way the units can compare current status with the past history of events and so learn the dynamic properties of a set of moving inputs.

Time invariant learning in TDNN units is achieved by forcing the neural network to develop useful hidden units regardless of the temporal position of a relevant feature in the utterance. During learning, the network is exposed to sequences of patterns and allowed to learn about the most powerful cues and sequences of cues among them. The time-delay arrangement of TDNN enables the network to discover acoustic-phonetic features and the temporal relationships between them.

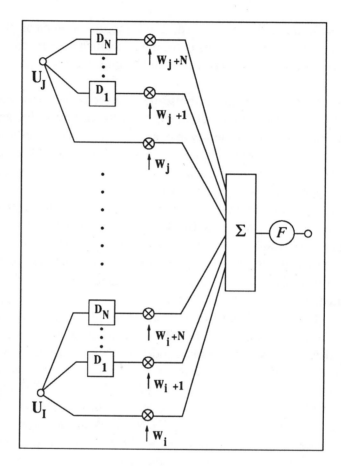

Figure 7.3: **A time-delay neural network unit.**

By linking the weights of time-shifted copies of the net during a scan through the input token, the relative timing information can be removed.

Through extensive performance evaluation, the TDNN approach has shown robust recognition results (Waibel et al. 1988a; Lang 1989). The TDNN in Waibel et al. 1989 has been found to "reinvent" well-known acoustic-phonetic features as useful abstractions, and learned to form alternate representations linking different acoustic events with the same high-level concept.

A different neural network approach to speech processing is to use the nets as nonlinear signal predictors. In other words, such a network would perform speech recognition by signal prediction instead of classification. Linked predictive neural networks (LPNNs) (Tebelskis and Waibel 1990), which follow this approach in the application of large vocabulary recognition, are described further in Section 7.5.1.

Neural network technology can also be applied to areas of speech-to-speech translation other than phoneme recognition tasks. For instance, a connectionist model is proposed in Wang and Waibel 1991 to track the semantic flow of a dialogue in the domain of registration for scientific conferences. This model, which is robust against certain input corruptions, tracks and identifies key semantic events in a dialogue for generation in another language.

7.2   Integrating Speech Recognition and Language Analysis

The simplest speech-to-speech KBMT architecture—essentially a pipeline—is diagrammed in figure 7.4.

This architecture, however compelling for its elegance and simplicity, lacks realism, at least with respect to the recognition and analysis components. Whereas speech synthesis is a process that can proceed accurately in open-loop mode, this is not so for speech recognition. The recognition accuracy at the word level, and especially the sentence level, depends crucially on tightly coupled interaction with higher-level language knowledge. To understand why this is so, let us introduce the notion of *perplexity*, namely the number of possible words that can legitimately follow a given word without violating linguistic or semantic constraints. For instance, in isolated word recognition, the perplexity is equal to the vocabulary size. In sentence recognition however, it can be much smaller. Consider an air-traffic control task:

(7.1)   This is Pan Am 105 calling Kennedy control _____ .

Now, very few words could legitimately fill the blank in example (7.1) (e.g., *tower*), and hence the perplexity at that point is low. In general, we measure average perplexity over many word transitions in different sentences in a task domain.

Perplexity is inversely correlated with recognition accuracy and speed. The fewer candidate words, the smaller the probability of error and the faster the overall processing. The key question, therefore, is how to reduce perplexity in speech recognition. The most effective answer is to exploit syntactic, semantic and pragmatic constraints, and even statistical co-occurrence preferences, whether specific to the task domain or general for the language in question.

The simplest approaches to perplexity reduction are primarily statistical—examining a large transcribed corpus of "typical" speech in the task domain to extract all word pairs or triplets (bigrams and trigrams, respectively, when augmented with their corresponding transition probabilities) (Jelinek et al. 1976;

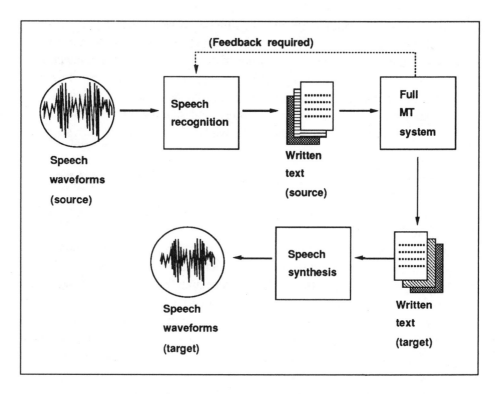

Figure 7.4: **A pipeline architecture for speech-to-speech machine translation. The speech recognizer outputs written text, which is translated and passed to speech synthesis. Unfortunately, recognition errors make this architecture unrealistic, and feedback from the language analysis component of the MT system to the speech recognizer is required to produce quality recognition before translation.**

Fujisaki 1985; Shikano 1987). Better results, however, are obtained by performing true linguistic analysis. Since for KBMT the source language analysis must be performed anyway, it proves useful to perform that very same analysis in a left-to-right manner to reduce perplexity in recognizing spoken language. Figure 7.5 zooms in on the speech recognition and analysis phase showing the tighter coupling currently investigated.

At the very least, integration requires that the analyzer provide constraints on possible subsequent words (a filter), or, better yet, the actual set of word candidates themselves, incrementally and on demand as the analysis proceeds in real time from left to right (tracking closely the temporal progression of the speech signal).

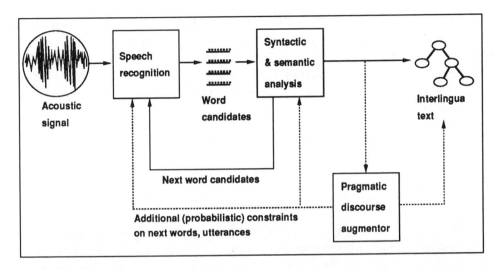

Figure 7.5: **Integrated speech recognition and language analysis. Acoustic signals are converted into probabilistically ranked word candidates which, along with syntactic, semantic and pragmatic constraints, produce the interlingua text. Constraints from all three knowledge sources may feed back to reduce perplexity in speech recognition.**

The next-word candidates are typically a small subset of the vocabulary, usually smaller than bigram or trigram expectations. Moreover, additional perplexity-reducing constraints can be derived from the pragmatic and discourse levels, as shown by Young et al. (1988).

7.3   SpeechTrans with-f Noise-Proof LR Parsing

The SpeechTrans project constitutes one of several efforts to integrate speech into a KBMT system at CMU's Center for Machine Translation. This project uses the Tomita algorithm (discussed in chapter 5) for language analysis with Matsushita experimental hardware for low-level phonemic speech recognition.

Much effort has been devoted to make the SpeechTrans parser more robust against noise in order to analyze sentences that suffer from accoustical recognition errors. The speech recognition device, which is a high-speed, speaker-independent system developed by Matsushita Research Institute (Morii et al. 1985) takes a continuously spoken Japanese utterance, for example *megaitai* ("I have a pain in my eye"), from speaker-microphone input and produces a sequence of phoneme symbols. Because the speech recognition device does not have any syntactic or semantic knowledge, recognition errors often produce illegal or *noisy* phoneme sequences, such as "ebaitaai" for *megaitai*.[1] Some more input/output examples of the speech device are presented in example (7.2), where the left-hand side of each line is the correct phoneme sequence and the right-hand side is what was recognized.

(7.2)   a. *igamukamukasuru* → "igagukamukusjuru"

        b. *kubigakowabaqteiru* → "kubigakooboqteiiru"

        c. *atamagaitai* → "otomogaitai"

The task then is to parse noisy phoneme sequences like those in example (7.2) and analyze the meaning of the original input utterances. A very efficient parsing method is crucial because the task's search space is much larger than that of parsing non-noisy sentences. In other words, one must attempt to parse variants of the input sequence to find the closest one that satisfies all lexical, syntactic and semantic well-formedness constraints. We adopt the generalized left-right (GLR) parsing algorithm discussed in chapter 5, together with a scoring scheme to select the most likely sentence from multiple candidates. The use of a *confusion matrix*, created in advance by analyzing a large set of input/output pairs to improve the scoring accuracy, is discussed below.

Note that some speech recognition devices (such as Matsushita's) produce a phoneme sequence, not a phoneme lattice; there are no other phoneme candidates available as alternates. Therefore, at analysis time, we must make the best guess based solely on the phoneme sequence generated by the speech device. Errors caused by the speech device can be classified into three groups:

- *Substituted phonemes:* phonemes recognized incorrectly. The second phoneme /b/ in "ebaitaai" is a substituted phoneme, for example.

- *Deleted phonemes:* phonemes which are actually spoken but not recognized by the device. For example, a phoneme /m/ is deleted at the beginning of "ebaitaai."

---

[1]We distinguish *noisy* from *ill-formed*. The former is due to recognition-device errors, while the latter is due to human users mistyping or misconstructing their sentences. Each phenomenon leads to different kinds of deviation from the correct or expected input.

- *Inserted phonemes:* phonemes recognized by the device but which are not actually spoken. The penultimate phoneme /a/ in "ebaitaai," for example, is an inserted phoneme.

To cope with these problems, we integrate two key technologies:

1. The GLR, a very efficient parsing algorithm, because our task requires much more search than conventional typed sentence parsing; and

2. A good scoring scheme, to select the most likely sentence from a multiple candidate set, as described in section 7.3.3.

SpeechTrans uses an augmented context-free grammar whose terminal symbols are phonemes rather than words. That is, the grammar contains rules like

```
Noun --> w a t a s i
```

instead of

```
Noun --> 'watasi'
```

Parsing therefore proceeds character by character (phoneme by phoneme). The grammar was developed for a doctor-patient communication task (see Tomita 1987a; Tomita et al. 1987) and consists of more than 2,000 rules including lexical rules like the one above.[2]

7.3.1 Handling Erratic Phonemes

To cope with substituted, inserted and deleted phonemes, the parser must consider these errors as it parses an input from left to right. While the basic algorithm described in chapter 5 cannot handle these noisy phenomena, it is well suited to consider many possible parses at the same time. Therefore, it can be modified relatively easily to handle various noisy phenomena:

---

[2]The runtime grammar, which contains both syntax and semantics, is compiled automatically from more abstract formalisms, namely the functional grammar formalism for syntax and frame representation for semantics. Further discussion about the universal parser architecture is offered in Tomita 1986a and in chapter 5 of this volume.

- *Substituted phonemes:* Each phoneme in a phoneme sequence may have been substituted and thus may be incorrect. The parser should consider all these possibilities. A phoneme lattice is created dynamically by placing alternate phoneme candidates in the same location as the original phoneme. Each possibility is then explored by each branch of the parser. Not all phonemes can be substituted for any other phoneme. For example, while /o/ can be misrecognized as /u/, /i/ can never be misrecognized as a consonant. This kind of information can be obtained from a *confusion matrix*, which we discuss in the next section. With the confusion matrix, the parser need not create an exhaustive set of alternate phoneme candidates, only the mutually confusible ones.

- *Inserted phonemes:* Each phoneme in a phoneme sequence may be an extra one, and the parser should consider the deletion of the current phoneme, assuming that at most one inserted spurious phoneme can exist between two actual phonemes.

- *Deleted phonemes:* Deleted phonemes can be handled by inserting potentially deleted phonemes between two actual phonemes. The parser assumes that at most one phoneme can be missing between two actual phonemes, and we have found the assumption quite reasonable. All possible legal insertions are considered if the current parse (without insertions) fails.

7.3.2   An Example: Integrating GLR Parsing with Speech Recognition

Let us consider the final configuration of the parser after a sample run. Here we use the grammar and LR table from chapter 5 (section 5.2.1) to try to parse the phoneme sequence "ebaitaai" represented in figure 7.6. (The correct sequence is *megaitai*, which means "I have a pain in my eye.")

For this example we make the following assumptions for substituted and deleted phonemes:

- /i/ may be misrecognized as /e/

- /e/ may be misrecognized as /a/

- /g/ may be misrecognized as /b/

- /m/ has a high probability of being missed in the output sequence

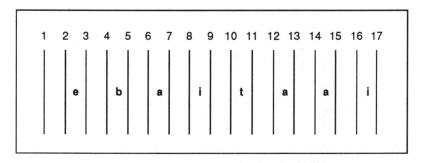

Figure 7.6: **An input sequence of phonemes.**

The final configuration of the parser is represented in figure 7.7. A step-by-step explanation can be found in Saito and Tomita 1988. Note here that the parser finds two successful parses: *megaitai* and *igaitai* ("I have a stomach ache").

7.3.3 Scoring and the Confusion Matrix

There are two main reasons for scoring each candidate parse. The first is to prune the search space by discarding branches during the parse whose score is hopelessly low and therefore clearly incorrect. The second is to select the best sentence of multiple candidates by comparing their scores after parsing is complete.

Branches of the parse that consider fewer substituted/inserted/deleted phonemes should be given higher scores. This is a form of "least-deviant-first search" for ill-structured input, first introduced by Fain et al. 1985. Whenever a branch of the parse handles a substituted/inserted/deleted phoneme, a specific penalty is applied to the branch. Unfortunately, the recognition device gives us neither the probability of each phoneme transition in the sequence nor the likelihood of finding substituted/inserted/deleted phonemes. Only the "best" phoneme sequence is given. Therefore we have to resort to a data structure called a *confusion matrix* for scoring purposes. A portion of the matrix is given in table 7.1.

The table shows part of the matrix produced by the manufacturer of the recognition device from sample word data. This matrix tells us, for example, that if the phoneme /a/ is input, the device recognizes it correctly 93.8% of the time, misrecognizes it as /o/ 1.1% of the time, misrecognizes it as /u/ 1.3% of the time and so on. The column (I) says that the input is missed 0.9% of the time.

Conversely, if the phoneme /o/ is recognized by the device, there is a slight chance that the original input was /a/, /u/ or /w/, but no chance of it being /i/, /e/ or /j/, as can be seen from the table. The baseline *a priori* probability of the original

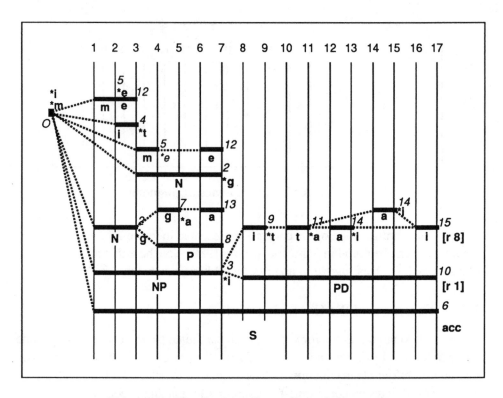

Figure 7.7: **The final configuration of the parser.**

input being /a/ is much higher than its being /w/. Thus, a substituted phoneme /w/ should be given a more severe penalty than /a/. A score for substituted phonemes can be obtained in this way, while deleted phonemes should be given a negative score, and inserted phonemes a zero or a negative score. With this technique, a score for a partial parse is calculated by summing the score of each constituent; the higher the score, the more likely the parse is correct.

Two methods have been adopted to prune partial parses by a score:

- Discarding the low-score, shift-waiting branches when a phoneme is applied; and

- Discarding the low-score branches in local ambiguity packing.

The former method, when strictly applied, is found to be very effective.

Note that the confusion matrix shows us only the phoneme-to-phoneme transition. It would seem that a broader-unit transition should also be considered, such

Output phoneme→ Input ↓ phoneme	/a/	/o/	/u/	/i/	/e/	/j/	/w/	...	(I)	(II)
/a/	93.8	1.1	1.3	0	2.7	0	0	...	0.9	5477
/o/	2.4	84.3	5.8	0	0.3	0	0.6	...	6.5	7529
/u/	0.3	1.8	79.7	2.4	4.6	0.1	0	...	9.7	5722
/i/	0.2	0	0.9	91.2	3.5	0.7	0	...	2.9	6158
/e/	1.9	0	4.5	3.3	89.1	0.1	0	...	1.1	3248
/j/	0	0	1.1	2.3	2.2	80.1	0.3	...	11.4	2660
/w/	0.2	5.1	5.8	0.5	0	2.6	56.1	...	11.2	428
.	.	.	.	.	.	.	.	.	.	.
.	.	.	.	.	.	.	.	.	.	.
(III)	327	176	564	512	290	864	212	...		

Table 7.1: **A portion of a confusion matrix. (I) denotes the possibility of deleted phonemes; (II) the number of samples; and (III) the number of times this phoneme has been spuriously inserted in the given samples.**

as the tendency for the /w/ phoneme in 'owa' or 'owo' to be missed, the tendency for the very first /h/ sound of an input to be missed, and the frequent transformation to 'h@' of the 'su' sound in 'desuka'. In other words, a better confusion matrix can be constructed by considering a larger context—such as entire words.

7.4 Sphinx-LR: Integrating HMMs with LR Parsing

Sphinx is a state-of-the-art HMM speech recognizer developed at CMU (Lee 1988). It is being tested as a front end to a machine translation system. The grammar compiler produces three knowledge files used by Sphinx-LR from the context-free grammar. They are the pure context-free grammar rules, the LR parsing table and the HMM net file, as depicted in figure 7.8.

The grammar compiler expects an input grammar to be in the same format as the parser. Thus, when the user develops a grammar for Sphinx-LR, he or she can test and debug the grammar with typed input sentences using the standard LR parser. Once the grammar is debugged, it can be fed into the Sphinx-LR grammar compiler.

As already noted, the analysis grammar for the translation system is written in augmented context-free grammar, while basic Sphinx uses only a bigram grammar

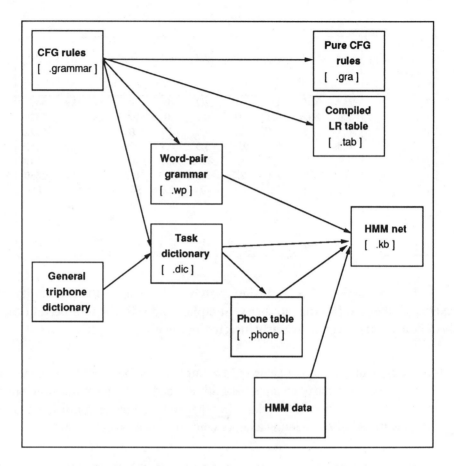

Figure 7.8: **Sphinx-LR's compiled knowledge files.**

to reduce perplexity and thereby constrain the search process. Since the bigram grammar is generally much looser than the context-free grammar, Sphinx will output many incorrectly recognized ungrammatical sentences, which cannot be handled by the translation system. It is therefore desirable to constrain Sphinx's search process with the same grammar as the analysis grammar in the translation system so that the probability of correct recognition is increased and all Sphinx output can be handled by the translation system. A side benefit of more constrained search is faster speech recognition. Therefore, grammar-constrained speech recognition provides net benefits on all counts. The addition of semantic constraints improves performance beyond that of context-free grammars.

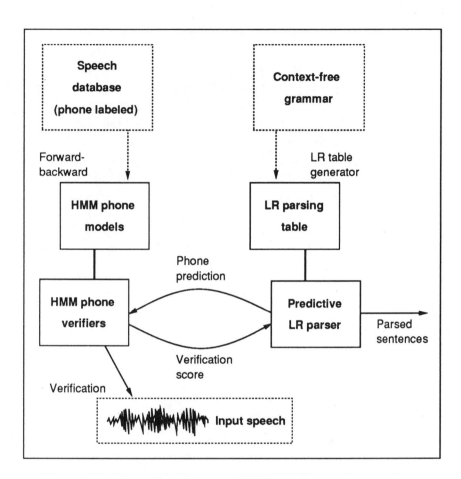

Figure 7.9: **Schematic diagram of HMM-LR speech recognizer.**

7.4.1 The HMM-LR Method

A technique called "HMM-LR" (Hanazawa et al. 1990; Kita et al. 1989), has been developed to integrate Hidden Markov Models and GLR parsing. This subsection gives a description of the HMM-LR method. We assume here that the HMM recognizer applies at the individual phone level, although it can also be applied at the syllable or word levels.

In standard LR parsing, any parser action (*shift, reduce, accept* or *error*) is determined by using the current parser state and the next input symbol. This parsing mechanism is valid only for symbolic data (at any level of granularity), but cannot be applied simply to continuous data such as speech.

In HMM-LR, the LR parser is used as a language source model for word/phone prediction/generation. Thus we call the LR parser in next-symbol-set prediction mode the *predictive LR parser*. A phone-based predictive LR parser predicts next phones at each transition and generates possible sentences as phone sequences. The predictive LR parser determines next phones using the LR parsing table compiled from the specified grammar, and splits the parsing stack not only for grammatical ambiguity but also for alternative or confusable phone variation. Because the predictive LR parser uses context-free rules whose terminal symbols are phone names, the phonetic lexicon for the specified task is embedded in the grammar. A very simple example of a context-free grammar rules with a phonetic lexicon is given here:

(a)	S	-->	NP VP
(b)	NP	-->	DET N
(c)	VP	-->	V
(d)	VP	-->	V NP
(e)	DET	-->	/z/ /a/
(f)	DET	-->	/z/ /i/
(g)	N	-->	/m/ /ae/ /n/
(h)	N	-->	/ae/ /p/ /a/ /l/
(i)	V	-->	/iy/ /ts/
(j)	V	-->	/s/ /ih/ /ng/ /s/

Here, rule (e) indicates the definite article *the* pronounced /z/ /a/ before consonants, while rule (f) indicates the *the* pronounced /z/ /i/ before vowels. Rules (g), (h), (i) and (j) phonetically indicate the words *man, apple, eats* and *sings*, respectively.

The HMM-LR continuous speech recognition system (see figure 7.9) consists of the predictive LR parser and HMM phone verifiers. First, the parser picks up all the phones predicted by the initial state of the LR parsing table and invokes the HMM models to verify the existence of these predicted phones. The parser then proceeds to the next state in the LR parsing table. During this process, all possible partial parses are constructed in parallel. The HMM phone verifier receives a *probability array* (see figure 7.10) which includes end-point candidates and their probabilities, and updates the array using a standard HMM probability calculation. This probability array is attached to each partial parse. Partial parses are pruned

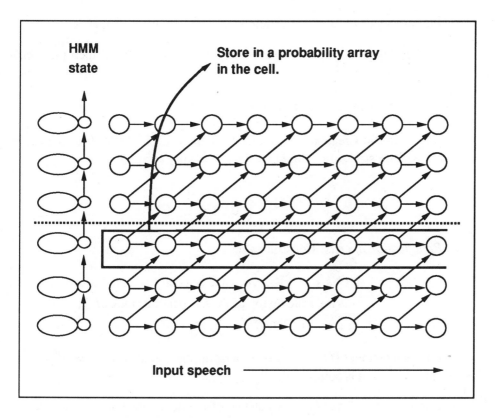

Figure 7.10: **Stacking of a probability array.**

when their probability falls below a predefined threshold. In case more than one partial parse reaches completion, the one with highest probability is selected. For semantically constrained domains and clean speech signals, only one parse typically reaches completion.

7.4.2 The Integrated Speech-Parsing Algorithm

This section presents the algorithm for HMM-LR recognition more formally. The extension of the algorithm to produce parse trees during recognition is straightforward.

First, we introduce a data structure called a *cell*. A cell is a structure with information about one recognition candidate. The following items are kept in the cell:

- *LR parsing stack*, with information for parsing control.

- *Probability array*, which includes end-point candidates and their probabilities.

LR recognition proceeds as follows:

1. *Initialization*: Create a new cell C. Push the LR initial state 0 on top of the LR parsing stack of C. Initialize the probability array Q of C;

$$Q(t) = \begin{cases} 1 & t = 0 \\ 0 & 1 \leq t \leq T \end{cases}$$

2. *Ramification of cells*: Construct a set

$$S = \{(C, s, a, x) | \exists C, s, a, x \ (C \text{ is a cell that is not accepted;}$$
$$s \text{ is the state on top of the LR parsing stack of } C;$$
$$\& \ x = ACTION[s, a] \ x \neq \text{``error''})\}$$

For each element $(C, s, a, x) \in S$, perform the operations below. If set S is empty, parsing is completed.

3. If $x =$ "*shift s',*" verify the existence of phone a. In this case, update the probability array Q of the cell C using the following computation:

$$\alpha_i(t) = \begin{cases} Q(t) & i = S_I \\ 0 & i \neq S_I \ \& \ t = 0 \\ \sum_j \alpha_j(t-1)a_{ji}b_{ji}(y_t) & i \neq 0 \ \& \ t > 0 \end{cases}$$

$$Q(t) = \begin{cases} 0 & t = 0 \\ \alpha_{S_F}(t) & t > 0 \end{cases}$$

If $\max_{1 \leq t \leq T} Q(t)$ is below a certain threshold, cell C is abandoned. Otherwise push s' on top of the LR parsing stack of cell C.

4. If $x =$ "*reduce $A \rightarrow \beta$,*" pop $|\beta|$ symbols off the LR parsing stack and push $GOTO[s', A]$ where s' is the current state on top of the stack.

5. If $x =$ "*accept*" and $Q(T)$ exceeds a certain threshold, cell C is accepted. If not, cell C is abandoned.

6. Return to 2.

Recognition results are kept in accepted cells. In general, many recognition candidates could exist, and it is possible to rank these candidates using $Q(T)$ of each cell.

In practice, however, the following two refinements of the above HMM-LR algorithm are useful:

1. Using beam-search technique:

   The *beam-search* technique was first used in the HARPY speech recognition system (Lowerre 1976; Lowerre and Reddy 1980). It is a modification of the breadth-first search technique, in which a group of near-miss alternatives around the best path are selected and processed in parallel, rather than retaining all candidates. The beam-search technique reduces search cost significantly and maintains accuracy. Generally, the set S constructed in step 2 in the algorithm is quite large. The beam-search technique is very useful for selecting the few most likely cells. The value $\max_{1 \leq t \leq T} Q(t)$ of each cell can be used as an evaluation score.

2. Using graph-structured stack:

   The *graph-structured stack* is one of the key ideas in GLR parsing (Tomita 1986a). In the above algorithm, when making a set S, virtual copies of the LR parsing stack are created. By using the graph-structured stack, it is not necessary to physically copy the whole stack. Copying only the necessary portion of the stack is sufficient and the amount of computation is reduced.

7.5 Speech Translation with Neural Networks

A speech-to-speech translation system combining connectionist and symbolic processing strategies is being developed at CMU (Waibel et al. 1991). The system translates continuously spoken English speech input in the domain of conference registration dialogues into corresponding Japanese or German utterances. The system consists of three major components and integrates statistical, connectionist and knowledge-based approaches: the speech recognition (SR) component, the machine translation (MT) component and the speech synthesis (SS) component. Two different approaches to machine translation are investigated in the MT component: a small-scale, pure connectionist approach and the standard, full KBMT method.

7.5.1   Speech Recognition with Linked Predictive Neural Networks

Speech recognition is provided by a connectionist, continuous, large-vocabulary system using linked predictive neural networks (LPNN) (Tebelskis and Waibel 1990). In this system, neural networks are employed as predictors of speech frames, maintaining a pool of such networks as phoneme models. High-level algorithms are used to connect these networks into sequences corresponding to the phonetic spellings of words. With this linking of phonemic networks, the system is vocabulary independent and is applicable to large-vocabulary recognition.

Figure 7.11 illustrates the basic idea of signal prediction behind an LPNN network. To predict the next frame of the speech signal, K, contiguous speech frames are passed through a hidden layer of units in the network (shown as a triangle in the figure). The predicted frame is then compared to the actual frame, with the difference between the two indicating how good a model the network is for that segment of speech. If the network is taught to make relatively good predictions with respect to a particular phoneme (say /a/), then it is effectively an /a/ phoneme recognizer. In this way, a collection of phoneme recognizers can be obtained, with one model per phoneme. Each phoneme is actually modeled by a total of three subnetworks corresponding to the beginning, middle and end of the phoneme; the sequentiality of these constituent subnetworks being enforced by the LPNN architecture.

To allow for word recognition, each word is associated with a "linkage pattern" which is a logically constrained sequence of models corresponding to the phonetic spelling of the word. For instance, suppose the phonemes /a/ and /b/ are modeled by the sequence of networks a1,a2,a3, and b1,b2,b3 respectively, then the word *aba* is represented by the network linkage pattern: a1,a2,a3,b1,b2,b3,a1,a2,a3. Note that multiple occurrences of networks (like a1,a2 and a3) are linked together; this allows LPNN to model phonemes from varying contexts and to recognize words that were not in the training set.

We briefly describe a three-step training algorithm of the LPNN on a word:

1. *Forward pass*: For each input speech frame at time t, the frames at time $t-1$ and $t-2$ are fed into all the networks that are linked into this word. Each of these nets then makes a prediction of frame(t), and the prediction errors are computed and stored in a matrix.

2. *Alignment step*: Dynamic programming is applied to the prediction error matrix to find the optimal alignment between the speech signal and the phoneme models.

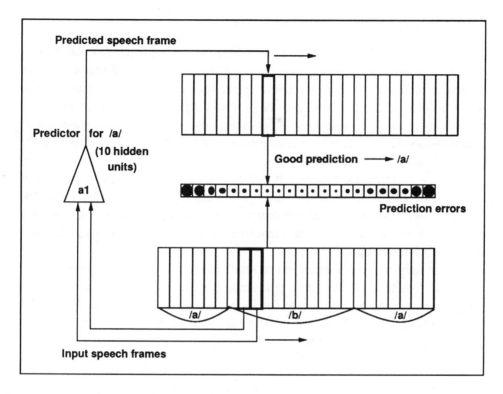

Figure 7.11: **Modeling a phoneme by signal prediction.**

3. *Backward pass:* Errors are propagated backward along the alignment path. For each frame, the error is back-propagated into the network that best predicted the frame according to the alignment. Note that this alignment-controlled back-propagation causes each subnetwork to specialize on a different section of speech, resulting eventually in a model for each phoneme.

The training is repeated for all the words in the training vocabulary. A variation on the standard LPNN architecture has demonstrated a positive effect on the modeling performance: it allows a limited number of alternate models (say two or three) for each phoneme to account for the different characteristics of the phonemes in different contexts

In the experiment described in Tebelskis and Waibel 1990, recognition rates of 94% for a 234-word Japanese vocabulary of acoustically similar words, and 90% for a larger vocabulary of 924 words, are obtained.

7.5.2   Integration of LPNN and KBMT

The LPNN speech recognition component is integrated with the full KBMT system via the GLR parser in a manner similar to the HMM-LR model discussed earlier. A difference, however, is that the LPNN generates the best n hypotheses for each word and the LR parser then selects the one with highest probability that satisfies syntactic and semantic constraints. After translation, speech synthesis is performed by DECTALK, a commercially available speech synthesis device, completing the speech-to-speech MT prototype.

The best performance obtained from the LPNN model to date is on a corpus of 12 English conference-registration dialogues containing a total of 204 sentences. Of these, 146 produced "legal" interlingua texts from the speech recognition and parsing components; 94% of these were correctly translated into both Japanese and German spoken dialogues.

In summary, speech recognition and KBMT technologies can be integrated successfully. Syntactic and semantic processing constraints reduce speech recognition perplexity, and hence provide for higher recognition accuracy. We expect speech-to-speech translation to be come a more widely investigated and exploited technology in the coming years.

Chapter 8

Machine-Aided Translation

It is widely supposed that research in knowledge-based machine translation is oriented exclusively to developing fully automated systems. This belief may lead one to the conclusion that the KBMT approach will bear fruit only in the not-so-near future. Such a conclusion is, in fact, wrong. While a major thrust of research in the KBMT tradition is indeed directed at full automation, many of the methods, techniques and tools of knowledge-based machine translation can be used immediately to build sophisticated tools for human translators.[1]

This chapter sketches one method of constructing a knowledge-based language processing environment supporting machine-aided translation. We believe it is possible to develop considerable synergy between the human translator and the current capabilities of automatic NLP using state-of-the-art human-computer interaction techniques. Depending on the needs and capabilities of a knowledge-based machine translation project, several different types of translator's workstations (TWSs) can be contemplated. We describe here two TWS configurations which differ by their level of sophistication.

A TWS and related tools will benefit translators and information processing specialists in two distinct but connected ways: through enhancing the *productivity* of translators and information specialists, and by supporting a wider range of

---

[1]Another area in which KBMT systems can have an immediate impact is the development of very high-quality translation for limited-domain systems for high-volume applications. These include specialized equipment manuals and highly structured documents.

practical *applications*, such as, for instance, multilingual abstracting and authoring documents intended for translation.

A basic translator's workstation must feature the following functionalities:

- An advanced human-computer interface to machine-readable monolingual, bilingual and multilingual dictionaries and machine-readable encyclopedias;

- An advanced *knowledge acquisition* interface for creating, maintaining and updating sophisticated knowledge sources such as domain models, multilingual corporate terminology banks and corporate translation archives;

- A set of utilities for search, retrieval and storage to support the above interfaces and enhance the translation process; and

- Capabilities for automatic morphological and small-scale syntactic analysis (part-of-speech determination) for one or more source languages.

An advanced workstation can feature the following added functionalities:

- Capabilities for deeper syntactic analysis (establishing functional structure) and partial semantic analysis (processing selectional restrictions);

- Specialized tools for producing controlled-language input for translation;

- Specialized tools to support interactive editing capabilities; and

- Capabilities for partially or fully automatic generation of target language texts.

As discussed in detail in chapter 3, the field of natural language processing is not yet able to produce complete interlingua representations of unrestricted source language texts in a fully automatic fashion. For instance, capabilities for automatic trans-sentential semantic and pragmatic analysis, including resolution of referential ambiguity, are among the central research topics in computational linguistics. At present, however, few general results can be introduced into a commercial setting. In addition, the requirements for deep analysis inherent in interlingua systems imply (i) designing and developing modules performing semantic and pragmatic analysis, (ii) designing the formalisms for representing linguistic and encyclopedic knowledge required by such systems and (iii) acquiring the vast repositories of such knowledge necessary to support deep text understanding. Finally, until recently, massive acquisition of knowledge for MT was considered a task insurmountable in practice. With the advent of new technologies (the size and speed of computers, convenient user interfaces, semi-automated text processing, etc.), this knowledge acquisition task has come within the realm of the possible, in practice as well as in theory.

With respect to attaining adequate levels of source text analysis, experimental interlingua machine-aided translation systems involve human help *of a kind radically different from postediting*. Instead of having posteditors, whose mission is to untangle the wrong guesses that a machine translation program made, advanced knowledge-based systems employ human users—*interactive editors*—to help the system understand the input text *during the process of analysis*. To support this functionality, the KBMT-89 machine translation project included the development of a special processing module, an *augmentor*. The KBMT-89 augmentor includes a specially designed user interface and a dialogue system to guide the human user through the disambiguation scenario.

An interactive editor engages in a dialogue with the MT system, in which the human resolves ambiguities that the machine is unable to resolve by itself. Building intelligent human-computer interfaces to support interactive editing (sometimes called *augmenting*) becomes a central concern in this approach. A dialogue between the augmentor program and the interactive editor can relate to lexical disambiguation, with the program asking the user to select among the several potential readings of a word in a given context. It can also relate to establishing dependency relations among components of text meaning representation (e.g., whether *IBM lecture* means a lecture *at* IBM or a lecture *sponsored by* IBM or maybe another of the set of the possible case role attachments). For a detailed description of augmentation capabilities see chapter 7 in Goodman and Nirenburg 1991, and Brown and Nirenburg 1990.

The main goal of building an interactive editing environment is to make the work of the human editor as easy as possible. There are two main ways in which this can be accomplished. The first is to present the choices to the user through menus, natural language messages and other user-oriented means instead of sets of computer-internal structures. The second method is helping the user to make a decision by providing him or her with a battery of reference materials—human-oriented, machine-readable dictionaries, encyclopedias and extensive text corpora in the subject domain of translation. Human translators will also benefit from selective access to translations already performed in this domain.

A module such as an augmentor opens new possibilities for machine-aided translation. As the starting point, the augmentor, taken separately, already provides a good platform for developing the initial version of a TWS. As the automatic analysis and generation capabilities are enhanced, they will be added to the basic set of functionalities in such a workstation, thus making the latter gradually more automated.

A major task in supporting automatic translation and related information-processing activities is *acquisition of knowledge*. Grammars and lexicons of adequate size and quality must be compiled for all languages involved. In order to support multilinguality and avoid the reduplication of effort inherent in the transfer-oriented, language-pair-based systems, it is necessary to acquire a *domain model*, a set of multiply indexed descriptive concepts relevant to the desired application. In KBMT-89 the application domain was the translation of IBM PC installation and maintenance manuals. Depending on the particular application, additional domain models may be integrated with the current one.

Technology already exists for speeding up the acquisition of domain knowledge. For example, using the Ontos system, members of the KBMT-89 project were able to create a large domain model—about 1,200 large knowledge frames, organized into an hierarchy with multiple inheritance—using only five person-months of effort. For comparison, a much smaller and shallower domain model (about 350 medium-sized knowledge frames in a flat list) used in the previous translation system built at CMT, for the domain of doctor-patient communication, took about three times as much effort to create. The Ontos system was also used in KBMT-89 project to support the acquisition of lexicons for English and Japanese.

To summarize, we believe that machine-aided translation systems can be developed for a commercial setting if they are

- Based on the interlingua, knowledge-oriented paradigm;

- Supported by state-of-the-art human-computer interfaces; and

- Have access to a large set of abundantly indexed electronic knowledge repositories, such as terminology banks, dictionaries, encyclopedias, corporate translation archives and so on.

Many components of such systems can be adapted from available technologies.

8.1   The TWS Configuration

The immediate objective of the developer of a knowledge-based machine-aided translation environment is to produce the basic set of tools for *translator productivity enhancement*. Advanced human-computer interface tools can be developed to allow multimode access to a variety of knowledge repositories in the environment. Large amounts of knowledge must be acquired—dictionaries for all languages selected for use and extensive, multiply indexed terminology banks for each of the chosen domains. The terminology bank knowledge bases must be multiply indexed by languages in the system, words and phrases in every language involved, sources (countries, corporations, industries, etc.), time of knowledge acquisition and other types of indices, as required by the domain. Tools for the support of knowledge acquisition must be either developed or adapted and integrated with the interface tools in a powerful working environment. This set of functionalities can form a first stage of the TWS.

An additional impetus to the development of TWS is given by the possibility of merging its capabilities with other intelligent text processing systems. If the input is obtained electronically, a TWS can routinely use results of the work of text processing systems such as message categorizing systems; these are exemplified by the TIS and PRECIS systems from Carnegie Group Inc., which categorize, route and extract key information from a wide range of short electronic texts in real time. More specifically, the former can serve to filter incoming stories, and the latter, to fill the structured fields in the story abstract. Since one of the central functionalities of TWS is assisting translators in filling "open" textual fields of a standard story abstract, it is clear that such systems are truly symbiotic.

More sophisticated TWSs must incorporate machine-aided translation of texts in one or more subject domains. This functionality requires additional knowledge acquisition efforts (notably, writing grammars for every language involved) as well as enhancement to the interface capabilities, for instance, creating a structured editor with the ability to display the source text interspersed with elements of its translation into the target language—to allow translators to use the "copy-and-edit" technique instead of having to type in the entire translation.

In what follows we describe the above functionalities in additional detail.[2] A crucial goal in modernizing an information-processing environment is enhancement of product quality. With respect to translation, quality includes such parameters as accuracy and speed of translation and its consistency over a large corpus of input texts. While the accuracy of translation in human-initiative environments depends largely on the translators themselves, the speed of translation and consistency over time and over the members of the translation team can be enhanced significantly with the introduction of state-of-the-art tools.

---

[2]In this initial description we proceed from the assumption that the input to the translation tasks that the translators perform is *not* available on-line. (Additional functionalities become possible if this is that case.)

8.1.1   The Basic Translator's Workstation

A sample screen of a base-level translator's workstation is illustrated in figure 8.1. The screen shows a double-pane TWS editor window, a dictionary lookup window, a word frequency window and a concordance ("key word in context") window. In the editor window, the source text appears in the left-hand pane (if the source text is not available on line, the window will have a single pane in which the target text will be processed by the translator; additionally, a TWS can support an overwrite mode in which the translator writes the target text directly over the original). The word *panel* is highlighted in the editor window because the translator decided to look it up in a dictionary. In this case, this is an English-English general dictionary, and the entry is displayed in a special window (titled "Dictionary Shell"). If the translator wants to check the usage of a particular word in a corpus (for instance, in the entire source text), a concordance program is used. The results of context retrieval on the word *panel* in the source text are represented in a special window. The frequency counts of words and especially phrases in a corpus are useful primarily as tools for building text-oriented glossaries; this is a very desirable functionality in general, and in particular for maintaining consistency in terminology when a translation task is carried out by a team of translators.

With respect to *speed*, the initial productivity enhancement due to the use of a TWS relates to the speed of the use of reference materials. The time of dictionary look-up can be dramatically cut if an on-line dictionary is made available to the translator. A dictionary support system must have a large number of navigational capacities. These include (but are not limited to) easy access for each word in the display window to its synonyms, antonyms, hyperonyms, hyponyms, semantically related words and, finally, translation examples from corpora of available translations. Examples may be taken from general texts, texts from the particular domain of translation and texts from corporate archives.

Consider, for example, the entry for *merge* in the *Collins Robert French-French English-French Dictionary* (Atkins et al. 1987, 418).

> **merge**   **1** *vi* **(a)** *[colours, shapes]* se mêler *(into, with* à*)*; se fondre *(into, with* dans*)*; *[sounds]* se mêler *(into, with* à*)*; se perdre *(into, with* dans*)*; *[roads]* se rencontrer *(with* avec*)*, se joindre *(with* à*)*; *[river]* confluer *(with* avec*)*.
>
> **(b)** *(Comm, Fin)* fusionner *(with* avec*)*.
>
> **2** *vt* **(a)** unifier. **the states were ~d (into one) in 1976** les États se sont unifiés en 1976, l'unification des États s'est réalisée en 1976.
>
> **(b)** *Comm, Fin* fusionner, amalgamer; *(Comput)* fusionner. **the firms**

> were ~d les entreprises ont fusionné; **they decided to ~ the compa-
> nies into a single unit** ils décidèrent d'amalgamer *or* de fusionner les
> compagnies.

The user must have an opportunity to obtain a list of synonyms or near-synonyms for any word in the display—at a touch of a key or a click of a mouse. Thus, for *merge*, {*unite, combine, join, amalgamate, consolidate*} will be displayed as synonyms and for *fusionner*, {*amalgamer, unifier*}. Additionally, antonyms must be easily reachable, as for instance to support the use of a negative construction in the resulting sentence. For *merge*, a possible list of antonyms will include {*disband, separate, divide*}. The list of hyperonyms for *firm* will include {*organization, producer, provider, manufacturer*}. Hyponyms for *sound* will include {*din, racket, noise*}. With respect to the semantically connected words, *merge* will, for instance, list {*company, corporation, firm*} as typical objects of merging. Translation examples may include the examples from the dictionary entry as well as from all the available text corpora, including the archives. As an additional feature, if the archives contain a sentence that is identical or almost identical to the one that has to be included by the translator into the document, the system must include means of copying it into the translation editor buffer from the interface buffer.

Retrieval of hyperonyms, hyponyms and semantically related words is facilitated by the existence of a domain model whose elements contain, among other links, connections to lexical units that realize their meaning in all the languages in the system. One example of such a knowledge base is the KBMT-89 domain model. Figure 8.2 shows a sample screen of the Ontos knowledge acquisition interface. The large window on the left is an editor window; frames representing concepts are displayed in it in a structured way. In this example, the concept `remove` is displayed in such a way that its local properties appear first, followed by properties inherited from its parents in the ontological network—`change-location`, `spatial-event` and so on. Note the presence of language realizations of the concept meanings as slot-value pairs in concept frames. In this example, the languages used are English and Japanese. The corresponding property names are `ehead` and `jhead`.[3]

A small browser window on the right shows a subset of the ontology which includes the concept `remove`. Any number of browser and editor windows can be used at any time; the only constraint is screen size. The topological arrangement

---

[3]Note that the lexical units in the two languages are indexed by their meanings and thus are not directly juxtaposed at the lexical level, as in standard bilingual dictionaries.

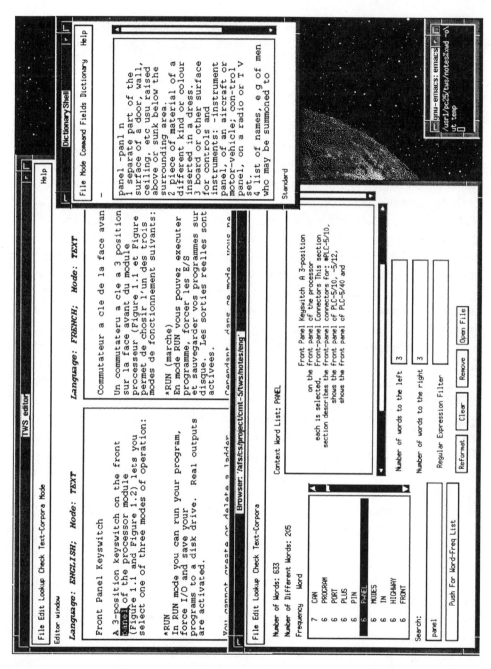

Figure 8.1: **A translator's workstation screen, with several windows, including a double-pane editor, a dictionary lookup, a word frequency facility and a concordance ("key word in context").**

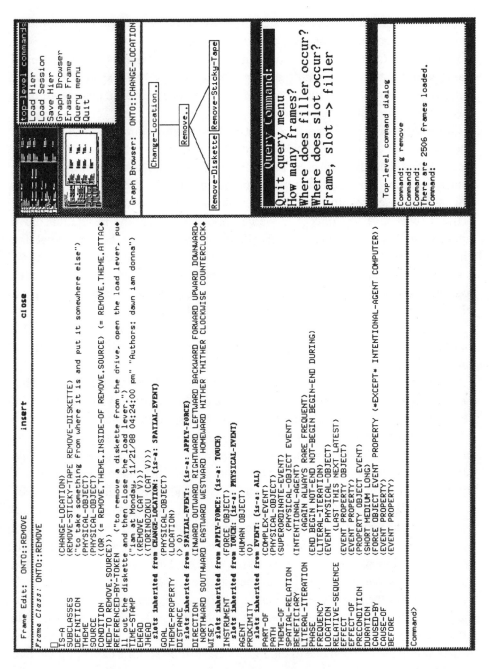

Figure 8.2: **An Ontos screen with dominant editor window. A small browser window at top shows a subset of the ontology. There are also two standing command menus and a command dialog window.**

of windows on the screen is completely free. They can be stacked, tiled, iconified, shrunk, expanded, moved around, buried or exposed.

Finally, the Ontos screen has two standing command menus and a command dialog window through which the user can interact with the system by typing commands. Thus, there are three ways of interaction supported in Ontos—through commands, menus and mouse clicks.

The nodes in the domain model network stand for concepts in the domain. These concepts are multiply interconnected on a large variety of named relation types. Using these relations, we can reach any set of connected concepts. Since domain concepts contain fields with words and phrases in each of the system's languages whose meaning this concept reflects, by traversing a conceptual link L from Concept A to Concept B we can find words standing in relationship L with one another, in any language. For instance, by traversing the conceptual link theme-of in the concept corporation we find that the concept of merge is among the set of processes in which a corporation can be an object. Since the nodes for both concepts also contain links to lexicon entries in various languages, relations can be established at the lexical level.

The task of maintaining *consistency* of translation among all members of a translation team over time is facilitated through the use of terminology banks and translation archives.

If the input texts can be provided on line then an additional functionality becomes possible. Even before the human translator starts to process the text, a special back-end program creates a small temporary corpus-based subset of the standard dictionaries and knowledge bases to speed up further or conceptually specialize the retrieval of information when the user requests it. These small dictionaries contain more information that is more focused than the general dictionaries, because it will become possible to display only the entries corresponding to the part-of-speech forms in which particular words were used in the text. For instance, if the word *set* were used in the text only as a verb, by default, then only verbal senses of this word are stored in the run-time dictionary. (The user is, of course, allowed to override the system's decision and retrieve the rest of the senses.) This functionality, supported by a simple trigram-based analysis of the input text, significantly cuts the search time and makes the display smaller and therefore more manageable. The trigram analysis is based on the observation that in most cases (at least in English) it is possible to determine a word's part of speech based on the context of one word to the left of it in the text and one to the right (see Giuse 1990 for a description of one such system). Of course, if the part of speech cannot be uniquely determined, all remaining entries are displayed.

The use of such application-constrained dictionaries enhances consistency by itself. However, a special consistency checker program can be developed to scan a complete translation in parallel with the original and flag all cases of potentially inconsistent terminology use by translators. Once such terms are flagged, the translator or an editor can substitute terminology or determine that the different selections were indeed appropriate.

8.1.2 An Enhanced Translator's Workstation

In many applications, reports must be compiled from a large number of sources. If such reports have to be disseminated in several languages, a translation workstation may be used productively. For such an application, a suggested method of operation of a TWS is as follows. First, using the basic functionalities, an information processing specialist produces abstracts of particular documents. At the next stage, an *automatic text analyzer* with an interactive augmentor module, as needed, is run with each such document as input; as a result, processed documents are stored in an on-line archive in the form of interlingua texts. Note that the presence of ILT-formatted documents in the archive enhances the quality of the knowledge bases because it allows an additional type of link among the conceptual elements in the domain models, namely, the `is-token-of` links, which are very useful in searching for pertinent textual examples (remember that the natural-language versions of every document are also stored in the archive, and the ILT version is interconnected with them). When a request comes in for information about a certain topic, the TWS performs a search in the database of ILTs and retrieves an ILT for generation in a desired target language. Finally, the *automatic generation component* of the TWS obtains the ILT representations of documents as input and produces required target texts.

The various functionalities of an advanced knowledge-based TWS can be used in different applications, such as, for instance, an electronic communications environment.

Among the obvious advantages of this approach are the following:

- The potential for multilinguality, due to the use of the interlingua paradigm; texts can be generated into every language for which the generation program is built. The source language from which the ILT was built is immaterial;

- The speed-up of the translation time due to the use of "prefabricated" interlingua representations which were produced off-line, when the text entered the system.

To support the analysis and generation stages of the machine-aided translation system in the advanced TWS, computational grammars and dictionaries for all the desired source and target languages should be constructed. The better the quality of these knowledge bases and the greater their size, the larger share of the overall processing could be done completely automatically. However, an augmentor-like user interface must be developed to facilitate human help. This functionality may be required even when the possible input text comes from a constrained domain, to ensure good-quality output (as was noted in chapter 1). The augmentor-like interface is used by the human translator, acting at this point in the capacity of *interactive editor*, to help the program reach decisions in difficult cases. A special back-end *error-processing* module must be developed and connected to the human-computer interface. A version of such a module was built for the KBMT-89 augmentor. A more sophisticated version would allow users to determine if the ILT were correctly and completely formed.

The general architecture of an advanced TWS is similar to a typical architecture of a knowledge-based machine translation system. The only differences lie in the expected level of automation. The level of automation is determined by the availability of programs and knowledge bases at every level of source language analysis and target language synthesis that guarantee high-quality results. While in earlier versions of the TWS the role of the human interactive editor and interactive editing tools is relatively high (essentially requiring human translator abilities), some functionalities required from the interactive editor will eventually be subsumed by computer programs. In this sense, TWS is an *open-ended* system. The level of automation in a TWS can grow, eventually reaching near-full- or full-automation levels of a knowledge-based machine translation system.

To support a mixed automatic and manual translation, a TWS must contain a structured screen editor facility in whose buffers elements of target language text will coexist with elements of source language text. The automatic components of the system will produce as much of the translation as they can, while attracting the attention of the interactive editors to the areas of difficulty in the source language text and, whenever possible, creating a menu with a list of candidate solutions. The interactive editor must be able, by choosing a solution from a menu, to cause its insertion into an appropriate place in the translation buffer. The interactive editor should type in a translation only if none of the solutions suggested by the computer is acceptable. In principle, the best way of enhancing the interactive editor's productivity is to insist on using menu selections and "copy-and-edit" techniques as much as possible in preference to typing text from scratch.

8.2   Other Multilingual NLP Environments

The tools discussed in the preceding can support more than translation. A wide variety of potential applications can be envisaged for them. In this section, we give brief sketches of three information-processing environments in which the benefits of using an environment such as TWS become evident.

8.2.1   Multilingual Electronic Communication Environments

One additional type of multilingual environment that can be supported by a TWS is that of communication among speakers of different languages in the context of an electronic conference (for instance, in an international organization). Conference participants could sit at computer terminals in their respective offices and write messages in their own languages. Messages they receive from other participants appear on their screens in the language of their choice. At every node only one language analyzer and one language generator are active. When a participant creates a message, it is locally transformed into an interlingua text form. It is then transmitted over the net to other sites. When such processed messages arrive at another node in the network, they are generated into the target language chosen at that node. In such an environment, transfer-based machine translation systems that require postediting become grossly inefficient for two main reasons. First, in a transfer environment, every node must contain *all* the transfer and generation modules for the chosen target language. Second, the messages must be postedited after they are received and generated. Even though it is sometimes claimed that it is not necessary for the posteditor to know the source language from which the text was translated, in practice the poor quality of the target text often necessitates reference to the source text. In the environment pictured here, this is impractical if not impossible.

We believe that the source texts must be adequately analyzed at the source. If it is not possible to do this in a completely automatic fashion, then the sender of the message will serve as an interactive editor in a machine-assisted machine translation environment and thus help the program to come up with an adequate interlingua text. As a result, the generator at the receiving end will be able to produce target language texts that do not require postediting. (This is not to say that interactive editing is needed only once, at the source, and can be done monolingually, even if multiple target languages are produced.) This approach is useful in any environment in which relatively fast communication is required and in which postediting is not a viable option. In addition to the international conference setting, this type of system can also support communication among joint armed forces speaking different languages, information flow in a multinational corporation and so forth.

8.2.2   Information Processing and Abstracting

Yet another type of translation-related activity supportable by TWS involves the production of news story abstracts. The stories can come from a variety of printed sources in a large number of languages. In many cases a single abstract is produced for a set of connected stories, or information about a particular news item is collated from a number of sources in a number of languages.

The output of this procedure is an abstract of a news story. The format of such an abstract typically includes a number of structured information fields, such as source(s), country, topic, date and others. However, in addition to the structured fields the abstract must also contain at least one "open-text" field, in which a synopsis of the story is recorded. The synopsis is manually composed by the translator after the original material is completely scanned and understood.

In this environment, the translator becomes also an editor whose task is not simply to translate a given set of input texts into a target language but, in fact, to produce an added value by *selecting* what to translate, *merging* different sources and *translating* the selected passages. Users of this service include information-gathering and information-disseminating institutions, such as intelligence agencies and news services.

8.2.3   A Translation Shop

The mandate of machine-aided translation is not to supplant human translators but rather to enhance their productivity, especially for multilingual translation tasks. It is clear that the main beneficiary of such efforts should be the translation industry. Translation departments of large corporations and independent translation agencies can benefit both from the machine-aided translation capabilities and the interface functionalities to be developed in the framework of a translator's workstation. In fact, the needs of the specialized applications, such as the ones described above, should be viewed as a subset of the automation and computerization needs of a general-purpose translation shop.

Chapter 9

The Future of Machine Translation

Scientists, engineers, entrepreneurs, corporations, government agencies and members of the general public repeatedly pose the question, "What is the future of machine translation?" The question is partially answered by recalling that the global translation market has been estimated at $20 billion U.S. in 1989, and its annual growth rate at 20% (JEIDA 1989). The need for faster, higher-quality and less expensive translation will continue to lead to investment in research and development of MT systems. It is hoped that MT systems will gradually enter the mainstream, day-do-day translation market.

Predicting the distant future of machine translation is futile, since the development of any high-technology field is dependent on discoveries yet to be made. We realize that our projections will most probably suffer from a horizon effect—not being able to see beyond the current horizon of knowledge. However, we will examine some present trends in MT and extrapolate from them into the near future. Naturally, we will feel more secure extrapolating from the trends in knowledge-based machine translation. We will try to be conservative and, whenever possible, suggest conclusions based on the confluence of several threads, or those supported by demonstrated pilot research projects.

9.1   From the Mainframe to the Desktop

Early MT systems required expensive equipment; mainframe computers were the only adequate source of computational power and necessary memory in the 1960s and 1970s. Both commercial systems (e.g., SYSTRAN and the early version of LOGOS) and academic ones (e.g., GETA and Mu) were implemented on large central computers. At present, a majority of new machine translation systems are being developed on single-user machines, typically engineering-level workstations, and often delivered on even less expensive personal computers. Thus, the KBMT-89 project, with its in-depth semantic processing and consequent need for processing power, was developed and delivered on IBM PC/RTs.

Not every MT research and development team has hopped on the workstation/PC bandwagon, however. The most notable holdouts are the most obvious ones—IBM and Fujitsu, the two giants of the computer world. IBM developed and runs all its MT systems (SHALT in Japan, the LMT system and the statistical MT project) on large IBM mainframes. Similarly, Fujitsu developed its ATLAS-I and ATLAS-II systems on its own mainframes. The hardware giants, of course, have substantial in-house mainframe capacity. Their clients both present and future, however, cannot be satisfied with expensive hardware, and we predict that even IBM and Fujitsu will move toward workstations/PCs and distributed computing in machine translation, if they have not already started in that direction. This prediction is a fairly safe one. After all, computing in general is moving inexorably towards the inexpensive, powerful, user-friendly networked workstation and PC environment, and MT will ride the wave.

9.2   From Monolithic Systems to Interactive Symbiosis

The first- and second-generation MT systems (direct and transfer approaches) were essentially hands-off, batch-processing processes. Since it was expected that MT output would contain errors, the posteditor was also supplied with the source text, in order for her or him to understand what the target text was supposed to say. The posteditor, typically an experienced translator, would mark up all the corrections offline, retranslating the more obscure passages, and these corrections would be later entered, again offline, producing the final translation. Later improvements, such as the connection of PCs with editing capabilities to the mainframe computer, facilitated data entry and, more importantly, permitted the posteditor to perform corrections directly in the translated text. But the basic MT process remains to this day essentially a monolithic black box, where human judgment can enter only before input to the central MT process or after output. However, human judgment would be extremely welcome *during* the MT process itself.

Recent developments in the transfer-based approach have started to chip away at the proverbial monolith. For instance, a search for unknown words in the source text, followed by an interactive lexical entry phase prior to translation, is becoming commonplace—compare the ALEX facility in the LOGOS translation system or the user environment in the TOVNA system; these systems were demonstrated at MT Summit III in Washington in July 1991.

This book discussed in some detail how to incorporate semantics into the translation processes in an automated way. Equally important is the question of how to do so in an interactive, symbiotic way. The essential idea is for the translation system automatically to make the myriad of low-level semantic judgments (such as matching selectional restrictions to case fillers for prepositional-phrase attachment or simple lexical disambiguation), but to interact with the human user in making the more difficult judgments. A quick interaction at analysis time may save a much more costly correction down the road, especially if the result of the interaction is reused in several places throughout the source text. Moreover, the new knowledge imparted to the system can be accumulated for future use in translating texts in the same subject matter, and thus the system will require progressively less human intervention with accumulating experience.

The notion of interactive disambiguation for machine translation has only recently been analyzed in some depth, and its use for difficult disambiguations in a KBMT system was first introduced systematically in the KBMT-89 project. The automated accumulation of knowledge as a result of on-line user interaction, however, has not yet been incorporated into a working MT system. We believe, however, that it is only a matter of time, and not too much time, before performance of KBMT systems incrementally improves through on-line coaching and integration of user interaction and the knowledge-based approach.

A human posteditor working with erroneous and stylistically deficient target text is essentially performing a janitorial service: cleaning up the mess that the machine made. However, a human interactive disambiguator is performing the role of consultant or tutor, as he or she imparts knowledge that the machine lacks, and receives the satisfaction of observing improved performance over time. This does not totally obviate the need for human postediting as a final verification of the translation (a standard procedure in better translation agencies even for translations performed by top-notch human translators). We predict that the role of human participation in machine translation will gradually change to that of consultant and tutor, and in the long term the student (the MT system) will be largely on its own, producing highly accurate and increasingly autonomous translations.

9.3 From "MAT versus MT" to "M(A)T"

In contrast with classical MT, the machine-aided translation (MAT) philosophy endeavors to retain human control at every stage of the translation process, providing such help as rapid electronic access to mono- and bilingual dictionaries, terminology banks, multilingual word processing, spelling checkers, aligned source and target windows for text editing, fast access to previously translated passages and other such conveniences. MAT became commercially viable only with the advent of inexpensive desktop word processors and personal computers.

Since classical transfer-based MT is a batch process, and MAT is a totally user-driven interactive process, the two have been viewed as mutually exclusive alternatives to the partial automation of the translation process. With the advent of KBMT, where human interaction is an integral part of the translation process, the demarcation between MT and MAT blurs into M(A)T. One can envision an entire spectrum of increasingly automated MT workstations, starting from present-day MAT, and gradually automating more and more of the translation process, progressively reducing human intervention until it reaches the point of an occasional consultancy.

In particular, a MAT system can be augmented with increasingly sophisticated analysis and generation functionalities, such as the following:

- *Morphological decomposition* to aid in dictionary search by addressing inflectional, derivational and compounding morphology.

- *Morphological production* to aid in the composition of the target text by conjugating the selected verb, selecting the appropriate declension and gender agreement, compounding words correctly, and so on.

- *Lexical selection* to aid the translator in selecting the most appropriate term in the target language, using context-sensitive corpus statistics, such as collocation tables.

- *Syntactic analysis* of the source language to help in the comprehension process if needed, and to provide the first step towards automating the translation.

- *Syntactic verification* of generated target sentences to catch grammatical errors or stylistic deficiencies.

- *Sentence generation* from the representation of a functional structure of a sentence into target text, possibly querying the user on difficult lexical selections or other problems.

- *Sentence-level semantic analysis* of the source text to resolve most lexical and prepositional-phrase attachment ambiguities, querying the user to resolve the more difficult residual ambiguity.

As one can see, this list progresses gradually from a translator-driven process (in which the computer provides essentially clerical background help), to a mixed-initiative task (where the simpler aspects of translation are fully mechanized), to the standard knowledge-based method (where the system performs the bulk of the work, and consults the user only on those occasions where its knowledge proves deficient). The scenario briefly sketched above is not yet a technological reality; it is our projection that it will come to pass in the not-too-distant future. Laboratory work in this direction is already under way.

9.4 From Knowledge-Free to Knowledge-Based Machine Translation

Machine translation in its early heyday was viewed primarily as a transduction task. Sentences in the source language were merely character strings to be decoded into the corresponding sentences in the target language. As discussed in chapter 1, this approach failed to take any principled account of linguistic structure or semantic content, and was essentially discarded.

However, the spirit of doing as little linguistic and semantic analysis as possible survived well beyond ALPAC in the MT community. After all, comprehensive analysis of arbitrary text is arbitrarily difficult. Therefore, the name of the game became one of performing the minimal amount of analysis to permit transfer to the target language. Over time, however, the analysis process became more and more comprehensive in order to improve the low accuracy of early MT systems. Most modern transfer approaches recognize the need for in-depth morphological and syntactic analysis—but not yet the equally important need for in-depth semantic analysis. This final barrier has proven more formidable for scientific and perhaps even psychological reasons. With respect to the latter, at the first Conference on Theoretical and Methodological Issues in Machine Translation, Victor Raskin remarked on the hesitancy of MT researchers to address semantics head on, and coined the word *semantophobia*—"fear of meaning." Full semantic analysis is indeed an extremely knowledge-intensive and computationally expensive process, but we prefer to view it as a great challenge, rather than an obstacle.

Although the proponents of the interlingua approach, present authors included, have argued the need for in-depth semantic analysis, that need can be fully recognized and decoupled from the transfer-versus-interlingua debate. That is, transfer systems require semantic analysis for accurate translation just as much as interlingua systems, even if the former have no intermediate "pivot" representation. With considerable reluctance, the transfer-based MT projects are indeed starting to add an initial measure of semantic analysis, but still fall far short of the depth of analysis we believe required for accurate MT. One important example is the argument for feature-based semantic processing in the transfer-based METAL translation system (Bennett 1991). Manifold increases in computing power and memory capacity have reduced significantly the run-time efficiency penalty for in-depth analysis, whereas the accuracy penalty for shallow analysis remains forever with us.

We believe that the trend toward increasing depth and sophistication of source-language analysis will continue at an accelerated pace in the coming decade. Driven by the desire for translations of better quality, many of the better transfer-based MT systems will perform increasingly deep semantic analysis.

9.5   From Monomedia to Multimedia Machine Translation

Although the primary commercial requirement for MT is to translate significant volumes of printed text, there is an acute need for simultaneous translation of spoken language. Speech recognition technology, coupled with language analysis, is starting to emerge from the laboratory. Such technology permits translation of spoken language in domains limited by vocabulary size, semantic complexity and relatively clean acoustic input. The additional constraints imposed by speech recognition are twofold. First, any recognition system will make acoustic recognition errors; even the well-tuned human ear does not recognize words with 100% accuracy. Second, spoken language is necessarily unedited. Sentence fragments, false starts, corrections, mispronunciations and grammatical errors abound. Lexical, grammatical and semantic constraints are called upon to help select among different candidate words hypothesized by the acoustic recognizer from the input signal. The tighter these constraints, the more acoustic recognition ambiguity may be tolerated. And, for spontaneous speech, KBMT is a requirement, as noted, even by the proponents of transfer-based, minimal-semantic systems. When faced with weaker grammatical constraints, a strong semantic model must be present to take on the task of resolving recognition ambiguities.

At present there are no viable commercially available, speech-to-speech MT systems, but several laboratories around the world are working to produce them (ATR, NEC and Matsushita in Japan, and CMU in the United States, for instance). But speech-recognition technology is rapidly improving, partially driven by faster hardware. Speech synthesis is generally simpler than recognition. We expect that for well-defined tasks, such as telephone assistance, airline reservations and office automation functions, speech recognition integrated with MT will be developed in the near future. General-purpose speech-to-speech machine translation, however, must await continued scientific progress well into the 21st century.

In addition to pure speech-to-speech MT, one can envision other translation modalities, such as speech-to-text, text-to-speech and mixed-mode, wherein both source and target can be a combination of textual and spoken language. In particular, as hypermedia moves from the laboratory to the office environment, documents will combine text, diagrams, images, speech and executable programs. Only the language-oriented parts of these documents will require translation: text, speech, labels on diagrams, output messages from the programs and so forth. However, these translation tasks must be unified, as context from one can constrain the analysis of another. At present, there is no large-scale effort in multimedia MT, as multimedia documents are just starting to emerge and become accepted. We nevertheless expect that multimedia machine translation will not trail the diffusion of multimedia documents by very much time.

9.6 Transfer or Interlingua?

Let us reexamine the basic trends in MT:

- *Increased demand:* The volume of textual material in need of translation is increasing inexorably, partly driven by commercial needs (e.g., by globalization of markets), partly by international organizations (e.g., the EEC), and partly by the information revolution (e.g., on-line network access to volatile and archival information).

- *Increased linguistic diversity:* Translation is needed among a growing pool of languages.

- *Increased low-cost computational resources:* The techno-economic barrier to widespread deployment of MT systems is coming down with amazing rapidity.

- *Increased electronic integration:* Multiple tasks are being integrated. These include authoring of manuals, document production, multilingual translation and maintenance and revision. In information-management applications, such tasks include document entry (OCR-based, conversion from other electronic forms, etc.), filtering for relevance, automated routing, content extraction for database storage and translation from diverse source languages.

The above trends identify a universal bottleneck recognized by all MT researchers: the time and effort required to include new languages, extend the coverage of existing ones and improve translation quality. The methods most efficient in terms of minimal development effort and maximal quality of translation will prevail. Run-time machine efficiency is less a concern than reusable components of the translation system (those that do not depend on a particular pair of source and target languages). The analysis and generation phases will assume an increasing share of the overall MT effort and the weight of the transfer component will be minimized. Interlingua approaches will continue to be developed, but engineering improvements and attention to meaning analysis will keep advanced transfer-based systems in business for a long time.

9.7   From Standalone MT to Situated MT

Now that MT technology is gradually coming of age, we predict a new direction of research and development of systems whose task includes machine translation as a component. Thus, MT can be integrated with document production by combining an MT system with an authoring support system (an advanced word processor), a desktop publishing system or both. As another example, MT can be integrated in a message understanding system, where the message (or document) traffic will first be automatically categorized, then the messages in each category will be ranked with respect to the urgency and importance and will be fed into an MT system in a corresponding order. In fact, two types of MT systems can be envisaged in this environment. First, a "quick and dirty" translator whose result will help a human analyst decide whether it is worthwhile to generate a high-quality translation of a given message. If the decision is made to translate a document completely and accurately, then the MT system of the second type will be used. Such an environment can, of course, include an automatic text-abstracting system, in which case selected messages could be routed through the abstracter and the resulting abstracts could be, possibly selectively, sent to the high-quality translation system.

Many more configurarions of an MT system coupled with other text processing technologies will be formulated and designed in the future, as the high-technology office becomes a norm.

Appendix A

KBMT Glossary

Analysis A stage in the machine translation process in which a source language text is obtained and an internal representation of it is produced. Stages in analysis may include morphological (*q.v.*), syntactic (*q.v.*), semantic (*q.v.*), discourse (*q.v.*) and possibly some additional system-dependent ones. The actual set of analysis stages differs among machine translation systems. Knowledge-based machine translation involves all of the above components since it requires the most detailed text representation. Depth of analysis required for successful machine translation is one of the hottest topics of debate in the field.

Analysis, discourse A component of the analysis stage in machine translation. Recognizes and represents various devices for expressing text cohesiveness, relations among sentences in a text and the various rhetorical devices.

Analysis, morphological Morphological analysis is needed to determine the citation form of lexical units in the input text to facilitate dictionary look-up. In some languages the number of word forms can be very large. Without morphological analysis, the size of the dictionary will have to grow dramatically, since instead of indexing entries by the citation form, they will have to be indexed through all the forms of a lexical unit.

Analysis, semantic Also known as "interpretation." A component of the analysis stage in machine translation. Required in knowledge-based machine translation. Using the lexical-semantic information from the dictionary, semantic analysis procedures seek to produce a meaning representation for an input text. This process includes selection of the most appropriate word senses for all polysemous words in the input. This selection is governed by contextual co-occurrence provisions (selectional restrictions, collocation information, etc.) listed in each lexicon entry. When violations of co-occurrence rules occur, a good-quality semantic analysis program enters metaphor- and metonymy-processing modes and attempts to come up with a realistic interpretation of the input, even if some of the constraints on components have to be relaxed.

Analysis, syntactic Also known as "parsing." A component of the analysis stage. Required in knowledge-based machine translation. Using the syntactic information encoded in the grammar and in the dictionary, produces a representation of the syntactic structure of the input text.

Anaphora A linguistic phenomenon in which short constituents such as pronouns (the "anaphors") are used to refer to more detailed descriptions elsewhere in the text.

Anaphora Treatment A component of both analysis and generation in machine translation. In analysis, this component finds antecedents for anaphoric elements, thus determining relations of coreferentiality. In generation, coreferentiality relations are given at input, and the task of the anaphora treatment component is to generate the appropriate anaphoric realization for an element of a coreference set.

Artificial Intelligence (AI) A field of study in computer science. Deals with building functional models of tasks considered to require human intelligence. Natural language processing (including knowledge representation and inference) is one of the areas of study in artificial intelligence.

Augmentation The process of improving the results of the analysis stage of a knowledge-based machine translation system when there remain residual ambiguities. This module is necessary when the system operates with an unrestricted input language. Augmentation can have an automatic component in which disambiguation can be achieved through further relaxation of various constraints from the grammar and the dictionary. Interactive augmentation uses a special program that detects residual ambiguities and gaps in the interlingua text and asks a human user intelligent questions, answers to which lead to the production of a canonical interlingua text.

Blackboard A publicly accessible data structure where results of knowledge sources (*q.v.*) are posted.

Control The sequencing of operations in a computer system. Crucially influences the efficiency of a system.

Controlled Input Input text that includes only words and syntactic constructions that are covered by a particular dictionary and grammar. Producing such a text is a result of pre-editing (*q.v.*) or controlled authoring.

Dictionary A collection of lexical units in a language with information about them typically including their morphological, syntactic or semantic properties. In bilingual dictionaries, translations of lexical units into lexical units of another language are listed. In knowledge-based machine translation, dictionaries (often called "lexicons") are used as a major static knowledge source in both analysis and synthesis. In transfer-oriented machine translation systems, a bilingual transfer dictionary is also used.

Dictionary, concept A collection of knowledge units describing an ontology (*q.v.*) and a set of domain models (*q.v.*) supporting a knowledge-based machine translation system. The meanings of source language and target language lexical units are expressed in terms of the elements of the concept dictionaries.

Dictionary, machine-readable (MRD) A regular, human-oriented dictionary available in a medium that can be directly manipulated by a computer.

Dictionary, machine-tractable (MTD) A dictionary useful for tasks in natural language processing. Machine-readable dictionaries need to be transformed in order for them to become machine-tractable dictionaries.

Dictionary, source language A dictionary supporting analysis (*q.v.*) of source language (*q.v.*) in a machine translation system. In knowledge-based machine translation systems, typically contains semantic and pragmatic information necessary for deriving an interlingua text (*q.v.*) as the result of the analysis stage. In transfer-oriented systems, there is less semantic information, and pragmatic information is typically not present.

Dictionary, target language A dictionary supporting generation (*q.v.*) of target language (*q.v.*) in a machine translation system. In knowledge-based machine translation systems, typically contains semantic, collocational and pragmatic information necessary for generating good-quality target language text from an interlingua representation. Information in the target language dictionary has a large intersection with the information in a source language dictionary for the same language. As a result, in some systems a single lexicon is used instead of two separate ones.

Dictionary, transfer A dictionary of correspondences between source language and target language lexical units in a transfer-oriented machine translation system.

Dictionary Acquisition A kind of knowledge acquisition (*q.v.*). The process of compiling the concept lexicon and the machine-tractable dictionaries. Typically performed manually, at best, using an acquisition interface. Studies are under way to allow for at least partial automation of the dictionary acquisition process through automatic conversion of machine-readable dictionary entries into machine-tractable dictionary entries.

Disambiguation The process of resolving the cases of polysemy (multiple meanings of lexical items) and multiple variants of syntactic structures in the input text. In knowledge-based machine translation, most disambiguation is performed at the semantic analysis phase.

Discourse Analysis see Analysis, discourse.

Discourse Representation A knowledge representation formalism that captures the information about discourse in a natural language text and is the result of discourse analysis (*q.v.*).

Domain A field of activity with its typical concepts (objects, relations, events), such as, for instance, chemistry, advertising, sports or shipbuilding.

Domain Model A computer representation of a domain (*q.v.*). Typically represented as a network of interconnected concept representations merged with an ontology (*q.v.*).

Ellipsis Gaps in a natural language text due to rhetorical and stylistic parameters. References to omitted material should be found during the analysis or augmentation (*q.v.*) stages of machine translation.

Generation A final stage in the machine translation process. In knowledge-based machine translation, the input to generation is an interlingua text. In transfer-based systems the input to generation is the result of structural and lexical transfer, usually a target language syntactic tree with lexical insertion. Knowledge-based machine translation generation involves text planning (*q.v.*) in addition to the realization (*q.v.*) stage.

Grammar A set of syntactic rules and constraints determining allowed combinations of syntactic categories in a language. Many grammar formalisms are used in machine translation.

Heuristic Rules Knowledge units encoding human knowledge in symbolic form, usually as condition-action rules: If the condition is satisfied, the action is applied. In machine translation, many heuristic rules are by nature *abductive*, that is, their conclusions can in principle be wrong (unlike those of *deductive* rules, which guarantee the correctness of the action once initial conditions have been met).

Ill-Formed Input Natural language text that violates any of the rules and constraints in a grammar or dictionary.

Interactive Machine Translation A paradigm in which a human is used as a knowledge source to help disambiguate (*q.v.*) the source text in analysis (*q.v.*) or augmentation (*q.v.*). Interactive disambiguation often reduces or eliminates the need for pre- and postediting (*q.v.*).

Interfaces, human-computer Computer programs that support interaction with human users. Used in knowledge-based machine translation systems and environments for augmentation (*q.v.*) and knowledge acquisition (*q.v.*).

Interlingua (IL) A knowledge representation language used for representing the set of meanings of a natural language text. Sets of interlingua expressions representing the meaning of natural language texts are called interlingua texts (ILTs). Terms in interlingua are instances of entities in the concept dictionary (*q.v.*).

Interlingua-Based Machine Translation See Machine Translation, interlingua.

Knowledge A blanket term for any kind of information used in an artificial-intelligence-related computer system. In knowledge-based machine translation, knowledge includes knowledge about the world, contained in the concept dictionary (*q.v.*); and knowledge about the languages, contained in the respective dictionaries and grammars.

Knowledge Acquisition The process of acquiring the knowledge needed for the support of knowledge-based machine translation. Dictionary acquisition (*q.v.*), including concept dictionaries (*q.v.*), is the primary type of knowledge acquisition; another is grammar acquisition.

Knowledge Base A collection of knowledge units organized in a humanly and computationally tractable manner.

Knowledge-Based Machine Translation (KBMT) The process of analysis (*q.v.*) of a source language (*q.v.*) text, augmentation (*q.v.*) if necessary, and generation (*q.v.*) into a target language (*q.v.*) text, using all required knowledge sources (*q.v.*) to extract and represent the meaning of source language texts, to disambiguate (*q.v.*) this input and produce an accurate translation. KBMT systems typically use an interlingua (*q.v.*) approach, though a deep transfer approach is possible.

Knowledge Representation (KR) Language A language specially designed to capture certain types of knowledge. Thus, interlingua (*q.v.*) is a knowledge representation language for text meaning. Dictionary entries, heuristic rules and grammars are all written using special knowledge representation languages. Frame-based languages are the most common for KBMT. (See also Representation, knowledge.)

Knowledge Source Generally, a synonym for a knowledge base or part of a knowledge base. In an area of artificial intelligence (*q.v.*) called "blackboard models of control," a knowledge source is a program that posts its results on a *blackboard* (*q.v.*). In knowledge-based machine translation, programs are often called *dynamic* knowledge sources, while knowledge bases are called *static* knowledge sources.

Lexical Selection See Selection, lexical.

Lexical Unit A word or a phrase used to index an entry in a dictionary.

Lexicon see Dictionary.

Machine-assisted Human Translation A human translation environment that involves the use of more-or-less sophisticated computer tools. Distinguished from human-assisted machine translation (see Machine Translation, human assisted).

Machine Translation (MT) The process of translating one natural language text (a source language (*q.v.*)) into another natural language text (a target language (*q.v.*)) by computer.

Machine Translation, human assisted A machine translation environment that calls for some involvement of human translators, either during or after the translation. Distinguished from Machine-assisted Human Translation (*q.v.*).

Machine Translation, interlingua A type of machine translation that involves analyzing the source language text and representing the results of analysis in a specially designed knowledge representation language (*q.v.*), the interlingua (*q.v.*). The second stage of the process involves generating a text in one or more target languages from the interlingua text. The interlingua paradigm (see Machine Translation Paradigms) is usually associated with knowledge-based machine translation.

Machine Translation, knowledge-based See Knowledge-Based Machine Translation.

Machine Translation, transfer-oriented A type of machine translation based on finding correspondences between source language and target language lexical units and syntactic structures. Typically, transfer-based machine translation systems do not perform involved semantic and pragmatic analysis of the input text, relying on the possibility of retaining any possible ambiguities in the target text and, failing that, on postediting (*q.v.*).

Machine Translation Generations Workers in machine translation typically refer to three generations in machine translation research and development. The first generation dealt with "direct replacement" systems, which did not involve any scientifically systematic syntactic or semantic analysis of input text, but rather consisted of a huge number of *ad hoc* rules of translation. The second generation is associated with transfer systems, in which syntactic analysis is performed according to the precepts of a scientific theory of syntax. Third-generation systems feature treatment of meaning.

Machine Translation Paradigms Types of overall machine translation system designs. The major paradigms are knowledge-based machine translation (*q.v.*) and transfer (*q.v.*). There is also some work on statistics-based machine translation and on machine translation in a "direct replacement" mode.

Morphological Analysis see Analysis, morphological.

Morphology Sometimes referred to as *inflectional* morphology. The study of the composition of a lexical unit and its form-formation rules, including pluralization, verb conjugation and so on. *Derivational morphology* involves rules for word formation (e.g., *worker = work + er*).

Multilingual Machine Translation Machine translation among multiple source and/or target languages (*q.v.*). The interlingua (*q.v.*) paradigm is often well suited for multilingual applications.

Natural Language Processing (NLP) An area of artificial intelligence (*q.v.*) that deals with automating the various language-related tasks that are currently performed predominantly by humans. These tasks include machine translation, information retrieval, natural language interfaces to database and expert systems and so on.

Ontology In knowledge-based machine translation, refers not to a branch of philosophy but rather to a computational model of a system's general "view of the world." It includes symbolic representations of the most general concepts (objects, relations, events, attributes) and serves as a detailed index for the attachment of the various domain models (*q.v.*).

Postediting Stage at which mistakes are corrected, usually by hand, in machine translation output. It is an essential stage in transfer-oriented machine translation systems. Knowledge-based machine translation systems seek to avoid the need for postediting, at the expense of having to build a more sophisticated natural language processing substrate.

Pragmatics A branch of linguistics that deals with the relationship between language and the speaker/hearer in a speech situation. Such phenomena as presupposition, speech acts, focus, conversational postulates and so forth traditionally have been studied in pragmatics.

Pre-editing The preparation of text for machine translation. Involves simplifying the syntax and making sure that the vocabulary used in the text is indeed covered in the system's dictionaries. Pre-editing can also include spelling checking. Sometimes pre-editing is performed as a part of a separate text-processing task, such as writing (authoring) or preparing abstracts or entire documents.

Primitives, semantic Minimal units from the combinations of which the meanings of various language units are produced.

Realization A module in the generation stage of a machine translation process. Takes as input the specification of the syntactic structure of the output text, with lexical items already selected, and, using a grammar of the target language, produces the final output target text.

Representation, knowledge (KR) The study of the ways of encoding data in a symbolic form manipulable by computer programs. Knowledge representation schemata specify the format of units in knowledge bases, and include the specification of the meaning of atomic knowledge elements, semantic primitives (*q.v.*) and operators. (See also Knowledge Representation Language; Ontology; and Dictionary, concept.)

Representation, syntactic structure The encoding of syntactic relations among words in sentences, usually into parse trees or feature structures.

Representation, text-meaning A kind of knowledge representation. It deals with representing the meaning of a natural language text. Text-meaning representation schemata must be able to describe both the propositional content of the text and the discourse and pragmatic meanings, including speaker attitudes, speaker goals and stylistic parameters of the text. (See also Interlingua.)

Selection, lexical A module in the generation stage of a machine translation process. In knowledge-based machine translation, for selecting open-class lexical items (e.g., nouns, verbs), takes as input the representations of event, object and property instances in the text meaning and, using the dictionary, finds among the available lexical units the best lexical realization for the meanings in input. Various closed-class lexical items (prepositions, conjunctions, particles, etc.) are selected at appropriate points in the text planning (*q.v.*) and realization (*q.v.*) processes. In transfer-oriented machine translation, lexical selection consists in replacing a lexical unit in the source language with the most appropriate of its translations in the target language, as specified in the bilingual lexical-transfer dictionary.

Semantics A branch of linguistics that deals with the meaning of text and text constituents.

Semantics, contextual Deals with deriving the meaning of a segment of natural language text from the meanings of its components. Knowledge of contextual semantics of a language is encoded in co-occurrence rules (selectional restrictions, collocation information, etc.) for lexical items and is used in semantic analysis (*q.v.*) to select the most appropriate combination of lexical unit senses.

Semantics, lexical A subdiscipline that deals mainly with the meanings of words. It also studies the meanings of set expressions such as idioms. Lexical-semantic knowledge in knowledge-based machine translation is encoded in the dictionary.

Source Language Natural language in which the input texts to a machine translation system are written.

Speech Recognition The mapping of acoustic wave forms of spoken language into the corresponding written forms.

Speech-to-Speech Translation The machine translation of spoken language. Speech recognition produces a text; the text is translated by machine; and that text is synthesized as speech in the target language.

Sublanguage A subset of a natural language with a constrained syntax and dictionary. Texts in a sublanguage are considered controlled input (*q.v.*).

Subworld See Domain.

Syntactic Analysis see Analysis, syntactic.

Syntax The syntax of a natural or artificial language is a set of rules prescribing a correct format of expressions in this language. Does not take into account the meanings of open-class lexical items.

Target Language The natural language into which the texts given to a machine translation system are translated.

Text Planning A module in the generation stage of knowledge-based machine translation. Obtains an interlingua text as its input and makes decisions on sentence boundaries and cohesiveness devices in the target language text. Results of the text planning can be recorded in a special text structure language, in a syntactic structure with lexical insertion or in both of them in turn (the text structure representation serving as an intermediate result).

Transfer A stage in the transfer-oriented machine translation systems. Finds target language correlates for lexical units and syntactic constructions of source language.

Bibliography

Abrett, G. 1987. The BBN Knowledge Acquisition Project Phase I—Final Report; Functional Description; Test Plan. Technical Report (6543), Bolt, Beranek, and Newman, Cambridge Mass.

Ahlswede, T. and M. Evens. 1988. Parsing vs. Text Processing in the Analysis of Dictionary Definitions. In Proceedings of the 26th Annual Meeting of the Association for Computational Linguistics (ACL-88), Buffalo, 217-224.

Aho, A. and J. Ullman. 1977. *Principles of Compiler Design*. Reading, Mass: Addison-Wesley.

Allen, J.F. 1984. Towards a General Theory of Action and Time. *Artificial Intelligence* 23:123-154.

ALPAC (Automatic Language Processing Advisory Committee). 1966. *Language and Machines: Computers in Translation and Linguistics*. Washington, D.C.: National Academy of Sciences, Publication 1416.

Amano, S. 1989. On Interlingua Approaches—from the Point of View of *traduttori traditori*. Presented at the MT Workshop "Into the '90s." Manchester, UK.

Amsler, R. 1980. The Structure of the Merriam-Webster Pocket Dictionary. Ph.D. dissertation, Department of Computer Science, University of Texas, Austin.

Amsler, R. 1987. Words and Worlds. In Proceedings of the Third International Workshop on Theoretical Issues in Natural Language Processing (TINLAP-3), Las Cruces, N. Mex., 16-19.

Amsler, R. Forthcoming. Deriving Lexical Knowledge Base Entries from Existing Machine-Readable Information Resources. In D. Walker, A. Zampolli and N. Calzolari (eds.), *Automating the Lexicon: Research and Practice in a Multilingual Environment*. Cambridge: Cambridge University Press.

225

Anderson, J. and G. Bower. 1973. *Human Associative Memory.* Washington, D.C.: Hemisphere Press.

Anscombre, J.C. and O. Ducrot. 1983. *L'argumentation dans la langue.* Brussels: Mardaga.

Appelt, D. 1985. *Planning English Sentences.* Cambridge: Cambridge University Press.

Arnold, D. and L. des Tombe. 1987. Basic Theory and Methodology in Eurotra. In S. Nirenburg (ed.), *Machine Translation: Theoretical and Methodological Issues.* Cambridge: Cambridge University Press, 114-135.

Arnold, D., S. Krauwer, L. des Tombe and L. Sadler. 1988. Relaxed Compositionality in MT. In Proceedings of the Second International Conference on Theoretical and Methodological Issues in Machine Translation, Pittsburgh, Pa.

Arnold, D. and L. Sadler. 1990. The Theoretical Basis of MiMo. *Machine Translation* 5:195-222.

Arnold, D. and L. Sadler. 1991. Some Formal Issues in Transfer. *Machine Translation* 6:193-200.

Atkins, B., A. Duval, R. Milne et al. 1987. *Collins Robert French-English English-French Dictionary.* London: Collins.

ATR Interpreting Telephony Research Laboratories. 1989. Research Activities of the Natural Language Understanding Department and the Knowledge and Data Base Department for 1988. ATR Technical Report, TR-I-0070, Tokyo.

Bar-Hillel, Y. 1959. Report on the State of Machine Translation in the United States and Great Britian. Technical Report, Hebrew University, Jerusalem.

Bar-Hillel, Y. 1960. The Present Status of Automatic Translation of Languages. In F.L. Alt (ed.), *Advances in Computers*, Volume I. New York: Academic Press, 91-163.

Baum, L., T. Petrie, G. Soules and N. Weiss. 1970. A Maximization Technique Occurring in the Statistical Analysis of Probabilistic Functions of Markov Chains. *The Annals of Mathematical Statistics* 41.

Ben Ari, D., M. Rimon and D. Berry. 1988. Translational Ambiguity Rephrased. In Proceedings of the Second International Conference on Theoretical and Methodological Issues in Machine Translation, Pittsburgh, Pa.

Bennett, W.S. 1991. METAL: Past, Present, and Future. In Proceedings of the Machine Translation Workshop, Hsinchu, Taiwan, 25-26.

Bennett, W.S. and J. Slocum. 1985. The LRC Machine Translation System. *Computational Linguistics* 11:111-121.

Benson, M., E. Benson and R. Ilson. 1986. *The BBI Combinatory Dictionary of English.* Amsterdam and Philadelphia: John Benjamins.

Bienkowski, M. 1986. A Computational Model for Extemporaneous Elaborations. CSL Report 1, Cognitive Science Laboratory, Princeton University, Princeton, N.J.

Boguraev, B. and E. Briscoe. 1987. Large Lexicons for Natural Language Processing: Utilizing the Grammar Coding System of LDOCE. *Computational Linguistics* 13:203-218.

Bourlard, H. and C. Wellekens. 1989. Speech Dynamics and Recurrent Neural Networks. In Proceedings of IEEE International Conference on Acoustics, Speech and Signal Processing (ICASSP-89), Glasgow, 33-36.

Brachman, R. 1979. On the Epistemological Status of Semantic Networks. In N.V. Findler (ed.), *Associative Networks*. New York: Academic Press, 3-50.

Brachman, R. and R. Levesque (eds.). 1985. *Readings in Knowledge Representation*. San Mateo, Calif.: Morgan Kaufmann.

Brachman, R. and J. Schmolze. 1985. An Overview of the KL-ONE Knowledge Representation Language. *Cognitive Science* 9:171-216.

Brown, P., J. Cocke, S. Della Pietra, V. Della Pietra, F. Jelinek, R. Mercer and P. Roossin. 1988. A Statistical Approach to French / English Translation. In Proceedings of the Second International Conference on Theoretical and methodological Issues in Machine Translation, Pittsburgh, Pa.

Brown, P., J. Cocke, S. Della Pietra, V. Della Pietra, F. Jelinek, J. Lafferty, R. Mercer and P. Roossin. 1990. A Statistical Approach to Machine Translation. *Computational Linguistics* 16:79-85.

Brown, R. 1991. Automatic and Interactive Augmentation. In K. Goodman and S. Nirenburg (eds.), *The KBMT Project: A Case Study in Knowledge-Based Machine Translation*. San Mateo, Calif.: Morgan Kaufmann, 189-229.

Brown, R. and S. Nirenburg. 1990. Human-Computer Interaction for Semantic Disambiguation. In Proceedings of 13th International Conference on Computational Linguistics (COLING-90), Helsinki, 42-47.

Burstein, M. 1990. BBN Knowledge Acquisition Project: Phase Two. Technical Report (7190), Bolt, Beranek and Newman, Cambridge, Mass.

Butts, R. 1969. Kant's Schemata as Semantical Rules. In L.W. Beck (ed.), *Kant Studies Today*. La Salle, Ill.: Open Court, 290-300.

Byrd, R., J. Klavans, M. Aronoff and F. Anshen. 1986. Computer Methods for Morphological Analysis. In Proceedings of the 24th Annual Meeting of the Association for Computational Linguistics (ACL-86), New York, 120-127.

Carberry, S. 1985. A Pragmatics-based Approach to Understanding Intersentential Ellipsis. In Proceedings of the 23rd Annual Meeting of the Association for Computational Linguistics (ACL-85), Chicago, 188-197.

Carbonell, J.G. 1982. Metaphor: An Inescapable Phenomenon in Natural Language Comprehension. In W. Lehnert and M. Ringle (eds.), *Strategies for Natural Language Processing*. Hillsdale, N.J.: Lawrence Erlbaum Associates, 415-434.

Carbonell, J.G. 1983. Derivational Analogy and Its Role in Problem Solving. In Proceedings of the Second Annual Meeting of the American Association for Artificial Intelligence (AAAI-83), Washington, D.C., 64-69.

Carbonell, J.G., M. Boggs, M. Mauldin and P. Anick. 1985. The Xcalibur Project: A Natural Language Interface to Expert Systems and Data Bases. In S. Andriole (ed.), *Applications in Artificial Intelligence*. Princeton, N.J.: Petrocelli Books.

Carbonell, J.G., R. Cullingford and A. Gershman. 1981. Steps Towards Knowledge-Based Machine Translation. *IEEE Transactions on Pattern Analysis and Machine Intelligence* 3:376-392.

Carbonell, J.G. and P. Hayes. 1983. Recovery Strategies for Parsing Extragrammatical Language. *American Journal of Computational Linguistics* 9:123-146.

Carbonell, J.G. and P. Hayes. 1987. Natural Language Understanding. In S.C. Shapiro (ed.), *Encyclopedia of Artificial Intelligence*. New York: Wiley & Sons, 660-677.

Carbonell, J.G. and R. Joseph. 1985. The FRAMEKIT Reference Manual. Internal Paper, School of Computer Science, Carnegie Mellon University, Pittsburgh, Pa.

Carbonell, J.G., S. Morrisson, M. Kee, M. Boggs and M. Mauldin. 1983. Xcalibur Working Document 5: The Semantic Representation II. Internal Paper, School of Computer Science, Carnegie Mellon University, Pittsburgh, Pa.

Carbonell, J. and M. Tomita. 1987. Knowledge-Based Machine Translation, the CMU Approach. In S. Nirenburg (ed.), *Machine Translation: Theoretical and Methodological Issues*. Cambridge: Cambridge University Press, 68-89.

Carlson, L. and S. Nirenburg. 1990. World Modeling for NLP. Technical Report, Center for Machine Translation, Carnegie Mellon University, Pittsburgh, Pa.

Carroll, J. 1966. An Experiment in Evaluating the Quality of Translations. *Mechanical Translation* 9 (3/4):55-66.

Charniak, E. 1983. Parsing, How To. In K. Sparck Jones and Y. Wilks (eds.), *Automatic Natural Language Parsing*. Chichester, U.K.: Ellis Horwood, 156-181.

Chodorow, M., R. Byrd and G. Heidorn. 1985. Extracting Semantic Hierarchies from a Large On-Line Dictionary. In Proceedings of the 23rd Annual Meeting of the Association for Computational Linguistics (ACL-85), Chicago, 299-304.

Chow, Y., M. Dunham, O. Kimball, M. Krasner, G. Kubala, J. Makhoul, S. Roucos and R. Schwartz. 1987. BYBLOS: The BBN Continuous Speech Recognition System. In Proceedings of IEEE International Conference on Acoustics, Speech and Signal Processing (ICASSP-87), Dallas, 89-92.

Cole, R., R. Stern, M. Phillips, S. Brill, P. Specker and A. Pilant. 1983. Feature-Based Speaker Independent Recognition of English Letters. In Proceedings of IEEE International Conference on Acoustics, Speech and Signal Processing (ICASSP-83), Boston, 731-783.

Courtney, R. 1983. *Longman Dictionary of Phrasal Verbs*. Harlow, UK: Longman.

Creary, L. and C. Pollard. 1985. A Computational Semantics for Natural Language. In Proceedings of the 23rd Annual Meeting of the Association for Computational Linguistics (ACL-85), Chicago, 172-179.

Cullingford, R. 1981. SAM. In R. Schank and C. Riesbeck (eds.), *Inside Computer Understanding*. Hillsdale, N.J.: Lawrence Erlbaum Associates, 75-119.

Cumming, S. 1986. The Lexicon in Text Generation. Paper presented at the Linguistic Society of America, Linguistics Institute Workshop on Lexicon, New York.

Cumming, S. Forthcoming. The Lexicon in Text Generation. In D. Walker, A. Zampolli and N. Calzolari (eds.), *Automating the Lexicon: Research and Practice in a Multilingual Environment*, Cambridge: Cambridge University Press.

Cumming, S. and R. Albano. 1986. A Guide to Lexical Acquisition in the JANUS system. Research Report (ISI/RR-85-162), ISI, University of Southern California, Marina del Rey.

Dahlgren, K. 1988. *Naïve Semantics for Natural Language Understanding*. Dordrecht: Kluwer.

Danlos, L. 1984. Conceptual and Linguistic Decisions in Generation. In Proceedings of 10th International Conference on Computational Linguistics (COLING-84), Stanford, Calif., 501-504.

Defrise, C. and S. Nirenburg. 1989. Aspects of Text Meaning: Using Discourse Connectives and Attitudinals in Natural Language Generation. Technical Memo, Center for Machine Translation, Carnegie Mellon University, Pittsburgh, Pa.

de Kleer, J., J. Doyle, G. Steele and G. Sussman. 1978. AMORD, A Deductive Procedure System. AI Memo (435), MIT, Cambridge, Mass.

Delavenay, E. 1960. *An Introduction to Machine Translation*. London: Thames and Hudson.

Derr, M. and K. McKeown. 1984. Using Focus to Generate Complex and Simple Sentences. In Proceedings of 10th International Conference on Computational Linguistics (COLING-84), Stanford, Calif. 319-326.

DiMarco, C. and G. Hirst. 1988. Stylistic Grammars in Language Translation. In Proceedings of 12th International Conference on Computational Linguistics (COLING-88), Budapest, 148-153.

DiMarco, C. and G. Hirst. 1990. Accounting for Style in Machine Translation. In Proceedings of the Third International Conference on Theoretical and Methodological Issues in Machine Translation of Natural Language, University of Texas, Austin, 65-73.

Dorr, B. 1988. UNITRAN: A Principle-Based Parser for Machine Translation. In S. Abney (ed.), *The MIT Parsing Volume, 1987-88*, Parsing Project Working Papers No. 1, Center for Cognitive Science, MIT, Cambridge, Mass., 128-150

Dostert, L. 1963. Machine Translation and Automatic Language Data Processing. In P. Howerton and D. Weeks (eds.), *Vistas in Information Handling: The Augmentation of Man's Intellect by Machine*, Volume I. Washington, D.C.: Spartan Books, 92-110.

Durand, J., P. Bennett, V. Allegranza, F. van Eynde, L. Humphreys, P. Schmidt and E. Steiner. 1991. The Eurotra Linguistic Specifications: An Overview. *Machine Translation* 6:103-147.

Earley, J. 1970. An Efficient Context-free Parsing Algorithm. *Communications of ACM* 6(8):94-102.

Emele, M. and R. Zajac. 1990. Typed Unification Grammars. In Proceedings of the 13th International Conference on Computational Linguistics (COLING-90), Helsinki, 293-298.

Englemore, R. and T. Morgan (eds.). 1988. *Blackboard Systems*. Reading, Mass.: Addison-Wesley.

Fain, J., J.G. Carbonell, P. Hayes and S. Minton. 1985. MULTIPAR: A Robust Entity-Oriented Parser. In Proceedings of the Seventh Cognitive Science Society Conference, Irvine, Calif., 110-119.

Farwell, D. and Y. Wilks. 1991. ULTRA: A Multilingual Translator. In S. Nirenburg (ed.-in-chief), Proceedings of Machine Translation Summit III, Washington and Pittsburgh: Center for Machine Translation, Carnegie Mellon University, 19-24.

Fass, D. 1988. Collative Semantics: A Semantics for Natural Language Processing. Technical Report (MCCS-88-118), Computing Research Laboratory, New Mexico State University, Las Cruces, N. Mex.

Fass, D. and Y. Wilks. 1983. Preference Semantics, Ill-Formedness, and Metaphor. *Computational Linguistics* 9:178-187.

Firth, J. 1957. *Papers in Linguistics, 1934-1951*. London: Oxford University Press.

Fong, S. and R. Berwick. 1991. The Computational Implementation of Principle-Based Parsers. In M. Tomita (ed.), *Current Trends in Parsing Technology*, Boston: Kluwer, 9-24.

Forney, G. 1973. The Viterbi Algorithm. *Proceedings of IEEE* 61:268-278

Franzini, M., K.-F. Lee and A. Waibel. 1990. Connectionist Viterbi Training: A New Hybrid Method for Continuous Speech Recognition. In Proceedings of IEEE International

Conference on Acoustics, Speech and Signal Processing (ICASSP-90), Albuquerque, N. Mex., 425-428.

Franzini, M., M. Witbrock and K.-F. Lee. 1989. A Connectionist Approach to Continuous Speech Recognition. In Proceedings of IEEE International Conference on Acoustics, Speech and Signal Processing (ICASSP-89), Glasgow, 425-428.

Fu, K.S. 1974. *Syntactic Methods in Pattern Recognition.* Orlando: Academic Press.

Fujisaki, T. 1985. Handling of Ambiguities in Natural Language Processing (in Japanese). Ph.D. dissertation, Department of Information Science, University of Tokyo.

Gachot, D. 1989. The SYSTRAN Renaissance. In Proceedings of MT Summit II, Munich, 60-66.

Gal'perin, I.R. (ed.). 1972. *The New English-Russian Dictionary.* Moscow: Sovetskaja Enciklopedia.

Gates, D., D. Haberlach, T. Kaufmann, M. Kee, R. McCardell, T. Mitamura, I. Monarch, S. Morrisson, S. Nirenburg, E. Nyberg, K. Takeda and M. Zabludowski. 1989. Lexicons. *Machine Translation* 4:67-112.

Gazdar, G., E. Klein, G. Pullum and I. Sag. 1985. *Generalized Phrase Structure Grammar.* Cambridge, Mass.: Harvard University Press.

Gervais, A. 1980. Evaluation du système pilote de traduction automatique TAUM-AVIATION. Ottawa: Bureau des Traductions.

Giuse, D. 1990. The Reading Assistant. Project Report, Robotics Institute, Carnegie Mellon University, Pittsburgh, Pa.

Giuse, D. 1991. In-Context Foreign Language Learning in the Reading Assistant. In Proceedings of the Ninth Annual Conference on Interactive Instruction Delivery, Society for Applied Learning Technology, Orlando, Fla., 91-93.

Goldman, N. 1975. Conceptual Generation. In R. Schank (ed.), *Conceptual Information Processing.* Amsterdam: North Holland, 289-372.

Goodman, K. and S. Nirenburg. Forthcoming. To Save the Semantic Phenomena: Machine Translation and Interlingua Texts. *Philosophy and Computing.*

Goodman, K. and S. Nirenburg (eds.). 1991. *The KBMT Project: A Case Study in Knowledge-Based Machine Translation.* San Mateo, Calif.: Morgan Kaufmann.

Goodman, K. and S. Nirenburg. Forthcoming. To Save the Semantic Phenomena: Machine Translation and Interlingua Texts. *Philosophy and Computing.*

Granville, R. 1983. Cohesion in Computer Text Generation: Lexical Substitution. Technical Report (MIT/LCS/TR-310), Laboratory for Computer Science, MIT, Cambridge, Mass.

Grishman, R. and R. Kittredge (eds.). 1986. *Sublanguage Description and Processing.* Hillsdale, N.J.: Lawrence Erlbaum Associates.

Grosz, B. and C. Sidner. 1986. Attention, Intentions and the Structure of Discourse. *Computational Linguistics* 12:175-204.

Hampshire, J. and A. Waibel. 1989. Connectionist Architectures for Multi-Speaker Phoneme Recognition. Technical Report (CMU-CS-89-167), School of Computer Science, Carnegie Mellon University, Pittsburgh, Pa.

Hanakata, K., A. Lesniewski and S. Yokoyama. 1986. Semantic-Based Generation of Japanese-German Translation System. 1986. In Proceedings of 11th International Conference on Computational Linguistics (COLING-86), Bonn, 560-562.

Hanazawa, T., K. Kita, S. Nakamura, T. Kawabata and K. Shikano. 1990. ATR HMM-LR Continuous Speech Recognition System. In Proceedings of IEEE International Conference on Acoustics, Speech and Signal Processing (ICASSP-90), Albuquerque, N. Mex.

Hausser, R. 1988. Left-Associative Grammar: An Informal Outline. *Computers and Translation* 3:23-67.

Hausser, R, 1989. *Computation of Language.* Berlin: Springer Verlag.

Hayes, P., A. Hauptmann, J.G. Carbonell and M. Tomita. 1987. Parsing Spoken Language: A Semantic Caseframe Approach. Technical Report (CMU-CMT-87-103), Center for Machine Translation, Carnegie Mellon University, Pittsburgh, Pa.

Hayes, P. and J.G. Carbonell. 1983. A Framework for Processing Corrections in Task-Oriented Dialogues. In Proceedings of the Eighth Annual Meeting of the International Joint Conference for Artificial Intelligence (IJCAI-83), Karlsruhe, Germany, 668-670.

Hayes, P. and S. Weinstein. 1990. CONSTRUE/TIS: A System for Content-based Indexing of a Database of News Stories. In Proceedings of the International Conference on Innovative Applications of AI, Washington, 1-5.

Heidorn, G., K. Jensen, L. Miller, R. Byrd, M. Chodorow. 1982. The EPISTLE Text Critiquing System. *IBM Systems Journal* 21:305-326.

Henisz-Dostert, B. 1979. Users' Evaluation of Machine Translation. In B. Henisz-Dostert, R. Ross McDonald and M. Zarechnak (eds.), *Machine Translation*, Trends in Linguistics: Studies and Monographs, Volume XI. The Hague: Mouton, 147-244.

Henisz-Dostert, B., R. Ross McDonald and M. Zarechnak (eds.). 1979. *Machine Translation*, Trends in Linguistics: Studies and Monographs, Volume XI, The Hague: Mouton.

Hirst, G. 1987. *Semantic Interpretation and the Resolution of Ambiguity.* Cambridge: Cambridge University Press.

Hobbs, J., W. Croft, T. Davies, D. Edwards, K. Laws. 1987. Commonsense Metaphysics and Lexical Semantics. *Computational Linguistics* 13:241-250.

Hovy, E. 1985. Integrating Text Planning and Production in Generation. In Proceedings of the Ninth Annual Meeting of the International Joint Conference for Artificial Intelligence (IJCAI-85), Los Angeles, 848-851.

Hovy, E. 1987. Generating Natural Language under Pragmatic Constraints. Research Report (521), Department of Computer Science, Yale University, New Haven, Conn.

Hovy, E. 1988a. Planning Coherent Multisentential Text. In Proceedings of the 26th Annual Meeting of the Association for Computational Linguistics (ACL-88), Buffalo, 163-169.

Hovy, E. 1988b. Two Types of Planning in Language Generation. In Proceedings of the 26th Annual Meeting of the Association for Computational Linguistics (ACL-88), Buffalo, 179-186.

Hovy, E. 1988c. Three Approaches to Planning a Coherent Text. Presentation at the Fourth International Workshop on Natural Language Generation, Santa Catalina Island, Calif.

Hovy, E. 1988d. Generating Natural Language Under Pragmatic Constraints. Ph.D. dissertation, Yale University, New Haven, Conn.

Hutchins, W.J. 1986. *Machine Translation: Past, Present, Future.* Chichester, UK: Ellis Horwood.

Hutchins, W.J. 1987. Prospects in Machine Translation. In M. Nagao (ed.-in-chief), *Machine Translation Summit* (proceedings of MT Summit I, Hakone, Japan, 1987). Tokyo: Ohmsha, 48-52.

IBM Speech Recognition Group. 1985. A Real-Time, Isolated-Word, Speech-Recognition System for Dictation Transcription. In Proceedings of IEEE International Conference on Acoustics, Speech and Signal Processing (ICASSP-85).

Ingria, R. Forthcoming. Lexical Information for Parsing Systems: Points of Convergence and Divergence. In D. Walker, A. Zampolli and N. Carzolari (eds.), *Automating the Lexicon: Research and Practice in a Multilingual Environment.* Cambridge: Cambridge University Press.

Isabelle, P. 1987. Machine Translation at the TAUM Group. In M. King (ed.), *Machine Translation Today.* Edinburgh: Edinburgh University Press, 247-277.

Isabelle, P. and L. Bourbeau. 1985. TAUM-AVIATION: Its Technical Features and Some Experimental Results. *Computational Linguistics* 11:18-27.

Itakura, F. 1975. Minimum Prediction Residual Principle Applied to Speech Recognition. *IEEE Transactions on Acoustics, Speech and Signal Processing* 23:67-72.

Jackendoff, R. 1983. *Semantics and Cognition.* Cambridge, Mass.: MIT Press.

Jacobs, P. 1985. A Knowledge-based Approach to Language Production. Ph.D. dissertation, University of California, Berkeley.

Jain, A. and A. Waibel. 1990. Robust Connectionist Parsing of Spoken Language. In Proceedings of IEEE International Conference on Acoustics, Speech and Signal Processing (ICASSP-90), Albuquerque, N. Mex., 593-596.

JEIDA (Japan Electronic Industry Development Association). 1989. *A Japanese View of Machine Translation in Light of the Considerations and Recommendations Reported by ALPAC, U.S.A.* Technical Report (TR-031), JEIDA, Tokyo.

Jelinek, F. et al. 1976. Continuous Speech Recognition by Statistical Methods. In Proceedings of the IEEE, 64(4).

Jensen, K. and J.-L. Binot. 1987. Disambiguating Prepositional Phrase Attachments by Using On-Line Dictionary Definitions. *Computational Linguistics* 13:251-260.

Johnson, R., M. King and L. des Tombe. 1985. EUROTRA: A Multilingual System under Development. *Computational Linguistics* 11:155:169.

Johnson-Laird, P. 1983. *Mental Models.* Cambridge, Mass.: Harvard University Press.

Joshi, A., L. Levy and M. Takahaski. 1975. Tree Adjunct Grammars. *Journal of Computer and System Sciences* 10:136-163.

Kaji, H. 1989. HICATS/JE: A Japanese-to-English Machine Translation System Based on Semantics. In M. Nagao (ed.-in-chief), *Machine Translation Summit* (proceedings of MT Summit I, Hakone, Japan, 1987). Tokyo: Ohmsha, 101-106.

Kaplan, R. and J. Bresnan. 1982. Lexical Functional Grammar: A Formal System for Grammatical Representation. In J. Bresnan (ed.), *The Mental Representation of Grammatical Relations.* Cambridge, Mass.: MIT Press, 173-281.

Karttunen, L. 1983. KIMMO: A two-level morphological analyzer. *Texas Linguistic Forum* 22, 165-186.

Katz, J. 1978. Effability and Translation. In F. Guenthner and M. Guenthner-Reutter (eds.), *Meaning and Translation: Philosophical and Linguistic Approaches*, London: Duckworth, 191-234.

Katz, J. 1988. The Refutation of Indeterminacy. *The Journal of Philosophy* 85:227-252.

Katz, J. and J.A. Fodor. 1963. The Structure of a Semantic Theory. *Language* 39:170-210.

Katz, J. and P. Postal. 1964. *An Integrated Theory of Linguistic Descriptions.* Cambridge, Mass.: MIT Press.

Kawabata, T., K. Shikano and K. Kita. 1989. Task Entropy and Phone Perplexity (in Japanese). In Proceedings of The Acoustic Society of Japan, Spring Meeting, Tokyo.

Kay, M. 1973. The MIND System. In R. Rustin (ed.), *Natural Language Processing.* New York: Algorithmics Press, 155-188.

Kay, M. 1985. Parsing in Functional Unification Grammar. In D. Dowty, L. Karttunen and A. Zwicky (eds.), *Natural Language Parsing: Psychological, Computational, and Theoretical Perspectives.* Cambridge, Mass.: Cambridge University Press, 251-278.

Kay, M. 1989. Presentation at MT Summit II, Munich.

Kee, M., L. Levin and S. Morrisson. 1991. Source Text Analysis. In K. Goodman and S. Nirenburg (eds.), *The KBMT Project: A Case Study in Knowledge-Based Machine Translation*. San Mateo: Morgan Kaufmann, 165-188.

Kenschaft, E. 1988. Linearization in DIOGENES. 1988. Technical Memo, Center for Machine Translation, Carnegie Mellon University, Pittsburgh, Pa.

King, M. 1989. A Practical Guide to the Evaluation of Machine Translation Systems. An Interim Report to Suissetra. Geneva: ISSCO.

King, M. (ed.). 1987. *Machine Translation Today*. Edinburgh: Edinburgh University Press.

King, M. 1981. Design Characteristics of a Machine Translation System. In Proceedings of the Seventh Annual Meeting of the International Joint Conference for Artificial Intelligence (IJCAI-81), Vancouver, 43-46.

Kita, K., T. Kawabata and H. Saito. 1989. HMM Continuous Speech Recognition Using Predictive LR Parsing. In Proceedings of IEEE International Conference on Acoustics, Speech and Signal Processing (ICASSP-89), Glasgow, N. Mex., 53-56.

Kittredge, R. 1987. The Significance of Sublanguage for Machine Translation. In S. Nirenburg (ed.), *Theoretical and Methodological Issues in Machine Translation*, Cambridge: Cambridge University Press, 59-67.

Kittredge, R. and J. Lehrberger (eds.). 1982. *Sublanguage: Studies of Language in Restricted Semantic Domains*. New York: de Gruyter.

Kittredge, R. and I. Mel'čuk. 1983. Towards a Computable Model of Meaning–Text Relations within a Natural Sublanguage. In Proceedings of the Eighth Annual Meeting of the International Joint Conference for Artificial Intelligence (IJCAI-83), Karlsruhe, Germany 657-659.

Kittredge, R., A. Polguère and L. Iordanskaja. 1988. Generation Using the Meaning–Text Model. In Supplement to Proceedings of 12th International Conference on Computational Linguistics (COLING-88), Budapest.

Knight, K. 1989. Integrating Knowledge Acquisition and Language Acquisition. Ph.D. dissertation proposal, School of Computer Science, Carnegie Mellon University, Pittsburgh, Pa.

Kolodner, J. 1984. *Retrieval and Organizational Strategies in Conceptual Memory: A Computer Model*. Hillsdale, N.J.: Lawrence Erlbaum Associates.

Kolodner, J. and C. Riesbeck (eds.). 1986. *Experience, Memory and Reasoning*. Hillsdale, N.J.: Lawrence Erlbaum Associates.

Koskenniemi, K. 1983. Two-level Morphology: A General Computational Model for Word-form Recognition and Production. Publication No. 11, Department of General Linguistics, University of Helsinki.

Kroch, A. and A. Joshi. Forthcoming. The Linguistic Relevance of Tree Adjoining Grammar. *Linguistics and Philosophy.*

Kubala, G., Y. Chow, M. Derr, M. Feng, O. Kimball, J. Makhoul, P. Price, J. Rohlicek, S. Roucos, R. Schwartz and J. Vandegrift. 1988. Continuous Speech Recognition Results of the BYBLOS System on the DARPA 1000-Word Resource Management Database. In Proceedings of IEEE International Conference on Acoustics, Speech and Signal Processing (ICASSP-88), New York, 291-294.

Kuwabara, H., K. Takeda, Y. Sagisaka, S. Katagiri, S. Morikawa and T. Watanabe. 1989. Construction of a Large-Scale Japanese Speech Database and its Management System. In Proceedings of IEEE International Conference on Acoustics, Speech and Signal Processing (ICASSP-89), Glasgow, 560-563.

Lakoff, G. and M. Johnson. 1980. *Metaphors We Live By.* Chicago: University of Chicago Press.

Landsbergen, J. 1989. The Rosetta Project. In Proceedings of MT Summit II, Munich, 82-87.

Lang, K.J. 1989. A Time-Delay Neural Network Architecture for Speech Recognition, Ph.D. dissertation, School of Computer Science, Carnegie Mellon University, Pittsburgh, Pa.

Laubsch, J., D. Rösner, K. Hanakata, and A. Lesniewski. 1984. Language Generation from Conceptual Structure: Synthesis of German in a Japanese/German MT Project. In Proceedings of 10th International Conference on Computational Linguistics (COLING-84), Stanford, Calif., 491-494.

Lea, W. (ed.). 1980. *Trends in Speech Recognition.* Engelwood Cliffs, N.J.: Prentice-Hall.

Leavitt, J. 1990. The DIBBS User's Guide. Technical Memo, Center for Machine Translation, Carnegie Mellon University, Pittsburgh, Pa.

Leavitt, J. and E. Nyberg. 1990. The DIBBS BlackBoard Control Architecture and Its Application to Distributed Natural Language Processing. In Proceedings of IEEE Tools for Artificial Intelligence Conference (TAI-90), Washington, D.C., 202-208.

Leavitt, J., E. Nyberg, S. Nirenburg and C. Defrise. 1991. DIOGENES-90. Technical Report (CMU-CMT-91-123), Center for Machine Translation, Carnegie Mellon University, Pittsburgh, Pa.

Lee, K.-F. 1988. Large-Vocabulary Speaker-Independent Continuous Speech Recognition: The Sphinx System. Ph.D. dissertation, School of Computer Science, Carnegie Mellon University, Pittsburgh, Pa.

Lee, K.-F., H. Hon and R. Reddy. 1990. An Overview of the SPHINX Speech Recognition System. *IEEE Transactions on Acoustics, Speech, and Signal Processing* 38:35-45.

Lehrberger, J. 1988. A Synthesis of Evaluations of Machine Translation Systems. In J. Lehrberger and L. Bourbeau (eds.), *Machine Translation: Linguistic Characteristics of MT Systems and General Methodology of Evaluation*. Amsterdam and Philadelphia: John Benjamins, 196-222.

Lenat, D. and R.V. Guha. 1988. The World according to CYC. MCC Technical Report (ACA-AI-300-88), Austin, Texas.

Lesser, V., R. Fennell, L. Erman and R. Reddy. 1975. The Hearsay-II Speech Understanding System. *IEEE Transactions on Acoustics, Speech and Signal Processing*23:11-24.

Leung, H. and V. Zue. 1988. Some Phonetic Recognition Experiments Using Artificial Neural Nets. In Proceedings of IEEE International Conference on Acoustics, Speech and Signal Processing (ICASSP-88), New York, 422-425.

Levin, L. 1991. Syntactic Theory and Processing. In K. Goodman and S. Nirenburg (eds.), *The KBMT Project: A Case Study in Knowledge-Based Machine Translation*. San Mateo, Calif.: Morgan Kaufmann, 49-70.

Levin, L., D. Evans and D. Gates. Forthcoming. The ALICE System: A Workbench for Learning and Using Language. *CALICO*.

Levinson, S., L. Rabiner and M. Sondhi. 1983. An Introduction to the Application of the Theory of Probabilistic Functions of a Markov Process to Automatic Speech Recognition. *Bell Systems Technical Journal* 62(4):1035-1074.

Linde, Y., A. Buzo and R. Gray. 1980. An Algorithm for Vector Quantizer Design. *IEEE Transactions on Communications* 28:80-94.

Lippmann, R. 1989. Review of Neural Networks for Speech Recognition. *Neural Computation* 1.

Lippmann, R. and B. Gold. 1987. Neural Net Classifier Useful for Speech Recognition. In Proceedings of IEEE International Conference on Neural Networks (ICNN-87).

Liro, J. 1989. The Intercoder as Central and Unique Component of the METAL System. *Quarterly Report* June: 1-13 (Linguistics Research Center, University of Texas, Austin).

Litman, D. and J. Allen. 1990. Discourse Processing and Commonsense Plans. In P. Cohen, J. Morgan and M.E. Pollack (eds.), *Intentions and Plans in Discourse*. Cambridge, Mass: MIT Press, 365-388.

Long, T. et al. (eds.). 1979. *Longman Dictionary of English Idioms*. Harlow, UK: Longman.

Lowerre, B. 1976. The HARPY Speech Recognition System. Ph.D. dissertation, School of Computer Science, Carnegie Mellon University, Pittsburgh, Pa.

Lowerre, B. and R. Reddy. 1980. The HARPY Speech Recognition System. In W. Lea (ed.), *Trends in Speech Recognition*. Englewood Cliffs, N.J.: Prentice-Hall, 340-360.

Lozinskii, E. and S. Nirenburg. 1986. Parsing in Parallel. *Journal of Computer Languages* 11:39-51.

Lytinen, S. 1987. Integrating Syntax and Semantics. In S. Nirenburg (ed.), *Machine Translation: Theoretical and Methodological Issues.* Cambridge: Cambridge University Press, 302-316.

Malpas, J. 1989. The Intertranslatability of Natural Languages. *Synthese* 78:233-264.

Mann, W. 1983. An Overview of the Nigel Text Generation Grammar. ISI Research Report (83-113), Information Sciences Institute, University of Southern California, Marina del Rey, Calif.

Mann, W. and S. Thompson. 1987. Rhetorical Structure Theory: A Framework for the Analysis of Texts. ISI Technical Report (ISI/RS-87-185), Information Sciences Institute, University of Southern California, Marina del Rey, Calif.

McArthur, T. 1981. *Longman Lexicon of Contemporary English.* Harlow, UK: Longman.

McDonald, D. 1983. Natural Language Generation as Computational Problem. In M. Brady and R. Berwick (eds.), *Computational Models of Discourse*, Cambridge, Mass.: MIT Press, 209-266.

McDonald, D. 1986. Description Directed Control: Its Applications for Natural Language Generation. In B. Grosz, K.S. Jones and B. Webber (eds.), *Readings in Natural Language Processing.* San Mateo, Calif.: Morgan Kaufmann.

McDonald, D. and J. Pustejovsky. 1985. A Computational Theory of Prose Style for Natural Language Generation. In Proceedings of the Second Meeting of the European Chapter of the Association for Computational Linguistics (EACL-85), Geneva, 187-193.

McDonald, D., M. Vaughan and J. Pustejovsky. 1987. Factors Contributing to Efficiency in Natural Language Generation. In G. Kempen (ed.), *Natural Language Generation.* Dordrecht: Kluwer.

McKeown, K. 1985. *Text Generation.* Cambridge: Cambridge University Press.

McKeown, K. and M. Elhadad. 1989. A Comparison of Surface Language Generators: A Case Study in Choice of Connectives. Manuscript, Columbia University, New York, N.Y.

Mel'čuk, I. 1974. *Towards a Theory of Linguistic Models of the Meaning–Text Type.* Moscow: Nauka (in Russian).

Mel'čuk, I. 1981. Meaning–Text Models: A Recent Trend in Soviet Linguistics. *Annual Review of Anthropology* 10:27-62.

Mel'čuk, I., and A. Polguère. 1987. A Formal Lexicon in Meaning–Text Theory (Or How to Do Lexica with Words). *Computational Linguistics* 13:261-275.

Meteer, M. 1989. The SPOKESMAN Natural Language Generation System. Technical Report (7090), Bolt, Beranek and Newman, Cambridge, Mass.

Meteer, M., D. McDonald, S. Anderson, D. Foster, L. Gay, A. Huettner and P. Sibun. 1987. Mumble-86: Design and Implementation. Technical Report (87-87), University of Massachusetts, Amherst, Mass.

Meyer, I., B. Onyshkevych and L. Carlson. 1990. Lexicographic Principles and Design for Knowledge-Based Machine Translation. Technical Report (CMU-CMT 90-118), Center for Machine Translation, Carnegie Mellon University, Pittsburgh, Pa.

Minami, Y., H. Sawai, M. Miyatake and K. Shikano. 1990. Large Vocabulary Spoken Word Recognition Using Time-Delay Neural Network Phoneme Spotting and Predictive LR-Parsing. Transactions of the Technical Group, Speech Acoustics Society of Japan, SP89-99 (in Japanese).

Mitamura, T. 1989. The Hierarchical Organization of Predicate Frames for Interpretive Mapping in Natural Language Processing. Ph.D. dissertation, Department of Linguistics, University of Pittsburgh, Pittsburgh, Pa.

Monarch, I. and S. Nirenburg. 1988. Ontos: An Ontology-Based Knowledge Acquisition and Maintenance System. In Proceedings of the Third AAAI Knowledge Acquisition for Knowledge-Based Systems Workshop, Banff, Alberta, Canada.

Monarch, I. and S. Nirenburg, 1989. Ontology-Based Lexicon Acquisition for a Machine Translation System. In Proceedings of the Fourth Workshop on Knowledge Acquisition for Knowledge-Based Systems Workshop, Banff, Alberta, Canada.

Moore J. and C. Paris 1989. Planning Text for Advisory Dialogues. In Proceedings of the 27st Annual Meeting of the Association for Computational Linguistics (ACL-89), Vancouver, 203-211.

Morii, S., K. Niyada, S. Fujii and M. Hoshimi. 1985. Large Vocabulary Speaker-independent Japanese Speech Recognition System. In Proceedings of IEEE International Conference on Acoustics, Speech and Signal Processing (ICASSP-85), Tampa, Fla., 866-869.

Morimoto, T., K. Ogura, K. Kita, K. Kogure and K. Kakigahara. 1989. Spoken Language Processing in SL-TRANS. ATR Symposium on Basic Research for Telephone Interpretation, Tokyo.

Muraki, K. 1989. PIVOT: Two-Phase Machine Translation System. In M. Nagao (ed.-in-chief), *Machine Translation Summit*, Tokyo: Ohmsha, 113-115.

Nagao, M. 1989a. *Machine Translation: How Far Can It Go?* Oxford: Oxford University Press.

Nagao, M. (ed.-in-chief). 1989b. *Machine Translation Summit*. Tokyo: Ohmsha (proceedings of the 1987 summit, Hakone, Japan).

Nagao, M., J. Tsujii and J. Nakamura. 1985. The Japanese Government Project for Machine Translation. *Computational Linguistics* 11:91-110.

Neff, M. and R. Byrd. 1987. Wordsmith Users Guide. Version 2.01. Manuscript, IBM T.J. Watson Research Center, Yorktown Heights, N.Y.

Newell, A. and H. Simon, 1972. *Human Problem Solving.* Englewood Cliffs, N.J.: Prentice-Hall.

Nirenburg, S. 1987a. Knowledge and Choices in Machine Translation. In S. Nirenburg (ed.), *Machine Translation: Theoretical and Methodological Issues.* Cambridge: Cambridge University Press, 1-21.

Nirenburg, S. 1987b. Introduction. In S. Nirenburg (ed.), *Machine Translation: Theoretical and Methodological Issues,* Cambridge: Cambridge University Press, xiii-xv.

Nirenburg, S. 1987c. A System for Natural Language Generation that Emphasizes Lexical Selection. In Proceedings of the Northeast Artificial Intelligence Consortium's Natural Language Planning Workshop, Blue Mountain Lake, N.Y., 124-152.

Nirenburg, S. 1987d. A Distributed System for Language Generation. Technical Report (CMU-CMT 86-102), Center for Machine Translation, Carnegie Mellon University, Pittsburgh, Pa.

Nirenburg, S. (ed.). 1987e. *Machine Translation: Theoretical and Methodological Issues.* Cambridge: Cambridge University Press.

Nirenburg, S. 1988. Resolution of Lexical Synonymy at the Word Level. Presentation at the Fouth International Workshop on Natural Language Generation, Santa Catalina Island, Calif.

Nirenburg, S. (ed.-in-chief). 1991. Proceedings of Machine Translation Summit III. Washington, D.C., and Pittsburgh, Pa.: Center for Machine Translation, Carnegie Mellon University.

Nirenburg, S. and J.G. Carbonell. 1987. Integrating Discourse Pragmatics and Propositional Knowledge in Multilingual Natural Language Processing. *Computers and Translation* 2:105-116.

Nirenburg, S. and C. Defrise. Forthcoming, a. Application-Oriented Computational Semantics. In R. Johnson and M. Rosner (eds.), *Computational Linguistics and Formal Semantics.* Cambridge: Cambridge University Press.

Nirenburg, S. and C. Defrise. Forthcoming, b. Lexical and Conceptual Structure for Knowledge-Based Machine Translation. In J. Pustejovsky (ed.), *Semantics and the Lexicon.* Dordrecht: Kluwer.

Nirenburg, S. and K. Goodman (eds.). 1989. KBMT-89. Project Report, Center for Machine Translation, Carnegie Mellon University, Pittsburgh, Pa.

Nirenburg, S. and K. Goodman. 1990. Treatment of Meaning in MT Systems. In Proceedings of the Third International Conference on Theoretical and Methodological Issues in Machine Translation of Natural Languages, University of Texas, Austin, 171-188.

Nirenburg, S. and V. Lesser. 1986. Providing Intelligent Assistance in Distributed Office Environments. In Proceedings of the Third International ACM Conference on Office Automation Systems, Providence, R.I., 104-112.

Nirenburg S., V. Lesser and E. Nyberg. 1989. Controlling a Language Generation Planner. Proceedings of 11th Annual Meeting of the International Joint Conference for Artificial Intelligence (IJCAI-89), Detroit, 1524-1530.

Nirenburg, S. and L. Levin. 1989. Knowledge Representation Support. *Machine Translation* 4:25-52.

Nirenburg, S., R. McCardell, E. Nyberg, P. Werner, S. Huffman, E. Kenschaft and I. Nirenburg. 1988a. DIOGENES-88. Technical Report (CMU-CMT 88-107), Center for Machine Translation, Carnegie Mellon University, Pittsburgh, Pa.

Nirenburg, S., I. Monarch and T. Kaufmann. 1991. World Knowledge and Text Meaning. In K. Goodman and S. Nirenburg (eds.), *The KBMT Project: A Case Study in Knowledge-Based Machine Translation*, San Mateo, Calif.: Morgan Kaufmann, 17-48.

Nirenburg, S., I. Monarch, T. Kaufmann, I. Nirenburg, and J. Carbonell. 1988b. Acquisition of Very Large Knowledge Bases. Technical Report (CMU-CMT 88-108), Center for Machine Translation, Carnegie Mellon University, Pittsburgh, Pa.

Nirenburg, S. and I. Nirenburg. 1988. A Framework for Lexical Selection in Natural Language Generation. In Proceedings of 12th International Conference on Computational Linguistics (COLING-88), Budapest, 471-475.

Nirenburg, S., I. Nirenburg and J. Reynolds. 1985. The Control Structure of POPLAR: a Personality-Oriented Planner. In Proceedings of Third Annual Conference on Intelligent Systems, Oakland University, Rochester, Mich.

Nirenburg, S. and J. Pustejovsky. 1988. Processing Aspectual Semantics. In Proceedings of Annual Conference of the Cognitive Science Society, Montreal, 658-665.

Nirenburg, S. and V. Raskin. 1986. A Metric for Computational Analysis of Meaning: Toward an Applied Theory of Linguistic Semantics. In Proceedings of 11th International Conference on Computational Linguistics (COLING-86), Bonn, 338-340.

Nirenburg, S. and V. Raskin. 1987a. The Analysis Lexicon and the Lexicon Management System. *Computers and Translation* 2:177-188.

Nirenburg, S. and V. Raskin. 1987b. The Subworld Concept Lexicon and the Lexicon Management System. *Computational Linguistics* 13:276-289.

Nirenburg, S., V. Raskin and A. Tucker. 1986a. On Knowledge-Based Machine Translation. In Proceedings of 11th International Conference on Computational Linguistics (COLING-86), Bonn, 627-632.

Nirenburg, S., V. Raskin and A. Tucker. 1987. The Structure of Interlingua in TRANSLATOR. In S. Nirenburg (ed.), *Machine Translation: Theoretical and Methodological Issues*. Cambridge: Cambridge University Press, 90-113.

Nirenburg, S., J. Reynolds and I. Nirenburg. 1986b. Studying the Cognitive Agent: A Theory and Two Experiments. Research Report (COSC 9), Colgate University, Hamilton, N.Y.

Nyberg, E. 1988. The FrameKit User's Guide. Technical Memo, Center for Machine Translation, Carnegie Mellon University, Pittsburgh, Pa.

Nyberg, E., S. Nirenburg and R. McCardell. 1988. The DIOGENES User's Guide. Technical Memo, Center for Machine Translation, Carnegie Mellon University, Pittsburgh, Pa.

Ogden, C. and I. Richards. 1923. *The Meaning of Meaning.* London: Routledge and Kegan Paul.

Paris, C. 1988. Tailoring Object Descriptions to a User's Level of Expertise. *Computational Linguistics* 14:64-78.

Pereira, F. and D. Warren. 1980. Definite Clause Grammars for Language Analysis—A Survey of the Formalism and a Comparison with Augmented Transition Networks. *Artificial Intelligence* 13:231-278.

Pericliev, V. 1984. Handling Syntactic Ambiguity in Machine Translation. In Proceedings of the 10th International Conference on Computational Linguistics (COLING-84), Stanford, Calif., 521-524.

Pollard, C. and I. Sag. 1987. *Information-Based Syntax and Semantics.* Volume I: Fundamentals. (CSLI Lecture Notes 13.) Stanford, Calif: CSLI.

Poritz, A. 1988. Hidden Markov Models: A Guided Tour. In Proceedings of IEEE International Conference on Acoustics, Speech and Signal Processing (ICASSP-88), New York, 7-13.

Procter, P. et al. (eds.). 1978. *Longman Dictionary of Contemporary English.* Harlow, UK: Longman.

Pulman, S.G. 1983. *Word Meaning and Belief.* London: Croom Helm.

Pustejovsky, J. and S. Nirenburg. 1987. Lexical Selection in the Process of Language Generation. In Proceedings of the 25th Annual Meeting of the Association for Computational Linguistics (ACL-87), Stanford, Calif., 201-206.

Quine, W.V.O. 1953. Two Dogmas of Empiricism. In *From a Logical Point of View.* Cambridge, Mass.: Harvard University Press, 20-46.

Quine, W.V.O. 1960. *Word and Object.* Cambridge, Mass.: MIT Press.

Quine, W.V.O. 1968. Ontological Relativity. *Journal of Philosophy* 65:185-212.

Quine, W.V.O. 1987. Indeterminacy of Translation Again. *Journal of Philosophy* 84:5-10.

Quirk, R., S. Greenbaum, G. Leech and J. Svartvick. 1985. *Comprehensive Grammar of the English Language.* London: Longman.

Rabiner, L., J. Wilpon and F. Soong. 1988. High Performance Connected Digit Recognition Using Hidden Markov Models. In Proceedings of IEEE International Conference on Acoustics, Speech and Signal Processing (ICASSP-88), New York, 1214-1225.

Raskin, V. 1987. What Is There in Linguistic Semantics for Natural Language Processing? In Proceedings of the Northeast Artificial Intelligence Consortium's Natural Language Planning Workshop, Blue Mountain Lake, N.Y., 78-96.

Rich, E. 1983. *Artificial Intelligence*. New York: McGraw-Hill.

Riesbeck, C. 1975. Conceptual Analysis. In R. Schank (ed.), *Conceptual Information Processing*. Amsterdam: North Holland, 83-156.

de Roeck, A. 1987. Linguistic Theory and Early Machine Translation. In M. King, ed., *Machine Translation Today*. Edinburgh: Edinburgh University Press, 38-57.

Rohrer, C. (ed. and chair). 1989. MT Summit II. Proceedings of the Conference, Munich, Germany.

Rösner, D. 1986. When Mariko Talks to Siegfried. In Proceedings of 11th International Conference on Computational Linguistics (COLING-86), Bonn, 652-654.

Rudolph, E., 1988. Connective Relations—Connective Expressions—Connective Structures. In J. Petöfi (ed.), *Text and Discourse Constitution*, New York: de Gruyter, 97-133.

Sacerdoti, E. 1977. *The Structure for Plans and Behavior*. New York: Elsevier.

Saito, H. and M. Tomita. 1988. Parsing Noisy Sentences. In Proceedings of 12th International Conference on Computational Linguistics (COLING-88), Budapest, 561-566.

Sanders, M. 1988. The Rosetta Translation System. Technical Report (15.103), Philips Research Laboratories, Eindhoven, The Netherlands.

Scha, R. and L. Polanyi. 1988. An Augmented Context-Free Grammar for Discourse. In Proceedings of 12th International Conference on Computational Linguistics (COLING-88), Budapest, 573-577.

Schank, R. 1975. *Conceptual Information Processing*. Amsterdam: North Holland.

Schank, R. 1982. *Dynamic Memory*. Hillsdale, N.J.: Lawrence Erlbaum Associates.

Schank, R. and R. Abelson, 1977. *Scripts, Plans, Goals and Understanding*. Hillsdale, N.J.: Lawrence Erlbaum Associates.

Schneider, T. 1989. The METAL System: Status 1989. In C. Rohrer (ed.), Proceedings of MT Summit II, Munich, 128-136.

Schubert, L., M. Papalaskaris and J. Taugher. 1983. Determining Type, Part, Color, and Time Relationships. *IEEE Computer* 16:53-60.

Shikano, K. 1987. Improvement of Word Recognition Results by Trigram Model. In Proceedings of IEEE International Conference on Acoustics, Speech and Signal Processing (ICASSP-87), Dallas, 1261-1264.

Simmons, R. 1973. Semantic Networks: Their Computation and Use for Understanding English Sentences. In R. Schank and K. Colby (eds.), *Computer Models of Thought and Language*. San Francisco: W.H. Freeman, 63-113.

Slator, B. 1988. PREMO: the PREference Machine Organization. In Proceedings of the Third Annual Rocky Mountain Conference on Artificial Intelligence, Denver, 258-265.

Slator, B. and Y. Wilks. 1991. PREMO: Parsing by Conspicuous Lexical Consumption. In M. Tomita (ed.), *Current Issues in Parsing Technology*. Dordrecht: Kluwer, 85-102.

Slocum, J. 1985. A Survey of Machine Translation: Its History, Current Status, and Future Prospects. *Computational Linguistics* 11:1-17.

Slocum, J. and M. Morgan. Forthcoming. The Role of Dictionaries and Machine-Readable Lexicons in Translation. In D. Walker, A. Zampolli and N. Calzolari (eds.), *Automating the Lexicon: Research and Practice in a Multilingual Environment*. Cambridge: Cambridge University Press.

Small, S. and C. Rieger. 1982. Parsing and Comprehending with Word Experts (A Theory and Its Realization). In W. Lehnert and M. Ringle (eds.), *Strategies for Natural Language Processing*. Hillsdale, N.J.: Lawrence Erlbaum Associates, 89-147.

Sondheimer, N., S. Cumming and R. Albano. 1990. How to Realize a Concept: Lexical Selection and the Conceptual Network in Text Generation. *Machine Translation* 5:57-78.

Sowa, J. 1984. *Conceptual Structures: Information Processing in Mind and Machine*. Reading, Mass.: Addison-Wesley.

Stentiford, F. and M. Steer. 1988. Machine Translation of Speech. *British Telecom Technology Journal* 6(2).

Tebelskis, J. and A. Waibel. 1990. Large Vocabulary Recognition Using Linked Predictive Neural Networks. In Proceedings of IEEE International Conference on Acoustics, Speech and Signal Processing (ICASSP-90), Albuquerque, N. Mex., 437-440.

Tebelskis, J., A. Waibel, B. Petek and O. Schmidbauer. 1991. Continuous Speech Recognition using Linked Predictive Neural Networks. In Proceedings of IEEE International Conference on Acoustics, Speech and Signal Processing (ICASSP-91), Toronto, 61-64.

Thomason, R. 1990. Accommodation, Meaning, and Implicature: Interdisciplinary Foundations for Pragmatics. In P. Cohen, J. Morgan and M. Pollack (eds.), *Intentions in Communication*, Cambridge, Mass.: MIT Press, 325-363.

Tomita, M. 1986a. *Efficient Parsing for Natural Language*. Boston: Kluwer.

Tomita, M. 1986b. An Efficient Word Lattice Parsing Algorithm for Continuous Speech Recognition. In Proceedings of IEEE International Conference on Acoustics, Speech and Signal Processing (ICASSP-86), Tokyo, 1569-1572.

Tomita, M. 1986c. Sentence Disambiguation by Asking. *Computers and Translation* 1:39-51

Tomita, M. 1987a. The Universal Parser Architecture for Knowledge-Based Machine Translation. In Proceedings of 10th Annual Meeting of the International Joint Conference for Artificial Intelligence (IJCAI-87), Milan, 718-721.

Tomita, M. 1987b. An Efficient Augmented-Context-Free Parsing Algorithm. *Computational Linguistics* 13:31-46.

Tomita, M. (ed.). 1991. *Current Trends in Parsing Technology*. Boston: Kluwer.

Tomita, M. and J.G. Carbonell. 1987. The Universal Parser Architecture for Knowledge-Based Machine Translation. In Proceedings 10th Annual Meeting of the International Joint Conference for Artificial Intelligence (IJCAI-87), Milan, 718-721.

Tomita, M., M. Kee, T. Mitamura and J.G. Carbonell. 1987. Linguistic and Domain Knowledge Sources for the Universal Parser Architecture, in H. Czap and C. Galinski (eds.), *Terminology and Knowledge Engineering*. Frankfurt am Main.: INDEKS Verlag, 191-203,

Tomita, M., M. Kee, H. Saito, T. Mitamura and H. Tomabechi. 1988a. Towards a Speech-to-Speech Translation System. *INTERFACE: Journal of Applied Linguistics* 3:57-77.

Tomita, M., T. Mitamura, H. Musha and M. Kee. 1988b. The Generalized LR Parser/Compiler, Version 8.1: User's Guide. Technical Memo, Center for Machine Translation, Carnegie Mellon University, Pittsburgh, Pa.

Tomita, M. and E. Nyberg. 1988. The Generation Kit and Transformation Kit Version 3.2 User's Manual. Technical Memo, Center for Machine Translation, Carnegie Mellon University, Pittsburgh, Pa.

Tsujii, J. and K. Fujita. 1990. Lexical Transfer Based on Bi-lingual Signs—Towards Interaction During Transfer. In Proceedings of ROCLING III, R.O.C. Computational Linguistics Conference, Hsinchu, R.O.C., 141-157.

Tucker, A. 1987. Current Strategies in Machine Translation Research and Development. In S. Nirenburg (ed.), *Machine Translation: Theoretical and Methodological Issues*. Cambridge: Cambridge University Press, 22-41.

Tulving, E. 1985. How Many Memory Systems Are There? *American Psychologist* 40:385-398.

Uchida, H. 1989a. ATLAS-II: A Machine Translation System Using Conceptual Structure as an Interlingua. In M. Nagao, M. (ed.-in-chief), *Machine Translation Summit*. Tokyo: Ohmsha (proceedings of the 1987 summit, Hakone, Japan), 93-100.

Uchida, H. 1989b. ATLAS. In C . Rohrer (ed.), Proceedings of MT Summit II, Munich, 152-157.

Uchida, H. 1990. Electronic Dictionary. In Proceedings of International Workshop on Electronic Dictionaries, Oiso, Kanagawa, Japan, 23-42.

Van Slype, G. 1979. Evaluation of the 1978 Version of the SYSTRAN English-French Automatic System of the Commission of the European Communities. *The Incorporated Linguist* 18:86-89.

Vasconcellos, M. 1986. Functional Considerations in the Postediting of Machine-Translated Output. *Computers and Translation* 1:21-38.

Vasconcellos, M. and M. Leon. 1985. SPANAM and ENGSPAN: Machine Translation at the Pan American Health Organization. *Computational Linguistics* 11:122-136.

Vauquois, B. 1975. *La traduction automatique à Grenoble*. Paris: Dunod.

Vauquois, B. and C. Boitet. 1985. Automated Translation at Grenoble University. *Computational Linguistics* 11:28-36.

Waibel, A., T. Hanazawa, G. Hinton, K. Shikano and K. Lang. 1988a. Phoneme Recognition: Neural Networks vs. Hidden Markov Models. In Proceedings of IEEE International Conference on Acoustics, Speech and Signal Processing (ICASSP-88), New York, 107-110.

Waibel, A., T. Hanazawa, G. Hinton, K. Shikano and K. Lang. 1989a. Phoneme Recognition Using Time-Delay Neural Networks. *IEEE Transactions on Acoustics, Speech, and Signal Processing* 37:328-339.

Waibel, A., A. McNair, H. Saito and J. Tebelskis. 1991. A Speech-to-Speech Translation System Using Connectionist and Symbolic Processing Strategies. Presentation to IEEE International Conference on Acoustics, Speech and Signal Processing (ICASSP-91), Toronto, 793-796.

Waibel, A., H. Sawai and K. Shikano. 1988b. Modularity and Scaling in Large Phonemic Neural Networks. Technical Report (TR-I-0034), ATR, Tokyo.

Waibel, A., H. Sawai and K. Shikano. 1989b. Consonant and Phoneme Recognition by Modular Construction of Large Phonemic Time-Delay Neural Networks. In Proceedings of IEEE International Conference on Acoustics, Speech and Signal Processing (ICASSP-89), Glasgow, 112-115.

Walker, D. 1987. Knowledge Resource Tools for Accessing Large Text Files. In S. Nirenburg (ed.), *Machine Translation: Theoretical and Methodological Issues*. Cambridge: Cambridge University Press, 247-261.

Waltz, D. 1982. The State of the Art in Natural Language Understanding. In W. Lehnert and M. Ringle (eds.), *Strategies for Natural Language Processing*. Hillsdale, N.J.: Lawrence Erlbaum Associates, 3-32.

Wang, Y. and A. Waibel. 1991. A Connectionist Model for Dialog Processing. Presentation to IEEE International Conference on Acoustics, Speech and Signal Processing (ICASSP-91), Toronto.

Ward, N. 1988. Issues in Word Choice. In Proceedings of the 12th International Conference on Computational Linguistics (COLING-88), Budapest, 726-731.

Warner, R. 1979. Discourse Connectives in English. Ph.D. dissertation, Ohio State University, Columbus, Ohio. (Revised with G. Richard and published under the same title by Garland Publishing Co., New York, 1985.)

Warwick, S. 1987. An Overview of post-ALPAC Developments. In M. King (ed.), *Machine Translation Today*. Edinburgh: Edinburgh University Press, 22-37.

Weaver, W. 1955. Translation. In W. Locke and A. Booth (eds.), *Machine Translation of Languages*. Cambridge, Mass.: MIT Press, 15-23.

Weischedel, R. 1987. A Personal View of Ill-Formed Input Processing. In Proceedings of the Northeast Artificial Intelligence Consortium's Natural Language Planning Workshop, Blue Mountain Lake, N.Y., 23-44.

Weischedel, R. and L. Ramshaw. 1987. In S. Nirenburg (ed.), *Machine Translation: Theoretical and Methodological Issues*. Cambridge: Cambridge University Press, 155-167.

Werner, P. and S. Nirenburg. 1988. A Specification Language that Supports the Realization of Intersentential Anaphora. In Proceedings of the AAAI Workshop on Natural Language Generation, Saint Paul, Minn.

Whitelock, P. 1989. Why Transfer and Interlingua Approaches to MT Are Both Wrong: A Position Paper. Presentation at MT "Into the '90s" workshop, Manchester, UK.

Wilensky, R. 1983. *Planning and Understanding*. Reading, Mass.: Addison-Wesley.

Wilks, Y. 1973. The Stanford Machine Translation and Understanding Project. In R. Rustin (ed.), *Natural Language Processing*, (Courant Computer Science Symposium, No. 8). New York: Algorithmics Press, 243-290.

Wilks, Y. 1988. Philosophy of Language and Artificial Intelligence, Technical Memorandum (MCCS-88-132), Computing Research Laboratory, New Mexico State University, Las Cruces, N. Mex.

Wilks, Y. 1990. Form and Content in Semantics. *Synthese* 82:329-351.

Wilks, Y., D. Fass, C. Guo, J. McDonald, T. Plate, B. Slator. 1988. Machine Tractable Dictionaries as Tools and Resources for Natural Language Processing. In Proceedings of the 12th International Conference on Computational Linguistics (COLING-88), Budapest, 750-755.

Wilks, Y., D. Fass, C. Guo, J. McDonald, T. Plate and B. Slator. 1990. Providing Machine Tractable Dictionary Tools. *Machine Translation* 5:99-154.

Wilpon, J., L. Rabiner and A. Bergh. 1982. Speaker-Independent Isolated Word Recognition Using a 129-Word Airline Vocabulary. *The Journal of the Acoustical Society of America* 72(2), August.

Winograd, T. 1972. *Understanding Natural Language*. New York: Academic Press.

Winograd, T. 1983. *Language as a Cognitive Process*. Volume 1: Syntax. Reading, Mass.: Addison-Wesley.

Witkam, T. 1983. DLT-Ditributed Language Translation—A Multilingual Facility for Videotex Information Networks. Technical Report, BSO (Buro voor Systemontwikkeling), Utrecht, The Netherlands.

Witkam, T. 1989. Interlingual Machine Translation—An Industrial Initiative. In M. Nagao, M. (ed.-in-chief), *Machine Translation Summit*. Tokyo: Ohmsha (proceedings of the 1987 summit, Hakone, Japan), 128-132.

Wolf, J. and W. Woods. 1980. The HWIM Speech Understanding System. In W. Lea (ed.), *Trends in Speech Recognition*. Englewood Cliffs, N.J.: Prentice-Hall, 316-339.

Woods, W., M. Bates, G. Brown, B. Bruce, C. Cook, J. Klovstad, J. Makhoul, B. Nash-Webber, R. Schwartz, J. Wolf and V. Zue. 1976. Speech Understanding Systems—Final Technical Report. Bolt, Beranek, and Newman, Cambridge, Mass.

Wright, J. and E. Wrigley. 1988. Linguistic Control in Speech Recognition. In Proceedings of the Seventh FASE Symposium, Edinburgh, 545-542.

Young, S., A. Hauptmann and W. Ward. 1988. An Integrated Speech and Natural Language Dialog System: Using Dialog Knowledge in Speech Recognition. Technical Report (CMU-CS 88-128), Computer Science Department, Carnegie Mellon University, Pittsburgh, Pa.

Younger, D. 1967. Recognition and Parsing of Context-free Languages in Time n^3. *Information and Control* 10:189-208.

Zarechnak, M. 1979. The History of Machine Translation. In Henisz-Dostert, B., R. Ross McDonald and M. Zarechnak (eds.), *Machine Translation*, Trends in Linguistics: Studies and Monographs, Volume XI. The Hague: Mouton.

Zeitz, C. 1987. Knowledge Organization and the Acquisition of Procedural Expertise. Technical Report (6633), Bolt, Beranek and Newman, Cambridge, Mass.

Zernik, U. and M. Dyer. 1987. The Self-Extending Phrasal Lexicon. *Computational Linguistics* 13:308-327.

Zue, V., J. Glass, M. Phillips and S. Seneff. 1989. Acoustic Segmentation and Phonetic Classification in the SUMMIT System. In Proceedings of IEEE International Conference on Acoustics, Speech and Signal Processing (ICASSP-89), Glasgow, 389-392.

Index

Abelson, R., 69
Abrett, G., 112
abstracting, 201, 204, 212
actions, 33, 66, 70, 77, 79, 82, 87
    planning, 137
Adriaens, G., 105
Aho, A., 121
Albano, R., 151
Allen, J., 81
Amano, S., 20, 49, 56
ambiguity, 21–26, 48–49, 66, 126, 127,
    193, 218
Amsler, R., 104, 105, 107
analogical inference, 73
analogical reasoning, 73
analysis, *see also* source language analy-
    sis,
    algorithms, 120–121
    discourse, 118–119, 215
    intersentential, 129
    morphological, 21, 117–118, 125,
    215
    pragmatic, 118–119
    semantic, 118, 216
    syntactic, 118, 215
anaphora, 67, 83, 118, 136, 152, 216
Apollinaire, G., 61
Apollo-Soyuz space mission, 6
Appelt, D., 136
Arnold, D., 20, 32, 48, 52, 61
aspect, 76, 83, 85
ATLAS-I MT system, 206
ATLAS-II MT system, 28, 29, 32, 52, 206
ATR Interpreting Telephony Research Lab-

    oratories, 167, 211
attitude, 68, 75–77, 83, 92–93, 148
    epistemic, 148, 149
    evaluative, 150
    lexically realized, 150
    realization, 150
augmented transition networks, 120
augmentor, 30, 36, 129, 193, 216, *see*
    also interactive editing
Automatic Language Processing Advi-
    sory Committee (ALPAC), 2, 5–
    6, 15, 209
automation, degree of, 108
Aymara, 59

BABEL MT system, 151
Bar-Hillel, Y., 1, 2, 4–5, 22, 49
Bell Labs, 166, 167
Ben Ari, D., 20, 47
Bennett, W., 54, 56, 105, 210
Benson, M., 106
Berwick, R., 118
blackboard architecture, 126, 131–132,
    160, 216
Bloomfield, L., 44
Boguraev, B., 103, 104
Boitet, C., 28, 30, 53–55
Bolt, Beranek and Newman (BBN), 112,
    167
Booth, A., 3
Bourbeau, L., 47
Bourland, H., 169, 171
Brachman, R., 78
breadth-first methodology, 83
Bresnan, J., 118, 123

249